**Praise for Leigh Steinberg
and *Winning with Integrity***

"Traditionally, nice guys get run over in the business world, because it is war. Only Leigh Steinberg could write a book which tells how to win the war while keeping personal integrity intact."
—*USA Today*

"The best professional decision that I've made with respect to my professional life has been to hire Leigh. He's negotiated two ground-breaking contracts where *everyone* came out smiling."
—DREW BLEDSOE, New England Patriots quarterback

"Negotiating with Leigh is an experience not to be missed. It is a highly charged mix of financial analysis, philosophy, and humor, all with a focused purpose—to make a deal, at which Leigh is a master, signing some of the most lucrative contracts in the sports world year after year."
—TED PHILLIPS, Chicago Bears general manager

"Leigh shows how he has mastered the art of negotiation and goes on to share his knowledge with readers."
—TROY AIKMAN, Dallas Cowboys quarterback

"Leigh is committed to using his success and the success of those with whom he works to strengthen community in America."
—RICHARD LOVETT, president, Creative Artists Agency

"Leigh Steinberg, who made 'agent' a respectable word and 'agency' a laudable profession, has written a book aptly subtitled 'Getting What You're Worth Without Selling Your Soul,' which should be required reading for every athlete and ten percenter in the business."
—JIM MURRAY, *Los Angeles Times*

"Leigh is a trendsetter and deserves his place at the forefront of his profession. He handles negotiations from a unique perspective, combining preparation, attention to detail, and carefully plotted strategy to work to the clients' advantage. Through Leigh, I've gained an understanding of the entire negotiation process."

—BRUCE SMITH, Buffalo Bills defensive end

"Leigh's success in negotiating is unparalleled. By putting in perspective the key elements of successful bargaining, this book is the bible of negotiating. Read it and win."

—RUSH LIMBAUGH, author of *The Way Things Ought to Be*

WINNING
WITH
INTEGRITY

LEIGH STEINBERG

———— *with* ————

MICHAEL D'ORSO

WINNING WITH INTEGRITY

Getting What You're
Worth Without
Selling Your
Soul

TIMES BUSINESS

RANDOM HOUSE

This work was originally published in hardcover by Villard Books,
a division of Random House, Inc., in 1998.

Library of Congress Cataloging-in-Publication Data

Steinberg, Leigh.
Winning with integrity: getting what you're worth
without selling your soul /
Leigh Steinberg with Michael D'Orso.
p.   cm.
Includes index.
ISBN 0-8129-3243-9 (pbk.)
1. Negotiation in business.   I. D'Orso, Michael.   II. Title.
HD58.6.S75   1998
658.4'052–dc21   98-24551

Random House website address: www.atrandom.com

Printed in the United States of America on acid-free paper

24689753

First Paperback Edition

Book design by JoAnne Metsch

SPECIAL SALES
Times Books are available at special discounts for bulk purchases for
sales promotions or premiums. Special editions, including
personalized covers, excerpts of existing books, and corporate
imprints, can be created in large quantities for special needs. For
more information, write to Special Markets, Times Books, 201 East
50th Street, New York, New York 10022, or call 800-800-3246.

To my father, Warren,
and my mother, Betty,
whose ideals and principles
have guided my life

Acknowledgments

I HAVE BEEN blessed over the course of my life and career by the guidance, companionship, and support of family, friends, teachers, and colleagues. They include:

- My wife, Lucy, whose love and understanding propel me through the world each day; and my children Jon, Matt, and Katie, who are the lights of my life.
- Steve Bartkowski, who had the faith to trust his career to an inexperienced twenty-five-year-old lawyer; and his parents, Roman and Helen, who nurtured and supported me in the early years.
- David Bateman, whose floor I slept on in the beginning; and Brian Kahn, my mentor in my very first contract.
- Jeff Moorad, my partner and soul mate for these last fourteen years; David Dunn, who keeps me sane and functioning on a day-to-day basis; and Scott Parker, the brains of the outfit.
- Warren Moon, my guiding light and dear friend; Rolf Benirschke, whose very existence is an inspiration; Steve Young, my surrogate younger brother; Troy Aikman, whose loyalty and courage have enriched my life; Greg Anthony, who opened up the world of basketball to me; and Drew Bledsoe, whose values are inspiring.

- My brothers James and Donald, two of three peas in the pod, who have sprouted in very different and exciting ways. Donald has led a courageous fight to rid the world of land mines.
- My uncle Larry Steinberg, who taught me that the unpopular view may still be the right one.
- My aunt Eleanor Blumenberg, my cousin David Hoffman, and all of my amazing extended family, who have strived so hard to make a difference in the world.
- Dave McElhatton, Wendy Tokuda, Wayne Walker, Jan Hutchins, Pete Wilson, and Anna Chavez, who introduced me to television news and brightened my life with their friendship.
- My high school social studies teacher Blanche Bettington, who taught me about passion and commitment.
- Julie Atkins, Joy Franich, Robert Hacker, Jill Dunn, Stefani Wanicur, Jill Peterson, Ben Francois, Kristi Ensign, Ashley Smith, Carmen Wallace, Scott Hensley, James Brown, Steve Baker, Tyler Goldman, Kelly Tomlinson, Edith Langley, Lynn Crawford, Mary Boies, Joby Branion, Cecilia Robinson, Andrea Bobinski, Ashley Smith, Jeff Williams, Josh Perttula, Brian Murphy, Todd Bollman, Domenic Mantella, Wm. David Cornwell, Sr., and Craig Richardson, who have helped me keep my life and law practice together over the years.
- Doug Katona, Arthur Rivin, and Charles Portney, who keep my beleaguered body in shape.
- Alan Epstein, Paul Heeschen, and Patrice Jeffries, who help me navigate the world of business.
- Adolph, Alma, Peter, and Margaret Landsberger, my second family.
- Artie Gigantino, Mike White, Paul Hackett, and Bill Walsh—my first and most enduring football friendships.
- Hugh Campbell, Jim Sochor, and June Jones—coaches who were successful and kept their ideals.
- Jack Friedman, my best friend through thick and thin.
- Buddy Epstein, Carl Stoney, and Jack Flanigan, true friends from way back.
- Marv Demoff, who helped and mentored me in the early days.

- Vin Scully, whose voice first drew me to sports.
- Jim Murray, whose gifted writings on sports and life inspired me.
- Sandy Koufax, my all-time sports hero; and Maury Wills, my second all-time sports hero.
- Boalt Hall School of Law at the University of California at Berkeley, for being there with acceptance at a vulnerable point in my life; and Professor Jesse Choper and Dean Herma Hill Kay, for their support and guidance.
- Mike D'Orso, whose talent and dedication helped me translate my vision into the words on these pages.
- Brian DeFiore, for believing in this project and nurturing it to fruition.
- Marty Weinberg, whose vision and brilliance are such a welcome addition to my life.
- David Black, my literary agent, who understands my dreams.
- And finally, all of the wonderful clients who have become a part of my life over the years, the many team executives with whom I have had the true pleasure of working, and the talented journalists who have understood and helped share the message and the meaning of what we are all trying to do.

To all of you, I give my thanks.

Contents

WINNING
WITH
INTEGRITY

PROLOGUE

THE FIRST TIME I ever did business with New England Patriots owner Bob Kraft began as if it would be the last.

It was the spring of 1995, in Phoenix, where the National Football League was holding its annual meeting. Dozens of team owners, general managers, coaches, and sportswriters had converged on the city, streaming in and out of the lobby of the Arizona Biltmore hotel as Bob and I took seats in a corner to talk about the contract of Patriots quarterback Drew Bledsoe.

Bob Kraft had bought the Patriots just the year before, and in that short time he had already rekindled great hope and excitement in the New England area for a franchise that had become somewhat moribund in recent years. His habit of strolling through Foxboro Stadium's parking lot on game day, mingling and shaking hands with the fans, had captivated the people of New England. He was obviously an astute businessman, a multimillionaire who had made his fortune in a variety of industries, including paper goods and communications, but upon buying the Patriots, he established himself as an NFL visionary as well, with a long-term view of football that transcended traditional approaches to ownership in the sport. He understood the value of a professional football team as an asset with more revenue potential than simply selling tickets and generating television revenue. There are countless ancillary uses to which the game and its players can be applied, and Bob Kraft could see these. He had bought the Patriots with a clear understanding of the rapidly expanding technological and communications market for this sport. He could see that the growth of multiple platforms for information delivery—hundreds of cable television stations, the Internet, video games, home computer and entertainment systems—had created a continuing need for programming and content, a need that few products can fill as effectively as professional sports.

Bob Kraft understood all this. He also understood how critically his organization's success depended on having a player like Drew Bledsoe at quarterback. If there is one marquee position in all of sports, one fulcrum around which the fortunes of an entire franchise can swing, it is that of an NFL quarterback. But not all quarterbacks have the combination of talent, leadership, and charisma both on and off the field that it takes to turn an entire operation around. There are starting quarterbacks in the National Football League, and then there are *franchise* quarterbacks. There are quarterbacks a team can be successful *with,* and then there are quarterbacks a team can be successful *because* of.

In just two seasons, after arriving in New England as a rookie in 1993, Drew Bledsoe had left no doubt that he was a franchise quarterback. Not only had he led the Patriots to their first play-off appearance in almost a decade and become the youngest quarterback ever selected for the Pro Bowl, but his off-the-field involvement in the community and his approachable personality had stirred great excitement and support in the region.

Drew's rookie contract with the Patriots, which I had negotiated with Bob Kraft's predecessor, a major Anheuser-Busch stockholder named James Orthwein, was due to expire after the upcoming 1995 season. Because the quarterback position is so critical, and because most owners do not want their quarterback to be destabilized emotionally or in any other way by the dynamics of an intense contract negotiation, teams make it a priority to approach the player well before his contract comes up; that way, a new contract can be worked out with minimal stress and tension. There is a reason that with all the controversial, acrimonious, headline-grabbing negotiation holdups and player holdouts that often occur in professional football, virtually none involve quarterbacks: Stability at that pivotal position is a priority.

Which was why Bob Kraft and I sat down that March morning in Phoenix. Bob had made a point a year earlier, at our Super Bowl party in Atlanta, which was held at that city's historic downtown Fox Theater, to come up and introduce himself to me and to Drew and Drew's parents. I liked him immediately. I had been looking forward to doing our first piece of business together, and now it was time.

The hotel lobby was perhaps not the shrewdest choice of a location for this negotiation. Every two or three minutes, another team's executive or a coach or a writer would stop by our table to say hello. But this was where we had decided to start our discussion, and so we began.

"I don't know how you negotiate," Bob said. "Would you rather we make an offer that's exactly what we propose to pay, or do you want to haggle and go high-low?"

"We'd rather have a number that you're prepared to pay," I said, "and we'll come in with one too."

So he made his proposal—a salary average of about $4 million a year for six years, with a signing bonus of about $5 million.

There was a significant difference between the Patriots' figures and ours. The essence of our position was that Drew was the trendsetter of the next generation of quarterbacks in the NFL, poised to inherit the mantle of Troy Aikman and Steve Young. Aikman's existing contract averaged $6 million a year. Young's averaged $5.5 million. Both those deals were several years old. If Drew was going to take his place in the company of those players, we reasoned, he deserved to be making those kinds of numbers, at current market value.

So we offered a counterproposal of $6.5 million a year in salary for six years, with a $12 million signing bonus.

And that essentially stopped the discussion.

I did not realize it at the time, but Bob Kraft was extremely upset by our proposal. He felt he had made his offer in good faith. From his standpoint, the fact that we had responded with numbers so drastically different from his violated that faith. He had expected us to accept his proposal, or at least to come close with our counter. When we did not, he was greatly offended.

Again, though, I had no idea. We said something about getting together again soon, and that was the end of our conversation that day. In the days that followed, subsequent discussions ensued by telephone between my partner Jeff Moorad and some of the staff in the Patriots' offices. But Bob Kraft and I did not speak. Weeks passed, then months. April, May, and June went by with absolutely no progress. What had started off as a warm, promising relationship between Bob Kraft and me had dissolved into distance and silence.

June turned to July, which is always a hectic month as a flurry of final agreements and signings typically precedes the opening of NFL training camps. The summer of 1995 was especially intense. Our roster of rookie clients included Ki-Jana Carter, a running back from Penn State, who was the first overall pick in that year's draft, and Kerry Collins, Penn State's quarterback, who was the league's fifth pick. In the middle of that month I booked a flight east from my office in Los Angeles to wrap up those signings. Before I left, I put in a call to Bob Kraft.

"Look, Bob," I said. "I'm getting ready to make an eastern swing. Doesn't it make some sense for us to get together?"

He was not overly enthusiastic, but he was amenable, and that was enough.

I arrived on a Saturday in Charlotte, where we signed Kerry Collins to a $23 million deal with the Panthers, including a $7 million signing bonus—the largest rookie bonus ever. Unfortunately, Kerry had left the keys to his car, which was parked at the Charlotte airport, as well as those to his home in Charlotte, back at my Newport Beach office in California. So we spent the day scrambling to find a way to get Kerry packed and to training camp on time.

That night I flew to Pittsburgh, where I spent Sunday wrapping up negotiations with the Steelers on a contract for their second pick, quarterback Kordell Stewart, as well as calling back across country to Seattle to finish a deal with the Seahawks for their second-round pick, tight end Christian Fauria. Monday we finished Kordell's contract and that of Christian, who was waiting with his packed bags at the Seattle airport for us to give him the word to leave for camp.

Then it was up to Columbus, Ohio, where I began final discussions on Tuesday with the Cincinnati Bengals for Ki-Jana's contract. Wednesday we made that deal, a $19 million package, with a $7.125 million signing bonus. Thursday morning I drove with Ki-Jana to the Bengals' camp, trying to explain his complex contract while the blast of rap music boomed from his state-of-the-art auto sound system at a volume that rattled the license plate on the back of his car. After getting Ki-Jana to camp, I flew to Boston late that afternoon.

Bob Kraft and I had no agreement. We had nothing. The same proposals that had been laid on the table in the Arizona hotel lobby back in March were the proposals we were looking at now. The Patriots' training camp had just begun, and Drew was there, focusing on his job. He was not overly concerned about this negotiation. Drew Bledsoe was a player who had not even cashed all his checks during his first two years in the league. His mother found one uncashed paycheck behind the visor in his car. She found another in his sock drawer. Drew's mother and father were both teachers, and they had raised him and his brother, Adam, with a sense of values that revolved around things besides money. To make $40,000 a year would have seemed like a tremendous amount of money to Drew. The $4.5 million he had received to sign seemed almost inconceivable. He and Adam would occasionally call the bank just to hear the balance in Drew's account. Then they'd hang up and laugh. It was funny to them, like visiting a foreign planet.

Drew appreciated the magnitude of these discussions, but we had bonded strongly during his first contract negotiation with New England, and he trusted me to do my job. In my mind, it was critical that this contract be done soon. If it was not, the entire preseason would become an endless series of public discussions and speculations about what Drew Bledsoe's future with the Patriots would be. It would become a circus, a sideshow.

So I checked into my hotel, then met Bob for a meal at a comfortable Italian restaurant near the waterfront in Boston. The place was dark and relatively uncrowded, giving us the kind of privacy that had been lacking during our first meeting in Phoenix. We began talking, just a general conversation about the future of the Patriots and where the league was headed. Very quickly it became clear that we really did see things the same way, that the feeling I had had when we first met was accurate: We were two reasonably kindred souls who had simply allowed too much time to pass without talking.

Bob told me why he had not been eager to speak with me. He explained the anger and disappointment he had felt during our first meeting. In the other industries in which he was accustomed to doing business, deals tended to happen quickly, he said. He had always been a man of action, and he had come to Phoenix presuming that our deal would be completed that day and that he would be able to announce the signing there at the league meeting. When it did not happen that way, he was more than frustrated. He began to suspect that I had other motivations, that perhaps I was waiting for the end of the upcoming season so I could use the free agency system to take Drew somewhere else.

Now that we were face-to-face, I was able to address those concerns, as well as other issues that had been troubling Bob. First, I said, there was no place in the National Football League that Drew Bledsoe would rather be than with New England. If he had not wanted to come there, I pointed out, all we would have had to do back in 1993 was say so to Bill Parcells, who was the Patriots' head coach at the time, and New England would then have drafted Rick Mirer instead of Drew. But Drew was eager to play under Parcells, who had demonstrated great skill at developing quarterbacks during his coaching career, the prime example being Phil Simms with the Giants. Parcells also had a commitment to the running game, which tends to lessen the pressure on a young quarterback. Drew was excited about the team the Patriots were building, and he was excited about living in Boston, with its long sports tradition and rabid fans, its rich culture and history, and its many colleges and universities, with the energy they bring. This was where Drew wanted to be, I told Bob. There had never been an issue of trying to leave.

As for Bob's feelings about our first meeting, I told him I had the utmost respect for him. I had great respect for his sense of family and charity. I thought he was a major source of creative energy for the NFL. It had been my mission for the last ten years to increase the revenue sources in the National Football League, and I was excited by the fact that he not only had the same goal but also had specific, imaginative ideas about how to achieve it. I wanted him to be successful in everything he did.

But, I pointed out, reasonable people can have a reasonable difference of opinion without it becoming an issue of ethics or faith. I talked about some of the other football negotiations I had conducted over the years, to show how NFL contract discussions often begin where ours did. Though it may look at first as if the two parties are worlds apart, I said, the process, particularly with franchise quarterbacks, will almost always pull them together.

"Look," I said, "this is the first time you and I have negotiated together. We haven't done business before. We've been friendly and had several good talks, but we haven't negotiated yet. I'm ready to do that now if you are."

He was. Our false start had been a matter of misunderstanding and miscommunication. Now we understood each other. Just as importantly, we now *trusted* each other. With that settled, we were able to talk about what was in the best interest of Drew and what was in the best interest of the Patriots. We were assisted in this process by a couple of bottles of red wine.

The evening went on, and we went back and forth, sketching out the concept of a long-term contract. Because the only guaranteed money a player receives in the National Football League is his signing bonus (salaries in the league are not guaranteed), and because of the construction of salary-cap economics, with a ceiling on how much money a team can spend on its payroll each year, actually paying a Troy Aikman or a Steve Young $5 or $6 million in salary in a single season is unacceptable for an NFL team. There would not be enough money left under the cap to pay the rest of the players. So those kinds of dollars are paid through a large up-front signing bonus, which counts against the cap in a smaller, amortized fashion. I have worked very hard to create a win-win situation for players and teams under the conditions created by the cap. Because we have represented large numbers of highly paid free agents, it became necessary for us to pioneer the field of "caponomics"—a process that would allow a contract for a player like Drew to be structured in a way that would enable his team to surround him with the strongest possible supporting cast. The word *caponomics* was one I coined in a conversation with Gordon Forbes, the football columnist for *USA Today.*

Bob and I talked about the cap. We also talked about the fact that the hardest thing to find in pro football is a quarterback of the caliber of Drew Bledsoe. I pointed out that in 1993, the year Drew was a rookie, there were just two quarterbacks drafted in the first round—Drew and Rick Mirer. The next year, there were two more—Heath Shuler and Trent Dilfer. In 1995 there were just two—Kerry Collins and Steve McNair. And it did not look as if many would be coming along anytime soon.

The attrition rate among quarterbacks because of injury was something else we discussed. The development of larger, faster, stronger defensive linemen and linebackers has exponentially magnified the physics of the hit. The increasingly violent force of quarterback sacks has resulted in a slew of concussions and other injuries that both foreshorten the long-term careers of these players and make it difficult for them to play injury-free through an entire season.

There is no position in the sport, I pointed out to Bob, to which the concept of scarcity applies more than that of quarterback. A team can have all the money in the world to spend, but it won't be able to buy a player of Drew Bledsoe's caliber if one does not exist. When one does appear, as was the case with Rob Johnson this year, there are twenty teams desperate to get him. In other words, the Patriots were ahead of the game by already *having* such a player. All it was going to cost them, I told Bob, was money—money that would prove to be more than well spent in the years to come.

I tried to prepare him for the predictable outrage that would arise when the contract was announced. I had seen this with every major "breakthrough" contract I had ever done, from Steve Bartkowski's record-breaking $650,000 deal back in 1975 to Troy Aikman's land-mark $11.2 million rookie contract in 1989, to Steve Young's $42 million 1984 contract with the USFL's Los Angeles Express. In every case, the apocalyptic hue and cry arose that this deal was the one that would push the NFL over the brink, that this was the "figure to end all figures." And in every case, the figures paled within a couple of seasons. Within three or four years after each of these signings, some of the same people who criticized a particular contract as being over-the-top were complaining that that same player was now under-salaried.

We went on until well past midnight. By the time the restaurant began to close, Bob Kraft and I had pretty much come to terms. The next morning, Friday, we met to refine the figures. We decided on a little more bonus and a little less in salary in the contract's first couple of years, to free up as much cap room as possible to allow the Patriots to aggressively sign other players and surround Drew with a top-quality team—a Super Bowl–quality team, as it would turn out two seasons later, when the Patriots won the 1996 AFC title and the right to meet the Green Bay Packers for the NFL championship.

By late that Friday morning, the deal was done—a seven-year $42 million package that included an $11.5 million signing bonus, the largest in league history.

I called Drew late that morning to tell him it looked like we had a deal. "Listen," I said. "Bob Kraft's just done a wonderful thing for you. Now's the time to do something for him." Drew was a step ahead of me. Besides pledging a million dollars to his Drew Bledsoe Foundation, which supports training centers in family counseling, Drew suggested that he pledge an additional million dollars to the Bob Kraft Foundation, which helps a variety of charities in the Boston area.

I gave Bob that news as he drove us from Boston to the team's training camp in Providence, Rhode Island. The concept that we could go from one state to another in forty-five minutes was com-pletely foreign to me: I could get in my car at my home in Newport Beach, California, and start driving north and not hit the Oregon border until the next day. We made up for the short distance, how-ever, by getting lost several times. The combination of our conversation about the future of the league and the fact that Bob had a discussion on his car phone with his mother, whom he calls every day, distracted us enough to put us off course.

But we finally made it. Drew signed the contract, we held a press conference, then Bob and I drove up to his home on Cape Cod, where he and his wife, Myra, and I went out to dinner. When we got back to their house, Bob and I ended the evening in his hot tub, toasting our agreement with a glass of champagne and a great view of the Atlantic.

As we were walking back inside, the television was on in the living room. ESPN was airing a story on the Drew Bledsoe signing that had taken place that day. They discussed the size and possible ramifications of the contract. Then the reporter concluded with an overview:

"What a week it's been for Leigh Steinberg. First he signs Kerry Collins to the biggest rookie bonus ever. Then Christian Fauria. Then Kordell Stewart. Then Ki-Jana Carter, to a bonus higher than Collins's. And now Drew Bledsoe's eleven-and-a-half-million-dollar bonus, half again the size of Carter's. All in the last five days.

"Leigh," the reporter finished, "it's time to take a *rest*!"

Bob and I looked at each other, laughed, and said good night.

INTRODUCTION

THIS IS A book about the process of negotiation—which means that this is a book about life.

If we have anything at all to do with other people, personally or professionally, whether as a society, as companies and corporations dealing with one another, as employees dealing with employers, or as husbands dealing with wives, the inescapable fact is that each of us every day is faced with a number of decisions that require some level of negotiation.

From buying a house or a car or a piece of land to approaching your employer for a raise, from setting curfew for your teenage son or daughter to deciding where your family will spend its vacation, in any situation where two or more people need to work out a mutually agreeable decision, some level of negotiation is required.

Too many people would rather simply give up what they want. They would rather avoid the discomfort of possible conflict by accepting a situation or terms without discussion, even when it means accepting less than they rightfully deserve or desire.

Just as unfortunate are the people who *do* negotiate but are ill equipped for it, arriving either unprepared or, worse, with a combative, warlike attitude.

We live in a time, at least in America, where the prevailing mood seems to be one of intense adversarial conflict. In politics, in public dialogue and discourse, on the pages of newspapers and magazines and on the airwaves of television and radio, everyone seems to be talking—*shouting*—with very few people listening. Rather than truly considering one another's thoughts and ideas, we seem to be a society entrenched in deeply dug positions, tightly clutching our agendas, shouting across the battlements at one another, hurling edicts and ultimatums, ruled more by our emotions than by carefully reasoned thoughts and responses.

The traditional thinking about the negotiating process is that it is this kind of adversarial showdown, a face-off, a matter of breaking another human being, destroying him, wiping his position out, conquering him personally. What people who carry this attitude into the negotiating process fail to understand is that war damages and destroys. It takes years to repair the damage done by a war, if it is repairable at all. And the damage is not done simply to the vanquished. The very act of war can turn the warrior into a monster. It can exaggerate and exacerbate those features of people's personalities that are most dysfunctional: animosity; hyperaggressiveness; the need to humiliate and dominate; dishonesty; manipulation.

Beyond that, a warlike stance is simply an ineffective way to negotiate. Effective negotiation is not about conflict. It is not about force. It is not about deviance or dishonesty. It is not about posturing or bullying or threatening.

Effective negotiation is about exhaustive preparation, utter clarity, heartfelt communication, and a sincere, demonstrated desire to fully understand not just your own needs but the needs of the other party.

Effective negotiation is the result of comprehensive research, of building a well-reasoned position, of studying and fully understanding the other party's position—perhaps more fully than he or she understands it—then bridging the gap between your position and the other party's with a persuasive, mutually satisfying proposition based upon facts, reason, and fairness rather than upon willpower, desire, or deceit.

Too many people separate the business of doing business from the business of being human. They adopt situational ethics, playing the role of unselfish, caring parent and congenial friend away from work while feeling that the law of the jungle prevails in the workplace. This is a fundamental mistake. Effective negotiation at any level, be it between governments, between business organizations, between individuals in the privacy of their own homes, or between a sports attorney and the owner of a National Football League team, is grounded in the ability to understand people and to treat them fairly. This begins with an understanding of *yourself*—a brutally honest assessment that is not always easy to attain.

There is no magic to effective negotiation. There are no mirrors. It is an entirely learnable process, a series of steps that can be broken down into clearly identifiable elements, that should, in almost every situation, lead to a resolution that satisfies everyone involved.

An understanding of these elements, the application of these specific skills and principles, is what will determine your level of success in any negotiating situation, personally or professionally. Even in those unfortunately common situations where a person might feel that he has very little leverage—facing an employer who has all the power; having no job options other than the job one has; dealing with a spouse who is obstinate and controlling—the application of the techniques contained in this book can help create alternatives and avenues of change that might not have seemed possible before.

A theme that runs throughout this book, and one that has always formed the basis of the way I do business, is that the ideal negotiating environment is one in which two reasonable people are able to communicate openly and honestly from the heart. Everything possible should be done to attain this environment. Sometimes, unfortunately, we must negotiate with someone who makes this impossible. In such cases, there are techniques and strategies that can be used to deal fairly and effectively.

Always keep in mind that time and again, throughout the course of any negotiation, there will come a point where the road forks and an ethical choice must be made between one action or response and another. A decision will have to be made between taking the high road or the low road. Sometimes it can appear to be more immediately beneficial to take the low road, to deceive, to dissemble, or in some other way to take advantage of a particular situation. The immediate rewards can be seductive, but they are also deceptive. Whatever benefits might result from dishonest or otherwise unethical actions will always be outweighed by the damage that is done—damage to your relationship with the other party, damage to your reputation, and damage to your own self-esteem and sense of honor. In the long term, it is *always* more advantageous to act ethically, to take the high road. Beyond the practical rewards that will eventually accrue, there is the immeasurable benefit of being able to wake up in the morning and know that you have done the right thing. That is a feeling that no amount of money or power or influence can measure.

There are people in this world who are driven by a need to dominate. There are others whose tendency is to capitulate. And then there are those who know how to negotiate, both in business and in life—or who *want* to know how.

This book is for them.

1

ORIENTATION

VALUES

I NEVER PLANNED on becoming a sports attorney. I was twenty-five years old when I essentially fell into this profession. But although it was not by design that I entered this business, neither was it completely an accident. My particular plans were unfocused when I found this career, but my values—what I believed in, what I cared about, what *mattered* to me—were not.

Defining and clarifying your own values—not your colleagues' values, not your family's values, not your friends' values or society's values, but *your* values—is, I believe, an essential first step toward effectiveness in any endeavor. A passionate belief in the worthiness of the work you do—or of the product you sell or of the client you represent—is a bedrock cornerstone of success. I am convinced that a sense of ethical or moral certainty about one's position or product can unlock an incredible amount of energy, enthusiasm, creativity, and commitment. A person can certainly do business without that sense of internal justification, but the person who lacks that sense of calling will rarely be a match for the individual who is fueled by a fundamental belief in the merit of what he or she is doing, selling, or representing.

A pivotal point in the film *Jerry Maguire* occurs when the main character, a sports attorney played by actor Tom Cruise, confronts his conscience and decides he no longer wants to do business in an insincere, manipulative way. He drafts a personal code of ethics for his profession—a "mission statement"—which he eagerly shares with his colleagues, assuming that they will join him as he steps toward this newly found high ground. None do, of course. The remainder of the film follows Cruise as he struggles alone to stay faithful to his freshly discovered values.

It might not be necessary to go so far as to write a mission statement for your profession, but I believe that this kind of precise definition of one's values is at the root of success and fulfillment in any field.

Unlike Cruise's character, whose values were discovered only after he was well into his career, mine were in place long before I entered this business, and they still guide my approach to my work each day. I was raised in Southern California in the 1950s and '60s by socially conscious parents who emphasized our obligation to be involved in an active way in the community around us. My father was a high school principal and head of the city of Los Angeles's human relations commission. My mother was an audiovisual librarian. As a young marine trainee and college student during World War II, my father wrote an editorial for the University of Southern California student newspaper condemning the relocation of Japanese-Americans to internment camps. He and my mother raised my brothers and me to have that same courage of our convictions.

We lived in a multiracial neighborhood about six blocks from a federal housing project. I grew up sleeping over at the houses of Chicano, Asian, and African-American friends, and they slept over at mine. Every night at the dinner table, our family would talk about issues and current events—politics, race relations, the Cold War, housing discrimination, the civil rights movement. I remember watching television reports of the dogs and hoses being turned on African-American children in Birmingham in 1963. I was so repulsed and disgusted by the fact that something like that could be happening in America that I joined CORE—the Congress of Racial Equality—as a fourteen-year-old.

During my undergraduate years in the late 1960s and early 1970s at the University of California at Berkeley, I became involved in campus politics and witnessed what can occur when the spirit of negotiation and consensus building breaks down. In 1969, as student body representative, I participated in negotiations between the university, the community, and the students over the use of the People's Park, where students were staging demonstrations against the war in Vietnam. When those talks broke down, the police were called in. The students refused to move.

The result was a nightmare: tear gas was dropped from helicopters, pepper fog sprayed from police cruisers; bird shot and buckshot fired into the crowds of students, who in turn hurled rocks and bottles. One student was killed, and another was blinded. The National Guard was called in. Troop carriers and tanks arrived.

That time in my life taught me some fundamental lessons. I learned the devastating consequences of an inability to understand that differences in points of view can reasonably exist and that it is not only possible but necessary to understand and accommodate viewpoints and positions different from one's own.

When I entered law school in 1971, it was with the intention of pursuing politics or, possibly, entertainment law. I had grown up with a fascination for films and filmmaking, and I understood the enormous power that both movies and television have in shaping people's perceptions. Three years later, after graduation, I took time off to travel and decide exactly what I wanted to do with my life. I went to the Watergate hearings, and was on the steps of the Supreme Court when the historic Nixon tapes decision was announced. Then I traveled overseas, to Israel, Greece, Italy, Egypt. It was a flush time in terms of jobs in the legal profession in the United States. I knew there would be something waiting when I returned, and there was.

I went through the interview process and received offers from a number of corporate litigation firms, but my heart was just not in it. Entertainment law intrigued me, as did environmental law. But I had grown up watching *Perry Mason* and reading books about Clarence Darrow. What really excited me was the idea of trials in the courtroom. So I tentatively lined up a job with the Alameda County District Attorney's Office. I wasn't certain that this would be my career direction, but I was sure about one thing: I was not going to succumb to the pressures of security, of economic expectations, or of the norms of society in making my decision.

Those pressures are very real. It is no small thing to face an onslaught of questions and opinions from family and friends when making an important decision. It was easy in my case, at that time, to make my decision with minimal pressure from others. I was single. I had no financial responsibilities. My decision would affect no one but myself. If I had not been in such an independent situation, my decision would have been more difficult to make. The problem many people face when making such decisions in the midst of pressures— and this is a problem faced often in negotiating situations—is that they rush into a bad choice. They feel themselves strongly torn between competing values. They feel confusion, tension, and stress.

Leon Festinger, a professor of psychology, developed a theory for this phenomenon—he called it cognitive dissonance. This principle suggests that the psyche can tolerate only so much indecision and wavering between the poles of a difficult choice. At a certain point, the strained psyche forces the conflicted person to make a decision simply to relieve the tension and anxiety. Unfortunately, this relief is short-lived, and the person then finds himself often facing the larger challenge and greater confusion of living with or working his way out of a bad move—a choice of the wrong career; a purchase of the wrong automobile; a marriage to the wrong person.

It is essential to think through your own value system, to clarify and prioritize the issues, considerations, and questions that matter to you *before* stepping into the process of decision making. It is critical to ask yourself what is going to make you happy *before* going out to pursue it. This is critically true in terms of the negotiating process. The time to be conceptualizing what exactly it is that you want is not three weeks into the discussions. Unless a person preparing to enter into a negotiation achieves the proper self-awareness, definition, and prioritization of values and goals long before the discussions begin, critical errors will be made. The entire approach to the process will be misguided. Commitments to the wrong positions will be made.

Acquiescence will be given to terms that turn out to be untenable. Unfortunately, it is often the negotiation process itself that clarifies those values. And by then it is too late.

Some people make the conscious choice to separate their personal values from their profession. They divorce their home life, where they may be warm and empathetic human beings, from their behavior in the workplace, where they become dog-eat-dog practitioners of social Darwinism, convinced that the ends justify the means—any means. This kind of personality split, this application of situational ethics, leads to moral confusion and, ultimately, a lack of fulfillment.

I grew up with a generation of people with a marked sense of ideals, who actively worked in many ways to make the world a better place. Today, thirty or so years later, we all feel squeezed—and, in many cases, trapped—by the competing necessities and economic realities of our obligations and responsibilities to our professions, to our families, and to ourselves. As a result of such pressure, it's easy for our fundamental values, which were so important to us when we were younger, to be compromised or pushed aside.

That is a dangerous thing to do. The amount of success, economic or otherwise, achieved by abandoning or ignoring one's values cannot compare to the degree of success, satisfaction, and fulfillment achieved by applying those values to the process.

- Identify, clarify, and prioritize your values before beginning the process of negotiation.
- Depend on your values as a guide throughout the process.
- Do not allow yourself to abandon, ignore or compromise your values.

PASSION

MY VALUES WERE well formed by the time I returned from my post-law-school travels. It was soon thereafter that I found a profession to which I could apply them.

During my first year in law school, I had taken a job as a dorm counselor at Berkeley. Among the students living in the dorm where I worked were Steve Wozniak, who later went on to form Apple Computer; Brian Maxwell, who founded the PowerBar company; and Bob Sarlatte, who became a nationally known actor and comedian. Also living there was the university's entire freshman football team, including a young quarterback named Steve Bartkowski. Steve and I became good friends. Not long after I got back from traveling in the spring of 1975, I got a call from him. By then he had wrapped up a storied college career and had become the first pick in that January's NFL draft, selected by the Atlanta Falcons.

Athlete representation was pretty much a fledgling profession at that time. Fewer than half the NFL's first-round picks were represented by agents. The others depended on family or friends for advice, or they simply conducted their own negotiations. Steve had an attorney to represent him, but by late that spring he had become unhappy with the course of their discussions with the Falcons. So he approached me and asked if I would consider representing him.

I knew nothing about this profession, but I knew Steve fairly well, and I liked him. I respected him. His values seemed to be essentially in concert with mine, which was no small consideration, as I will explain shortly.

Beyond the question of Steve's values in particular was the issue of whether this industry in general, the business of professional sports, was one I could put my heart into. Did I care about it? Did it excite me? Could it accommodate not just my values but my *passion*?

This question of passion is as important as that of values when it comes to preparing for a career or for a specific negotiation. Not only do you need to believe in the work you do, but you must love it; it must excite and energize you.

There was no question that sports did that for me. Just as the seeds of my values were planted early in my life, so was a deep passion for sports. My paternal grandfather, John Steinberg, managed Los Angeles's Hillcrest Country Club, which had been created in the middle of this century for Jewish show business figures who were outcast at the time, along with Catholics and blacks, by the established country clubs around that city. My grandfather was a personable, compelling man. Among my earliest memories was coming into the club one day and having him introduce me to Elvis Presley, who gave me an autographed guitar. I would often watch my grandfather play gin rummy in the afternoons with Jack Benny, George Burns, Groucho Marx, George Jessel. These men were all big baseball fans. It was George Burns who took me to see my first professional baseball game—the old Hollywood Stars of the Pacific Coast League, who played in a place called Gilmore Field.

Like tens of thousands of kids—and adults—in Los Angeles, I was ecstatic when the Brooklyn Dodgers moved west in 1958. I'll never forget how my grandfather got me out of school with a note about "urgent family business" so he could take me with him to attend the Dodgers' opening-day game that year, the first regular-season major-league baseball game ever played in the L.A. Coliseum. I was a Dodgers kid. I grew up listening to Vin Scully on the radio every day, that incomparable voice of his describing my heroes—Sandy Koufax, Maury Wills, Don Drysdale, and the rest.

The San Francisco Giants, with Willie Mays, Juan Marichal and Orlando Cepeda, were our archrivals. How ironic that I would be asked thirty-four years later by San Francisco mayor Frank Jordan to head an effort to stop the Giants from moving their franchise to Tampa Bay. Franchise movements have always seemed wrong to me. The sense of pain and loss felt by a community, especially by young kids, when a team leaves a city is enormous. I have always been concerned about this, which is why, after we were successful in saving the Giants, I helped Mayor Elihu Harris in Oakland find a local buyer for the Oakland A's in 1994 and led a less successful effort to save the Los Angeles Rams in 1995.

I've never forgotten being in the coliseum for "Roy Campanella Night," watching 90,000 people hold up lit matches as a tribute to the much-loved Dodgers catcher, who had been paralyzed by an automobile accident.

That's the kind of drama, the intense shared emotion with tens of thousands of other people, that makes sports so special. That's the kind of moment that makes someone a sports fan for life. Those early experiences—and dozens more like them—convinced me of the bonding power of sports, its capability to connect people to one another, in families, in a community, even across an entire nation. There are few forces in America as central to the social fabric of our society as the relationship between professional sports and its fans. There is nothing that comes close to touching the lives of as many American men and boys—and, increasingly, women and girls—as sports.

When Steve Bartkowski approached me about representing him, I considered what this opportunity might mean in terms of applying my values. I could see that whether they like it or not, athletes have an enormous effect on their audience—an effect that can be used to change lives for the better. More than any other public figures, professional athletes are totems in our society, triggering imitative behavior, especially among young people. Many young people have a perceptual screen that filters out certain authority figures, such as parents, teachers, principals, coaches, religious leaders, and politicians. But athletes are able to permeate that barrier and reach into the hearts of young people, capturing their admiration and adulation.

In my opinion, those in a position of such influence have not only an opportunity but an obligation to use it to affect lives for the better, to develop and nurture positive behavior, to display the qualities of focus, discipline, team work, and determination, and to show through their actions and attitudes the value of connecting and contributing to the community around them, the community around *all* of us.

It became quite clear to me that if I spent a life in politics or in public service, it would be hard to replicate the effect and impact that I could have through becoming involved in professional sports. This was an opportunity to extend the values I believed in into an industry that I adored.

· Seek opportunities to combine your values with your passion.

YOUR CLIENTS' VALUES

THE MID-1970S was a dizzyingly strange time to become a sports agent. I should say here that I am an attorney. I practice law. Bob Woolf, the founding father of the business of professional athlete representation, used to stop and correct every person who used the word *agent* to describe our profession. But the term has become ubiquitous, and there's no use fighting it.

When I began in this business twenty-five years ago, there was not a well-defined profession of sports law. It was chaotic, essentially unregulated, as lawless and filled with grifters and con artists as the Wild West. Teams were able to ignore agents—there was no guaranteed right for an athlete to be represented at all. Individuals calling themselves agents were everywhere. They went to college campuses, offered players money, cars and women, and induced athletes to sign binding representation contracts prior to the expiration of the players' collegiate eligibility. This was a violation of NCAA rules. Some players would sign with three or four agents and take money from each of them. Often these players signed over power of attorney to the agents, giving the agents the right to write checks out of the players' bank accounts. This practice led to fraudulent withdrawals and certainly did not prepare the players for the financial responsibilities they would need for the rest of their lives.

College All-Star games were the worst, virtual shopping malls. A player would come back to his hotel room after practice at one of these events and find two women waiting for him, bought and paid for by someone who called himself an agent. I remember one case where two agents got together and negotiated in a room at the Senior Bowl as to which one of them would ultimately represent a player who had signed with them both.

It became clear to me that if I was going to make this profession my career, I would have to set up and apply my own standards—not just for myself, but for the players I represented. The industry offered no standards. I made a decision to try and represent athletes who would serve as role models, who would be willing to retrace their roots to reward the high school, collegiate, and professional cities that had shaped and supported them, setting up programs that would enhance the quality of life in these communities. This decision—to adjust my work to accommodate my values, rather than vice versa—remains at the core of the success I have enjoyed. But it was by no means a difficult decision for me to make. Anyone whose profession involves representing clients knows that such work necessitates carving out a little piece of your life to share with each person you represent. Every athlete I choose to represent is a reflection of me and of my lifestyle. I want to make sure that I'm sharing my life with people whose values I respect, people who are going to make an impact in the world that is measured by more than how many dollars they earned or how many yards they gained on the football field.

Whatever the nature of your business, whatever type of client or product you might represent, the point is the same: It is critical that you find the right match of values in your client or product and yourself, that you do as much as you can to surround yourself in the workplace or any other environment with people who share your fundamental values.

1. Align yourself with people who share your values.

Focusing on "role models" greatly narrows the field of available clients. The professional athletes of today live, more than ever before, in a world of external adulation, to the extent that many of them do not generally build strong internal values. Too many of them are self-absorbed, convinced that they are the center of the world and that everyone else is there to serve them. Too many of them wind up disconnected from the rest of society, and that is dangerous in many ways.

I have watched this disconnection of athletes from society become increasingly pronounced in the past quarter century. By and large, the players I see today have not grown up with the same sense of idealism that their predecessors did. They think of sports much more as a business than as a game. From the time they first begin drawing attention for their talent—for some of them, before they are even in high school—that talent is equated with the riches and fame of professional sports. Early on, for many of these young athletes, the game becomes a means to an end as much as an end in itself. And their sense of competitiveness extends much further than the boundaries of the playing field. They see the world from a social Darwinist perspective, as a place with limited available resources where everyone fights for the largest piece of the pie. This every-man-for-himself approach bombards them from every direction, from what they see in the business world to the programming they watch on television.

Speaking of television, that medium has had as much effect on today's athletes as it has on the entire generation coming of age today. Two hundred competing stations, viewers armed with remote-control clickers, the cascade of colors and sounds splashed across big screens— all this has spawned a freneticism a world away from the sleepy black-and-white world of *Howdy Doody* and *Rin Tin Tin* that I grew up with. Young people now coming of age have markedly shorter attention spans and an overwhelming desire for immediate gratification. The external influences on them, from MTV to video games, have been much faster paced. They want what they want, and they want it now.

Too many athletes lack a sense of history and context, which is something that deeply concerns me. We are seeing a generation coming of age that knows alarmingly little about the individuals and events that shaped the world it has inherited. I remember driving with a client one day and passing a billboard that made reference to the Beatles. I began telling him what a revolutionary impact *Sgt. Pepper's Lonely Hearts Club Band* had had on our entire culture when that album was first released. When I was done, he looked at me and said, in all sincerity, "Leigh, who are the Beatles?"

With this understood, I would still maintain that most athletes today embody the best fundamental values of hard work, sacrifice, loyalty, and pursuit of excellence. It is hard for many sports fans to have that impression, given the daily catalog of athletes' misbehavior that is recorded in each morning's newspapers. The sports sections tend to read more like business sections or, even worse, crime sections. The media tends to feed the public appetite for scandal, and with the resultant tabloidization of news coverage, it is easy to lose perspective. If we tracked five thousand young lawyers, accountants, or steelworkers around for a year, subjecting them to the same scrutiny faced by professional athletes, I am certain that their rates of drunk driving, domestic abuse, and substance abuse would be higher than those of athletes. The average fan watching sports today has the sense that professional athletics has gone to the dogs in terms of behavior and values, that innocence and beauty have been taken out of sports by greedy, self-indulgent athletes. The reality is that most players wake up in the morning, drive themselves safely to the ballpark, gladly give autographs, go out and perform at peak levels even when injured, drive home in a safe, sober condition, play with their children, and go to sleep with their wives, none of which is news. Any deviance from that normal behavior *is* news, which is a distortion of reality and is not entirely fair to the majority of professional athletes, who lead normal, uneventful lives off the playing field.

It was with issues like this in mind that I created, back in 1975, a general profile of the type of person I wanted to represent—not the type of athlete, but the type of *person.*

Athletic ability is a given with my potential clients. That has to be there. But beyond probing athletic strengths and weaknesses, my partners and I scrupulously investigate a potential client's personal qualities as well.

We talk to scouts, coaches, teammates, family members, friends, neighbors, and reporters about what the player is like *off* the field—on campus, in class, around town. Then we go and spend time with the athlete, preferably at his home, with his family, among his buddies, in his neighborhood, hanging out, getting a sense of what kind of an individual he is and allowing him to get a feel for us as well.

To get to know Warrick Dunn his senior year at Florida State, I went home with him to Baton Rouge, where we explored his hometown from his perspective. He showed me his high school, took me to the hills he used to run up and down to build strength and stamina, showed me his favorite place to eat, shared some Creole food with me, then took me back to his house, where the living room was jammed with brothers and sisters and cousins, all of whom Warrick, along with his grandmother Willie Wheeler, had taken care of ever since his mother, Betty Dunn Smothers, a police officer, had been shot and killed during a robbery when Warrick was in high school. All I needed to know about Warrick Dunn's character became evident from the way I watched him treat his family and friends that day.

In a completely different environment, Ryan Leaf showed me the same kinds of qualities. I had concerns about Ryan. I had read a few stories during his college career in which he came across as somewhat brash. It turned out that he was apprehensive about me as well. He wondered if he would receive the time and attention he needed from an agent with as many high-profile clients as I have. The fears on both sides vanished after I spent a weekend with him and his family at their home in Great Falls, Montana. Ryan's parents, John and Marcia, sat with me in their dining room and quizzed me extensively about the fast-lane nature of professional football and talked about their concern that Ryan should maintain the values they had taught him. As for Ryan himself, we spent Sunday afternoon down in the family's basement watching the NFL games and talking. He referred to several older players, such as Warren Moon, in glowing, reverent terms. This was not the attitude of a young man wrapped up in himself. At one point he asked if I would give him one of my clients' telephone numbers, so he could call and talk a little bit. When I gave him Troy Aikman's number, his face lit up as if it were Christmas morning. "Mom," he said. "Can you believe it? I've got *Troy Aikman's* phone number!" So much for Ryan Leaf's brashness.

We all have stereotypes. I'll never forget flying up to Yakima, Washington, to meet Drew Bledsoe's family during his junior year at Washington State University. I checked into the Ramada Inn, called the Bledsoes, and was told that Drew's father, Mac, would meet me out front. I had spoken with Mac on the telephone. I knew he was a teacher, an expert on the subject of family dynamics and raising children. I knew he crisscrossed the country giving lectures and workshops on that subject. But we had never met in person.

When the time arrived, I walked outside the hotel and waited. A few people were gathered around a couple of pickup trucks by the front doors, a fellow was sitting on a motorcycle, and a couple of men in coats and ties came and went from their cars. But I didn't see anyone who vaguely fit my idea of the father of Drew Bledsoe.

Time passed, and no one showed. I went back in and called the Bledsoe home. Drew's mother, Barbara, told me Mac had to be there. He had left the house some time ago.

So I went back out. The only person now in sight was this guy on the motorcycle, still sitting there with his bushy hair and mustache.

I walked up and said, "Are you Mac Bledsoe?"

He didn't blink an eye. "That's me," he said.

Then I climbed on the back of his Harley and he took me to his home.

These are the ways I like to learn about people. Sometimes I don't have to go far. Tony Gonzalez, the tight end for the Kansas City Chiefs, who became my client last year after finishing his career at Cal, grew up in Huntington Beach. I can look out the window of my office to the north and virtually see Huntington Beach High School, where Tony played ball. A few miles to the south is Mission Viejo, where Rob Johnson, quarterback for the Buffalo Bills, grew up. Toby Bailey, the star UCLA basketball player, who was drafted by the Lakers and then traded to Phoenix Suns, is the son of John Bailey, who grew up in Los Angeles as I did. I've known about Rob and Tony and Toby since they were kids. By the time I formally spoke with them as prospective clients, I already knew that we shared the same culture and values.

If I decide that a potential client is indeed an individual we want to represent, and if he decides the same about us, then I let him know what will be expected of him, that we will be developing a long-term relationship, one aimed at the player developing him*self*—not just his athletic ability, but his quality and worth as an individual. I explain that when we can get our athletes to contribute to and get involved in society, in circles of people beyond the tight ring of coaches, other athletes, and the press that typically defines their existence, it exposes them to a larger, *realer* world than the one they know.

These kinds of activities—personal involvement in community, civic, and business organizations—force the athletes to look outside themselves, to use their brains, skills, and such qualities as dedication and determination in arenas beyond just the physical. It forces them to think about their role in the world as citizens, and it helps them realize that they will eventually have to move into that world once their playing career is over. I point out to them that in three to ten years, their athletic careers will be behind them and the rest of their lives will lie ahead. If they don't start preparing now—and money will be the least of their worries—they are going to have a shocking adjustment to make.

I am as gratified by the careers many of my clients have built after retiring from football as I am by the success they enjoyed during their time in uniform. Rich Martini, a former wide receiver with the Raiders, is now the CEO of a computer software company in Northern California. Rolf Benirschke, formerly a placekicker with the Chargers, has put together a successful investment and travel agency, as well as traveling the country giving motivational lectures and serving for a short time as the daytime host of *Wheel of Fortune*. Deron Cherry, a former safety with the Chiefs, has an Anheuser-Busch distributorship in Kansas City, which is essentially a license to print money. He also is a part owner of the Jacksonville Jaguars NFL franchise. Howie Long, whom we represented at the end of his career with the Los Angeles Raiders, has gone on to become an analyst and host for Fox Sports and to launch a motion picture acting career. Ken Ruettgers, former Green Bay Packers tackle, authored a children's book, and Jack Trudeau, former Colts quarterback, owns a golf course in Indianapolis. Among my clients who are still in the NFL but are already positioning themselves for postathletic careers is Raiders quarterback Wade Wilson, who has earned his stockbroker's license and will move into that field when he's finished with football. Steve Young has earned his law degree. Troy Aikman owns his own automobile dealership in Dallas.

Troy's business in particular represents a new trend in professional sports, one in which the athletes, beyond simply being licensed spokespeople doing endorsements for various businesses and products, are now becoming the equity owners of those businesses, using their skills and resources to build equity. Rather than earning a certain amount of income endorsing someone else's dealership, Troy endorses the Troy Aikman Auto Mall and pays himself.

These are the kinds of possibilities and potential I discuss with all prospective clients. But I insist that they accept my basic terms, which include a commitment to community involvement. Some refuse. One player I met with several years ago, an All-Pro running back who was available for free agency, laughed when I talked about charities. "My only charity," he said with a satisfied smile, "is me."

I showed him the door. He was a tremendously talented athlete, and he made some people a lot of money. But he was simply not the type of person I wanted to represent.

Neither was the All-American college quarterback who, I learned from talking to scouts, players, and coaches, cared only about his performance and statistics. When we met, he spent the entire session denigrating the other quarterbacks in the draft. Again, a tremendous talent—but just not my kind of human being.

Very few of the athletes who become my clients disappoint me or let me down with their attitude or behavior. I can count on one hand the number of players with whom I have had to phase out the business relationship because their values wound up clashing with mine. One was a talented defensive end who, besides being charged with assault in a bar fight—which is not an uncommon hazard of this profession—left his wife and began dating a Hollywood actress. His defiantly reckless public behavior—he and the actress had each other's name tattooed on their rear ends and displayed them for the press— was what bothered me most. It's a shame, because I think he wasted his future and his career.

Not that I am looking for saints or angels. None of us would like to be judged on the worst mistakes we made in our early twenties. Basically, all I want is someone with a good heart, with a little bit of a social conscience, usually with a strong family background behind him, someone who is ready to listen and to learn and to grow. He may come from the inner city of Miami or from a tiny town in the fields of Oklahoma—it makes no difference. The qualities I am interested in can be found anywhere.

Derrick Thomas, the linebacker for the Kansas City Chiefs, for example, was not immediately obvious as my kind of client when he called me in 1990, after his rookie NFL season, and asked if I would represent him. Derrick was raised on the tough streets of Miami. He had the hard edge that most young men who endure the type of environment he grew up in must have to survive. He had established himself after just one season as one of the premier linebackers in the NFL, but I had no idea of what kind of individual he was.

I was intrigued, however, by the fact that before Derrick called me, he had gone to the library and actually done research on agents. He wanted to adjust his contract with Kansas City, but he wanted more than that, he said. He wanted to expand his horizons and make an impact on the world.

Derrick listened carefully during our first telephone conversation. I explained my approach. I talked about the importance of getting involved in charitable and community activities. I told him how I felt about holdouts. I described my entire philosophy of a player's role in the NFL. At the end of the conversation, I asked him to keep in touch.

With some players, that might have been the last I heard of them. But Derrick followed through. He did stay in touch. And in the meantime he took every piece of advice I gave him. After having told the entire world that he was going to hold out from training camp, he swallowed his pride and went. That told me a lot about his courage.

Today, Derrick has become an influential part of the Kansas City community. He developed a novel concept for teaching young children to read, which turned into the Third and Long children's literacy foundation. He stood beside President Clinton not long ago and gave a very moving speech about his father, who was lost as a bomber over Vietnam. Derrick is an intense, emotional man, who plays an intense, emotional sport. Off the field, he shows great compassion for others. The NFL agrees. In 1995, he was named the league's Man of the Year for humanitarian services, following in the footsteps of my clients Rolf Benirschke, Warren Moon, and Troy Aikman.

Many of my clients' involvement in their communities has become fairly well known over the years: Steve Young's Forever Young Foundation, a Bay Area children's program that he started with seed money of $2 million; Troy Aikman's financing of new wings for two Dallas area hospitals; Warrick Dunn's purchase of new homes for single-parent families in the Tampa area; Ray Childress's Criminator Foundation, an organization that fights crime in the Houston area; John Starks's foundation, which has aided high schools in his hometown of Tulsa; Russell Maryland's foundation, which helps Chicago's and Oakland's inner-city youth; Greg Anthony's foundation, which helps kids in Las Vegas; Warren Moon's Crescent Moon Foundation, which gives grants to students to attend college; Eric Karros's endowment of a $100,000 baseball scholarship to UCLA; John Lynch and John Allred's program to help the San Dieguito Boys and Girls Club in San Diego; Carnell Lake's foundation to help underprivileged kids in Pittsburgh; Rolf Benirschke's Kicks for Critters, which raised more than $1 million for endangered species at the San Diego Zoo; as well as dozens of high school and college scholarships established by players I represent.

Not only do each of these efforts benefit the recipients, but there is no doubt that they also build my clients into better people, which makes them worth more to the people who pay their salaries—the team owners.

Values create value. That is a bottom-line, dollars-and-cents reality.

- Character counts.
- Values create value.
- Choose only clients whose core values you respect—and who respect yours.

GOALS

WHETHER YOU REPRESENT A company or are an employee, a parent dealing with children, or a husband or wife dealing with a spouse, before any effective discussion of a decision can even begin, it is crucial to sit down and think through exactly what you *want*. Not in vague terms. Not in half-baked general terms. As precisely and specifically as possible. It is necessary to be able to state to yourself just exactly what it is that would make you happy—in a particular job, in a career, in a marriage, as a family, in a car, in a home, on a vacation. Whatever the subject of an impending negotiation, the first step toward the discussion is defining your goals.

This is the first topic I discuss with a player once he becomes my client. We need to find out what is truly important to him, what his priorities are, what the shape of his life looks like—or what he would *like* it to look like—not just now, but in the future. I listen carefully. I ask questions. I push and probe, forcing him to think through issues he might never have thought through before, to ask himself questions he might never have asked. What we are doing is exploring his psychology, clarifying his hopes and dreams, working to help him understand what exactly it is that makes him happy.

Some, but not all, of the questions we consider are economic. Is he looking for short-term financial gain or long-term security? Is his family a factor? What might he consider in terms of a second career? Is it more important to him to be on a winning team or to make more money with a less successful club? Does he prefer a certain coaching system, a specific style of playing surface? Is the system the team plays one that the player's skills are adaptable to? How long does he see his career lasting? How important is the size of the city he will be living in? Does he prefer the East Coast or the West Coast? Does the climate matter to him? What about the availability of endorsements? The distance from his family? From his friends?

My partner Jeff Moorad, while negotiating a contract for Matt Williams, the All-Star third baseman of the Cleveland Indians, faced a unique paradox in early 1998. Matt had recently divorced and his three children were living with their mother in Arizona. Being cut off from his children made Matt miserable. He and Jeff approached Indians general manager John Hart about a possible trade to the new expansion Arizona Diamondbacks team.

Hart was happy with Matt as his third baseman and had no desire to trade him. But part of why Cleveland is a highly desirable team for players is the enlightened attitude of its management. Hart empathized with Matt and executed a trade with Arizona. The new $45 million, five-year contract that Jeff negotiated with the Diamondbacks was frosting on the cake. To Matt, being a full-time father was the most important priority in his life, and we knew that the dynamic Diamondbacks' owner, Jerry Colangelo, had built the nicest baseball stadium in the major leagues and would take care of Matt over time.

One of our clients, NBA point guard Greg Anthony, possesses an exceptional ability to reflect on his own feelings, to figure out precisely what will make him happy. As a teenager, Greg attended a world economic summit with then-President George Bush, and while at the University of Nevada at Las Vegas, he created his own sports-apparel company. Greg instructed me prior to the 1991 NBA draft to try matching him with a team in a major market so that he could play basketball *and* address some of his off-the-court goals. He wound up being drafted by the New York Knicks. Last year Greg decided that winning had become his top priority, so he joined the Portland Trailblazers, where teamwork rules and an NBA championship is realistic.

You need to ask yourself or your clients these same types of questions—regardless of your profession. The degree of autonomy a job offers may matter more to you than the money you earn. You may treasure working without feeling hovered over, finishing a task without having a tremendous fear of the consequences, using creativity and entrepreneurship without the limits of a prescribed structure. The money you make might matter less than being able to live in a particular part of the country. What matters most to you might be simply working for a corporation that you think is ethical or that produces a product that is beneficial to society, a product you believe in.

Timing also makes a difference in terms of one's goals. In some situations, you might be looking for security; in others, freedom. These priorities may differ depending on where you are in your career. If you're young, filled with ideas and energy and potential, security and a long-term contract may mean less than having the freedom and opportunity to explore and increase your abilities and your value.

If you're older, on the other hand, you might be at a stage in your career where security has become more important than growth, and so you will be looking for different, more stable, more defined, more committed terms in your contract than you might have desired at an earlier point in your career.

A large part of my job is to help people in very difficult, very tense, very time-sensitive decision-making situations avoid making mistakes in terms of satisfying their true interests. A key first stage in this process—in any negotiation process—is figuring out precisely what your true interests are.

Achieving this type of self-awareness and clarity is not always easy, but it has to occur. The couple out shopping for a car, for example, must understand whether it's the size and roominess of the automobile that matters most or the horsepower and performance. Maybe it's the ease of maneuverability in snow or ice. It might be the prestige of the name on the car that matters most or its lines and its color. Does its resale value concern you? Its safety record? All of these questions and considerations have to be looked at, discussed, and clarified *before* you step into the marketplace and begin haggling over price.

And when it comes to price, again it is important to consider, clarify, and prioritize competing values and goals. How important is the car you drive compared to the house in which you live or the clothes you wear or the food you eat or the vacations you take or the hobbies you have? In the workplace, how important is the amount of your salary compared to the location of your office, the size of your expense account, the availability of a company car, the comprehensiveness of your benefits package, or the flexibility of your working hours?

Always think these things through prior to getting involved in a negotiation. A simple but helpful exercise is to sit down with a pen and piece of paper and actually write down your values and goals, then prioritize them. You may be surprised by what that list reveals.

What do you want?

Once you have thoroughly and meticulously answered that question, you are ready to prepare for the negotiation.

· Identify, clarify, and prioritize your interests and goals *before* a negotiation begins.

2

PREPARATION

WHOSE REALITY WILL PREVAIL?

THE HIGHEST-SALARIED player in professional football today, Troy Aikman, currently earns $9.5 million per year.

Where does a number like that come from? How can Troy Aikman—or any football player, for that matter—be worth that much money?

This is a question continually asked by sports fans and commentators as one record-breaking contract follows another. People are astounded by the amount of money paid to professional athletes. The number of dollars seems unreal to them.

Reality—this is the underlying focus and the driving force of almost every negotiation: creating and presenting an assessment and interpretation of reality that is convincing to all parties involved.

In most negotiations, each party arrives with its own vision of the circumstances, its own interpretation of the facts, its own sense of what is relevant. Each party honestly and sincerely believes that its position accurately reflects the reality of the situation. Each side has its own sense of the way things are and the way they should be. And so the fundamental question of a negotiation then becomes, *Whose reality is going to prevail?*

An employer may consider a particular employee easily replaceable, someone who is lucky to have a job. The employee, on the other hand, may consider himself singularly valuable, irreplaceable, and deserving of increased compensation.

Whose reality is going to prevail?

A home seller may have no doubt that his house is rich with character, roomy, and solid, a bargain at the price he is asking. The potential buyer might agree that the old house has charm, but through his eyes it is a fixer-upper, with vast and costly improvements and repairs that must be made before it would be in a condition he considers livable.

Whose reality is going to prevail?

An NFL team's general manager may consider its veteran quarterback, whose statistical performance the previous year was the worst of his career, to be on the decline. The player, who missed several games that season due to injuries suffered because of lack of protection by the team's young offensive line and who feels that his statistics suffered because of sacrifices he made for the benefit of the team, has no doubt his best years are still ahead of him.

Whose reality is going to prevail?

In all of these situations, the supporting information each party assembles and the manner in which that information is interpreted and presented will determine the extent to which one party is able to persuade the other to agree with his vision of reality. How effectively, how thoroughly, how creatively, and how *honestly* such information is collected and communicated is the foundation of successful negotiation.

In any negotiation, information is power. That power is diminished by hyperbole, exaggeration, or outright dishonesty. The information on which you base your negotiating position must be accurate and reliable. If it is not, you will lose both the trust and respect of the other party. Your arguments will lose all validity. And your reality will not prevail.

The process of thorough and accurate preparation not only provides you with the foundation on which you will rely throughout the negotiation; it also shows respect for the other party. If you arrive at a negotiation prepared and armed with sound facts and valid arguments, the other party will see that you think enough of him and his capabilities to have done your research and homework.

On the other hand, to arrive unprepared—or to base your position on exaggerated or false information—is insulting to the other party. He may have to deal with you, but he will not trust or respect you. And the process, rather than being one of mutual problem solving, will become one of conflict and struggle.

It is always better to stay on the high ground of accuracy, reliability, and rational persuasion than to sink to dishonesty, dissembling, and force of will.

- Negotiation is a test of realities—yours and the other party's.
- Never forget that the other party believes in his reality as strongly as you believe in yours.
- Your goal in a negotiation is to convince the other party to accept your reality.
- The information on which you base your reality must be accurate and reliable.

VALUE

IN MOST NEGOTIATION situations, the bottom-line focus, the issue for which the concept of reality becomes the context, is the question of value.

How much is that house worth?

How much is that player worth?

How much are *you* worth?

In some instances, there are beginning guidelines for assessing value: area and neighborhood listing sheets for real estate; salaries of other players at the same position in the NFL; salaries of employees with similar jobs in a particular company or industry. But even such guidelines simply provide a general frame of reference, a starting point of comparison. In the end, it is *this* particular house you are talking about, *this* car, *this* player, *this* employee. The value of any of these items or individuals becomes, in the end, whatever the parties agree that it is.

Again, the bedrock question is: Whose reality is going to prevail?

In some situations, there is little or no frame of reference when it comes to the question of value. In the television industry, for example, reality is defined almost completely by the small number of participants—the networks. The least profitable television network in America made hundreds of millions of dollars last year. It said that this had been a *bad* year. That network is, in other words, defining its own reality.

Four years ago, when America's television networks agreed to pay $1.1 billion a year for the rights to broadcast NFL games, many people thought that amount was insanely high. But apparently that price was well within the bounds of reality for the networks themselves, since they agreed this year in their new contract with the league to pay *twice* that amount for the same rights.

Worth is a very loaded term in our society. It comes with a wide range of moral and ethical judgments attached. No one would argue that schoolteachers and police officers and doctors are critical to the health and safety and richness of our society—certainly more critical than a professional-football quarterback or a sports commentator or the Sunday-afternoon broadcast of an NFL game. There is a utopian theory that has been advanced by some economists whereby economic value would be assigned to jobs based on the undesirability of the work that is required. According to this concept, a garbage collector or a janitor would be compensated more than a bank president or an attorney. It's an interesting idea, but until another economic system is developed, we will continue to live and work with the one we have, a system defined by the dynamics of free enterprise, fair market value, and supply and demand.

That is what athletes' salaries are a function of—supply and demand.

That is what the television networks' contracts are a function of.

That is what a teacher's salary is a function of.

That is what *your* salary is a function of.

What is essential to understand as one prepares for a negotiation is that supply and demand—or the *sense* of supply and demand—can, like reality, be adjusted and shifted in a particular direction by building a thorough and convincingly presented case. One's value—or the value of one's product or of one's client—can be maximized by building a strong enough argument for it and by effectively presenting that argument in terms that convince the other party of the need for that product, that client, or you.

I can say, speaking from experience, that in the case of professional athletes' contracts, the salary figures that wind up as sports-page headlines are the result of carefully constructed and persuasively presented portraits of reality. They are based on exhaustively comprehensive factual information and on convincingly plausible projections and predictions about the future. These facts and projections involve the past, present, and future of the player, of the particular team he is negotiating with, and of the league—the industry—in general.

It is essential to understand that in any negotiation, value is always in the eye of the beholder. Whether it is a teenager discussing the amount of his allowance with his parents or a lawyer like myself discussing the terms of Steve Young's contract with the San Francisco 49ers, the goal is to convince the other party of the value of you, your product, or your client.

Beyond the fact that NFL players are the primary commodity of a thriving industry, something else I learned early on about professional football is the severe physical price the players pay to perform in this league. Beyond the short-term pain of their constant injuries, there is, in many cases, lifelong debilitation. Many people are not aware how short an NFL player's career is—3.2 years on average. The physical effects of those very few years on many of these athletes' entire lives can be devastating. Critics of the high salaries paid to professional athletes dismiss this industry as men being paid to play mere games. But it is no game at all when Steve Bartkowski has to struggle with knee pain for the rest of his life.

In 1981, I represented three top draft picks in the National Football League: Ken Easley, as talented and intelligent a player as I've ever represented, who came out of UCLA and had a tremendous career as a strong safety with the Seattle Seahawks before developing degenerative kidney damage, which required dialysis and, eventually, a kidney transplant; Curt Marsh, a warm and caring offensive tackle out of the

University of Washington, whose career with the Raiders left him with a left foot so damaged that it ultimately had to be amputated; and Neil Lomax, a witty and gifted quarterback out of Portland State University, who had to have his hip replaced after his career with the Cardinals was over.

None of these men, or the hundreds more like them, ask anyone for sympathy. But neither do they apologize for the money they earn during their careers. Part of what they are paid for, in addition to their performance, is the long-term physical cost required to make those contributions. As far as I am concerned, the athletes in the NFL earn every penny they are paid.

This is an issue that raises deep and troubling concerns for me. The worst dilemma I have as an attorney practicing in this field is the horrendous toll that professional football takes on the bodies of my clients. Caring for and being as personally invested in them as I am, I have to ask myself how I can continue to facilitate their entry into a game that may leave them crippled. How can I justify representing them?

The quick answer, of course, is that these are bright, aware individuals making knowing choices. Virtually any former NFL player living with injuries suffered during his football career will tell you that he would do it all over again if he were given the chance.

But at the same time, I still feel a queasiness at being an enabler in this process. Part of my response to that discomfort has been to campaign vigorously for better safety conditions in all sports, particularly in the area of concussions. We have worked hard in recent years to assemble the leading experts in head and brain injuries for seminars in which causation and better potential treatment for such injuries are discussed. This is still a frontier area of medical research. No one can precisely tell an athlete which concussion might be the one that will lead to Alzheimer's disease, Parkinson's disease, or premature senility. I have proposed a standardized regimen of grading concussions, along with new rules for mandatory sit-outs and better helmet designs.

It is not always comfortable to crusade for such changes in an industry as tied to tradition and the status quo as this one. I hear protests all the time from football purists, who claim I'm trying to put a dress on the quarterback.

That doesn't bother me. But I remain troubled, even with those efforts, by my own moral dilemma. There is no getting around the fact that there is a conflict here between the industry in which I do business and the detrimental effect of that industry on some of the clients I represent. Someone working in the fields of munitions, tobacco, or alcohol would have to ask himself these same questions. This is a dilemma many people can relate to in many professions, where their own moral standards and the standards of the company for which they work are sometimes contradictory.

There are no simple solutions to questions like these. The best we can do is remain aware of them and try our best to address them.

- *Value* is a relative term.
- Value is a function of supply and demand.
- Value is in the eye of the beholder.

SELF-ASSESSMENT

YOU ARE GOING to have a much better chance of getting to where you want to go if you have an accurate idea of exactly where you are.

We all have a vision of ourselves, a sense of our worth and value in the world. Some of us feel that we are properly appreciated and rewarded by the people in our lives—our employers, our friends, our loved ones. Some of us do not. In any case, one of the most critical, difficult, and awareness-raising steps in the negotiation process is putting that vision of ourselves to the test, laying ourselves bare, and objectively analyzing our strengths and our weaknesses.

This is not an easy thing to do. In many cases, it involves disassembling an image of oneself that has taken a lifetime to construct. But the fact may be that our own sense of ourselves is quite different from the way in which we are perceived by others. We may overrate our strengths and underrate our weaknesses—or vice versa. In either case, we are ill prepared to make a case for ourselves in a negotiation if we have not realistically assessed both our talents and our shortcomings.

Brutal honesty is required here, and you need to find people you trust and respect—from coworkers to supervisors to friends—to join in the process, to speak to you frankly about your skills, abilities, and attributes, *and* about your deficiencies and drawbacks.

It is not always easy to get this information about yourself from others. The natural tendency of most people, when asked to assess or rate the performance or skills of a friend or colleague, is to be "kind." Somehow you must convince them that you want and need the truth.

Are you assertive enough? Do you have a hard time pushing yourself in difficult circumstances? How do you deal with conflict? Do you have the motivation to spend the extra late night or weekend on a project that has to be finished? How well do you analyze situations under stress or a deadline? How do you respond to pressure? Are you a person who accepts responsibility for failures as well as successes, or do you tend to blame others when things go wrong? Are you better at carrying out orders from someone else or initiating action yourself?

These questions are the essence of determining your true market value. Even the answers that you might not like to hear are valuable. If you understand what and where your shortcomings are, not only can you work on strengthening them for the future, but you can also prepare to respond and defend them in the impending negotiation.

Be certain that you will need to address them. A mistake many people make as they approach a negotiation is to assume—or hope—that a troubling issue or question simply won't come up. This is a deadly mistake. Remember that while you are assessing your strengths and weaknesses, the other party is making the same assessment, and his focus will be on your weaknesses. Your assumption should be that the other party will leave no stone unturned, and so it is in your best interest to turn those stones over yourself—*all* of them.

If you do not acknowledge and address your weaknesses—if you avoid them or pretend that they don't exist—you will lose the trust and respect of the other party. If you are dissembling or evasive in any aspect of your arguments, then your entire presentation and position will be suspect.

In my business, the process of assessment is focused on the professional athletes I represent. The information I gather and base my calculations on in terms of a player's physical abilities and skills, of a rookie's draftability or a veteran's free agent value, is largely derivative. I would never pretend to be able to go out on a basketball court and tell you the difference between a great point guard and a mediocre one. I need someone else to tell me. I can judge character and background and determination, but as for pure athletic ability and potential, I depend on a range of reliable experts—scouts, coaches, directors of player personnel, and, in the case of rookies, draft prognosticators—to help me assess a player's talent and potential.

To effectively negotiate in any circumstances, a level of expertise and familiarity with both the product under discussion and the production process is necessary. When discussing the purchase of a car, it helps to understand the differences between a V-6 engine and a V-8. In negotiating for my media clients, I am expected to know that newscasters are called "talent" and a television station is called a "shop." When I discussed an endorsement deal for boxing champion Oscar De La Hoya, I needed to know all there is about the product being discussed and to understand the fundamentals of Oscar's sport. The same with the United States World Cup soccer team, which I represented during bonus and endorsement negotiations in 1994. A negotiator who is not well versed in the specifics of a product, a profession, or an industry will immediately be marked as uninformed, clearly over his head, and a rube to be taken advantage of.

When I started my football practice, I knew no more about football than the average fan. Fortunately, through friendships with people in the Cal and Stanford football programs, I found some great teachers, including coaches Bill Walsh, Mike White, Paul Hackett, Roger Theder, and Al Saunders, all of whom taught me about offensive football, and Gunther Cunningham and Artie Gigantino, who taught me about the defensive part of the game. I also spent extensive time with my clients, asking them about different aspects of the sport.

I would never claim to be an expert, but I have been able to gather enough knowledge to effectively do my job. Such fundamental knowledge is essential in negotiating in any industry.

GETTING A PROFESSIONAL athlete to acknowledge his shortcomings is a particularly difficult thing to do. A key ingredient in any athlete's success, at any level, is his degree of self-confidence. At the professional level, that confidence is supremely necessary. Every NFL running back believes he is as good as Barry Sanders—or could be if he were given the opportunity. The effective athlete totally believes in himself. He visualizes nothing but success.

For many of these players, especially rookies, it may well be the first time in their lives that anyone has ever asked them to consider their weaknesses. In such a case, what I often do is collect not just statistics that might point to a particular flaw or shortcoming; I also gather what other people in the industry—players, sportswriters, general managers—say or have said about my client. In this way, rather than my offending my client by telling him what *I* think, he is hearing it from people whose observations carry some professional and objective weight.

A prime example of this was the famous Kerry Collins "hitch." When Kerry arrived to play in the Senior Bowl in early 1995, he had just come off an undefeated season at Penn State, quarterbacking a very high-powered offense. He had won a number of individual awards, but by the end of Senior Bowl week, the professional scouts had magically discovered that he had a curious hitch in delivery. Since Kerry had been so prolific and successful, it seemed illogical that something like this would matter. But the issue was not whether or not we agreed that this was a problem. The league perceived it as a problem, and so it was. Rather than risk protest and defensiveness from Kerry by explaining the problem myself, I collected a number of coaches' and other experts' observations that had appeared in print. On the basis of this material, Kerry and I agreed that we had to correct this problem. At that point, we enlisted former 49ers head coach and noted offensive football tactician Bill Walsh to work with Kerry and, in essence, to "de-hitch" him.

When National Basketball Association scouts said that shooting guard Miles Simon, from the University of Arizona, had a shot that was "too low," we had him work intensely with basketball guru Howard Avery to correct it.

J. R. Henderson, the small forward with the Vancouver Grizzlies, had been used at center during his senior year at UCLA and needed to perfect his skills facing the basket. Toby Bailey, Henderson's teammate at UCLA, looked for help in addressing a perceived inconsistency of shooting mechanics.

A similar process occurred in early 1998 with Ryan Leaf. Every February, NFL teams hold a scouting combine in Indianapolis, where they closely scrutinize the top potential draft picks. All of the players are weighed and measured. Ryan weighed in at 261 pounds, which is a great weight for an offensive guard but a little heavy for a quarterback. I relayed the scouts' concerns about this to Ryan. He was initially defensive, which is natural. "I played in the Rose Bowl at 250," he said. "Who *wouldn't* gain ten pounds on the postseason banquet circuit?" The fact remained, however, that the issue had to be addressed. We enlisted the help of Chuck Williams, a nutritionist and bodybuilder, who put Ryan on a rigid no-carbohydrate diet. By late March, Ryan weighed a svelte 238.

The point in instances such as these is not to deflate or knock my client down. This is a process of *con*struction, not *de*struction. We all have our knocks. This is something I point out to each of my clients. I remind them that there has never been an athlete, not even a number-one draft pick, who has not had his detractors. Troy Aikman had plenty of critics his rookie season. Joe Montana was viewed early in his career as a player with no future at all: His legs were skinny, his arm was not strong enough. If there is one setting where all such shortcomings will be trotted out, it will be in a contract negotiation. And so we must be prepared with answers for everything, our strengths and our weaknesses.

· Do not overrate yourself.
· Do not underrate yourself.
· Do not ask others to assess you if you want to hear only praise.

· Be certain that your weaknesses will come up in a negotiation.
· Be prepared to address your weaknesses as well as your strengths.

THE MARKET

IN THE SPRING of 1975, when I agreed to represent Steve Bartkowski in his discussions with the Atlanta Falcons, the process of negotiation in the NFL was very rudimentary. There was no guaranteed right of representation, no assurance that a team would even talk to a player who had an agent. Some owners were openly disgusted by the notion of a sports attorney. Team executives would say they did not deal with agents, period, and slam the phone down. They would threaten a player who hired an agent by telling that player that he would be cut. With the "reserve clause" in effect, which made a player strictly the property of the team that had the rights to him, the athlete—and his agent—had few options.

Making matters even more difficult was how little information was available in terms of the market. Unlike today, where records of past and present salaries and offers are well publicized and readily available to be used as a basis for determining comparative worth— what we call comparables—in 1975 no one knew what anyone else was being paid. This was largely by the league's design. As much as possible, the teams kept such information in strict confidence. In most situations, a player had little or no idea what the player drafted in front of him or behind him was getting. There was virtually no concept of the market.

This practice of obscuring financial information has long been a tradition among employers in the American marketplace. By equating professionalism with an unwillingness to divulge salaries, managers and executives attempt to imbue in their employees the inviolable sanctity of revenue and salary figures. This is almost always an attempt to maintain a level of ignorance among employees. There is an in-grained American spirit of modesty and privacy about financial matters that I respect. But at the same time, the lack of information about such matters in the workplace has allowed enormous inequities to be maintained over generations. The revelation of these kinds of figures in any industry almost always has the effect of raising employees' salaries. The emergence of this information in professional sports has resulted in enormous, and justifiable, increases in player salaries.

It was difficult to get this kind of information twenty years ago. In 1976 I represented Steve Rivera, a wide receiver from Cal who was drafted by San Francisco in the fourth round. The 49ers' third-round draft pick had been Randy Cross, a center from UCLA who is now a CBS commentator. Since these were both mid-round draft picks, it would have helped me to know what Randy Cross had been paid in order to get a similar contract for Steve. I expressed this need to Jack White, the 49ers' general manager at the time, and he agreed to show me Randy Cross's contract. He then offered a proposal for Steve based on the signing bonus and salaries I had seen on Cross's contract. What Jack White had not shown me were a considerable set of incentive and roster bonus payments that were included in an addendum to Cross's contract. Fortunately, I found out about those before accepting White's offer.

In Steve Bartkowski's case, I did as much research as possible, calling other agents, talking to sports writers in various cities, talking to the few people I knew at the time working with various NFL teams. The information I was able to gather was relatively sketchy. The average NFL player's salary at the time was roughly $40,000, I knew that. The previous standard-bearers in terms of Steve's position in the draft were O. J. Simpson, who received $350,000 for five years with the Buffalo Bills, and Joe Namath, who was paid $412,000 for four years with the New York Jets.

That was essentially all I was able to learn about salaries at that point, but at least it was a start. And it is the same start anyone must make in beginning research to prepare for a negotiation. Typically, a negotiator must respond to a market that has already been defined. He must learn all there is to know about that market, not just as it exists at the moment, but also its recent history and its likely direction in the future. Gathering this information makes it possible to affect that direction, to create your reality. While in most situations a deal is limited by the context of the existing market (for home sales or car sales or kids' allowances or salaries at your particular position within a company), there is almost always room to push the boundary. *If* you come armed with information.

Unfortunately, most people enter a negotiation virtually unarmed. Men and women who don't do this for a living typically make the mistake of negotiating before they are ready. They've done little or no preparation. They have a vague, often arbitrary, notion of what they want, and they march forward with little in hand but that. They are not properly prepared to get the results they are seeking, and so they rarely get those results. Instead, they often feel disappointment and even resentment—against the other party, against *themselves*—once the deal is done and they must live with the less-than-satisfactory consequences.

A question you must answer long before you begin the negotiation itself is, What is the market?

Do your research. Find out what similar houses are selling for in your area—not just what people are asking, but what people are paying. Have your real estate broker check the listings and the city records office. Call other sellers. Call other buyers. Study the trend of prices in the past several years. Are they climbing? Are they falling? In which direction might they be headed in the next several years? Ask the same questions about a car you might buy or a job you might take or a raise in salary you might want.

It takes some digging, a bit of detective work, some effort, and perhaps some inconvenience. It helps to be comfortable calling people—sometimes strangers—and asking them questions. Whether you are comfortable doing this or not, it is a necessity for all that will follow. Without such fundamental information, you are crippled before you even begin.

- Research your "comparables"—what others in your market are paid for the same product or services you provide.
- Study not just where your market is but where it has been in the past and where it might go in the future.

THE COMPANY

THE NEXT STEP is to learn as much as possible about the particular company with whom you will be negotiating.

In my case, the company is whichever team I am planning to deal with in a particular situation. The factors I look at include the team's playing philosophy and off-field policies, the history of the franchise, the quality of management and the way it treats its people, past salaries, team performance, team needs as a whole and at specific positions, attendance, the size of the television market, the negotiating style of the other side, its short- and long-term goals, the dynamics of previous deals it has made. I study the team's payroll situation closely, to understand the organization's limits and to anticipate at what point its negotiator might say, "Look, we don't disagree with you that this amount of money is fair, but we just can't build the team if we do that." If I can see that statement coming, I can have a response to it, a possible solution.

When I was negotiating Darrell Russell's rookie contract with the Oakland Raiders, Bruce Allen, who was handling the agreement for the Raiders, responded to our proposal with one of the more entertaining faxes I have ever received. "After careful review of the current job market," he wrote, "I have decided not to accept your offer. Since I've been married for just over two years and my son is only seven months old, I believe it would be unfair to my family to start a new career at this particular moment."

Bruce's problem was the limitation imposed by the NFL's salary cap. So I pulled out a detailed Raiders budget, which we had already prepared—I have a team of "capologists," led by my partners Jeff Moorad and David Dunn, along with Scott Parker, whose job is to take every possible premise or concept or situation involving the league's salary-cap restrictions and figure out a way to work around it—and I showed Allen, using his team's own figures, how to construct bonus-heavy contracts with lower cap numbers that would allow him to keep his team together, satisfy his other players, *and* give our client what he wanted.

When I represented Ki-Jana Carter as a rookie running back out of Penn State, drafted first by the Cincinnati Bengals in 1995, a large factor in my approach to those discussions was knowing that the Bengals were going through the process of building a new stadium, which required voter support with a local referendum. The team's attendance was down, and the Bengals were struggling to convince the community that building this stadium was something the city should do.

This was a situation where a company's agenda worked in our favor. The Bengals were fighting to win the public's confidence. If they failed to sign their top draft pick, what would that say to the city that was deciding whether or not to build the team a new place to play? The Bengals needed to sign Ki-Jana Carter to convince the city of Cincinnati that they were moving in a positive direction. Mike Brown, the team's owner and general manager, is as good as they come, as bright and tough a negotiator as there is in professional football. But even the toughest have to respond to circumstances. In this situation, Mike Brown had far greater concerns than the size of Ki-Jana's signing bonus. Those marginal dollars were infinitesimal compared to the economic upside of a brand-new stadium that would ensure the Bengals' future in that city. Brown's priority was to be able to offer the fans of Cincinnati some excitement and real hope for that franchise. When we finally signed a $19.2 million package, which included a record rookie signing bonus of $7.125 million, we were fulfilling both Mike Brown's needs and those of our client—the Bengals won their referendum and proceeded with plans for a new stadium.

Besides learning all I can about specific team circumstances such as those faced by the Bengals with their stadium, I also study every city in the league, to get a sense of each community, its issues, and the climate of the general public in that particular place. I subscribe to two dozen daily newspapers from around the nation and the same number of magazines. In recent years, I have begun to use the Internet, which provides a wealth of instantly accessible information on virtually any subject.

Beyond such sources, I depend greatly on direct contact with people. We have friends and contacts across the country who call or fax us articles and information concerning our clients. Our clients themselves are full of information about their teams and the cities in which they live.

Two or three times a week I deliver speeches across the country to groups ranging from corporate conferences to business or law school seminars to civic organizations or schoolchildren. These appearances almost always involve a spirited exchange of information and opinions. I also cohost two weekly national call-in radio sports talk programs and regularly appear as a guest on several radio and television interview programs, all of which helps keep me in touch with public opinion, as do my own Web site (www.leighsteinberg.com) and my appearances on ESPN's "SportsZone" Web site.

In the fishbowl circumstances of high-level salary negotiations in my particular business, public perception—the team's relationship to its community, and the community's feelings about the team, its players, and its management—can be a critical factor. You need to be aware of such contextual elements going into any particular negotiation.

In the case of the Bartkowski negotiation in 1975, I found out everything I could about the Atlanta Falcons' situation. I learned that recent attendance had been extremely poor, that they had scored fewer points than anyone else in the league the previous season, that they had an enormous need for a quality quarterback, and that they had traded up in the draft order to get him. I learned that unlike most NFL teams, whose home games are typically sold out, the Falcons had a significant number of empty seats they needed to fill. That made a particular player's attraction as a drawing card to bring fans into the stadium a factor. And there is no position on an NFL team with more potential to become such a drawing card than quarterback—at least that was a point I prepared to make.

These are the same types of points anyone entering a negotiation must prepare to make, and they cannot be made without an analysis and understanding of the particular company you are dealing with, as well as the industry of which it is a part. What is the company's overall income situation, its profitability? Can you view this historically in terms of what its growth pattern has been? What is the reaction of other people in the industry to this company's product or to the company itself? Have there been any recent scandals or misadventures? How long has the company been in one location? What is its management structure, and how long has it been in place?

In the context of sports, some information about each team's economic circumstances is available because of the collective bargaining process. For a team to argue economic necessity, it's got to *show* economic necessity. One of the reasons that leagues are hesitant to use economic necessity as a rationale in the collective bargaining process is that they are then compelled to show their books.

As for other information about league and team finances, the sources are abundant. A league's television contract, attendance numbers and prices of seats in each stadium, the expenses involved with leases for those stadia—all these figures are public. The amount of money the owners receive from licensing and merchandise can be estimated fairly simply on a deal-by-deal basis and then added up overall.

The same kinds of numbers are typically available for almost any large company, especially if it is publicly traded. There are readily available materials that companies themselves often provide—annual reports, prospectuses, pamphlets, and brochures highlighting the organization's achievements. These materials can be useful—not so much for the rosy portraits they generally present of the company's health, but for information they offer about the structure of the company and the names of individuals within the organization. Some of these individuals may wind up being invaluable sources of information for you.

Within a company where you already work, it is useful to contact and befriend people who work in other divisions. In an indirect way, you may be able to gather valuable information about your particular department. When I negotiate contracts for television news anchors across the country, my clients may be the best source of information. An anchor like Dave McElhatton at CBS affiliate KPIX in San Francisco has been an institution in Bay Area news for so many years that he is a treasure chest of information. Pete Wilson, anchor at NBC affiliate KRON, also in San Francisco, is quickly approaching that status. A person working as a news anchor at any local television station may find that his friend in the advertising department has information about recent sales that the anchor can use in positioning himself for an upcoming discussion with management about his salary. A friend in the station's financial division could get him some precise figures he might well find valuable in his negotiation.

It is not necessary, of course, to have inside sources to gather such information. A person buying an automobile can, with a little footwork and a few phone calls, find out about the financial side of a particular dealership's operation—whether or not it is a high-volume/ low-premium operation or the other way around, whether it sells every automobile at sticker price, whether it has been having financial problems recently, whether its salesmen are under pressure to meet a quota, whether those salesmen are paid on a commission basis or earn a flat rate. All this information is immensely helpful in framing your approach to the negotiation.

Knowing the general health of an industry can be helpful as well, especially if that general health is tied closely to the performance of each particular company within that industry, as is true with professional sports. Because of the massive involvement and influence of television on the economic structure of professional sports, I need to know as much about the television industry as I do about the NFL, the NBA, the NHL, and major-league baseball.

Even the most casual observer of the NFL back in 1975 knew that the league's television income alone guaranteed a significant measure of profitability and that the profitability was likely to increase exponentially in the coming years—which it has. In 1976, the year after I began in this business, the NFL teams shared a national television contract that paid each of them $2 million. By 1989, they were getting $17 million apiece. Last year, each team made $40 million in TV money. The teams will average $73 million apiece per year over the next five years.

That is growth of more than 2,500 percent in just over twenty years. The most recent National Basketball Association television package doubled the figures for the previous agreement. That kind of growth alone is evidence that professional sports teams, which are in the *entertainment* business, can well afford what they are paying their performers—their athletes. If I, as a sports attorney—negotiating the multimillion-dollar packages that I do—were damaging these sports, I would stop. I would not want to represent the highest-priced players in a sport that was having financial problems.

But these teams have no such problems. And so I have always felt a bit like Robin Hood—taking from wealthy owners, who can well afford it, and distributing some of that wealth to the players, who, after all, are the attraction in this business. People don't pay money to see Jerry Jones, the owner of the Dallas Cowboys, play football against Al Davis, the owner of the Oakland Raiders (actually, people *might* pay to see that . . . once). People pay to see the games. And the players.

- Study the strengths and weaknesses of the particular company with which you will be negotiating.
- Study the general industry of which that particular company is a part.
- Identify the company's capabilities.
- Identify the company's limitations.
- Identify the company's needs.

VISION

FOR SOMEONE TO negotiate effectively for himself or for a client, he must not only understand where that company is at the moment, but he must be plugged into the larger vision of what that company, its product, and its industry can *become*. Part of what you can offer in a negotiating situation is a new vision of how the company's product might be packaged, marketed, and applied and how you or your client can contribute to these new directions.

In my business, for example, our firm was years ahead of everyone else in predicting and preparing for the phenomenal growth of naming rights in the NFL. We recognized the communication and marketing possibilities of the Internet very early and were turning those possibilities into reality, creating Web sites where fans can read weekly diaries posted by their favorite players or can shop for NFL products through an on-line "store." By the time other people in our business were just waking up to the potential of the worldwide personal computer network, we were already turning our ideas into actuality.

Envisioning new outlets and applications of your product, whatever that product might be, and bringing that vision into a negotiation can only enhance and strengthen your position. In the same way, envisioning your *own* growth and future value—or that of your client—is essential in shaping your negotiating strategy.

Kordell Stewart's place in the Pittsburgh Steelers organization was *not* clear when the Steelers drafted him as a rookie in 1995. Several teams were interested in Kordell and projected him into a variety of positions—safety, running back, wide receiver, and, of course, quarterback, the position he had played at the University of Colorado. Kordell desperately wanted to play quarterback. Despite his unorthodox array of extraordinary skills, we believed that his skills were such that, given the opportunity to display them, he could well convince the team to reshape the position to suit his abilities. After signing a new $9 million quarterback deal in 1997 to replace his $1.32 million rookie contract, Kordell went on to guide the Steelers to within one game of the 1998 Super Bowl.

This past off-season I was able to renegotiate Jake Plummer's contract and get him a record-breaking $15 million signing bonus. This was possible because Jake was one of the rising stars in the NFL, and the Cardinals knew they had to secure him for the future. It was also important to show the Cardinals that Jake was committed to them, and that they would not be developing a starting quarterback only to lose him at the end of the 1999 season.

Another example of our looking ahead was with Neil O'Donnell, who was Pittsburgh's third-round pick in 1990. The Steelers offered a four-year contract, but Neil did not want to lock himself in for that long. He believed in himself, and preferred taking a three-year deal for a significantly lower signing bonus. It was a gamble, but one based on our projections of Neil's future and what he would mean to the Steelers three years from then. In 1993 the gamble paid off; Neil played out those three years, became a restricted free agent, and went from a $300,000 salary to nearly $3 million a year.

The era of free agency has presented players entering the final year of their contracts with two options: sign contract extensions before their contracts expire (the secure option) or play out the final contract year (the high-risk/high-reward option). William Thomas, Pro Bowl linebacker from the Philadelphia Eagles, has twice chosen to accept lucrative contract extensions in the middle of final contract years instead of becoming a free agent. William's values of career stability and loyalty played a huge part in his decisions. On the other hand, cornerback Eric Davis had a choice between accepting a multiyear offer in the $1.5-million-per-year range from the 49ers before the 1995 season and playing out the season to attain free agency. He played out the season, won the Super Bowl, and played in the Pro Bowl, and we ultimately negotiated a deal for Eric with the Carolina Panthers that averaged $2.85 million a year. These choices are a reflection of client values and free agency dynamics.

A player in the process of free agency needs to have vision as well. Prior to the 1997 season, the Minnesota Vikings decided to replace Warren Moon as their starting quarterback with a younger player, Brad Johnson. The Seattle Seahawks expressed interest in signing Warren, but they made clear that they intended to stay with their incumbent starter, John Friesz, and would use Warren as the backup. They offered to pay Warren $750,000 for the season, compared to the $5 million a year Warren had been making with the Vikings.

Warren and I have been together for twenty years. I first met him right after he won the 1978 Rose Bowl for the Washington Huskies in a stirring upset of the University of Michigan. We have been through thick and thin. I consider him my closest friend and a critical adviser. I run most of my own important life decisions past Warren because of his incredible analytical ability and perspective. So when he was confronted with this decision last year, I knew he would make the right choice.

It would have been easy for Warren to say no to the Seahawks offer. He has a long and storied career behind him. He will be a certain inductee into the Hall of Fame whenever (if ever) he retires. Pride and ego could understandably have prevented him from even considering the deal. But Warren has enough confidence in himself, along with a strong sense of emotional security, that he took the deal. Unfortunately, Friesz, who is also my client, wound up becoming injured. While I felt terrible for John, this became an opportunity for Warren. He stepped in as the starter, and he ended up leading the league in pass completions. That put us in position to sign him in 1998 to a new contract that has returned him to a more competitive market level.

The moral? Sometimes it is necessary to take a half step back in order to take a step or two forward.

The point in all these cases is that we recognize what a player can *become,* and we shape his contract—or even the decision to negotiate at all—accordingly, with an emphasis on opportunity and future value rather than maximizing his current compensation.

Normally, the appeal of a new employee up front is not as high as it is going to be later, so it is important to look beyond the constraints of the current set of discussions to what the future will be. The best approach for a young attorney joining our firm, for example, would be to realize that the opportunities in sports law are unlimited and that rather than haggling about his starting salary, it would probably be more advantageous for him to focus on getting the chance to show what he can do to contribute to the overall performance and profitability of this law firm, knowing that whatever compensation he might have argued for when he first came through the door will be nothing compared to what he will be able to command once he has been able to demonstrate his value.

This kind of vision, of course, demands a fundamental faith in your own abilities or, if you are representing someone else, in your client's. With that kind of confidence, sometimes it makes sense not to push for the most money at the moment but to take the best offer you can get, knowing that by the time the *next* deal comes, your value will have multiplied many times over.

- Envision where your industry is headed in the future.
- Envision new outlets and applications of the services or product you have to offer.

- When shaping your negotiating strategy, envision your own growth.
- Remember that one negotiation always leads to the next, and keep that *next* negotiation in mind while planning for this one.
- Have confidence in your abilities.

THE OTHER PARTY

ONCE YOU HAVE assessed your own present and future value and learned all you can about the particular company with whom you will be negotiating, it is time to focus on the individual or individuals you will be facing in the actual discussion.

In any negotiation, information is a prerequisite—the more you have, the better. That includes information about the party with whom you will be negotiating. Understanding that individual's needs is as critical as understanding your own. That's what negotiation is fundamentally about—needs. The best negotiators are aware of and responsive to all needs of all parties; the worst are only aware of their own. An ethical negotiator thinks more about the person he is talking to than about himself. He absorbs himself in the other party's feelings, priorities, and needs in order to be able to respond to them effectively. His goal is not to manipulate or exploit those needs. His goal is to address them fairly, honestly, and, often, creatively.

Consider, for example, an employee for a small company who wants and *deserves* to be paid $75,000. The company is growing, but right now it can only afford to pay her $50,000. The company values this employee. It wants to keep her. It wants her to be part of its growth. With this in mind, the company might create a contract that pays her a salary of $50,000 but that also includes a clause providing for bonus payments based on increases in the company's earnings. In other words, as the company earns more money, so does she. The benefits that accrue from this arrangement extend beyond mere dollars. They include loyalty on the part of that employee, a feeling of support and a sense of personal investment, pride, and belonging. All this comes from the company's truly considering and responding to that employee's needs.

In a one-on-one business negotiation, the same understanding of needs is crucial. To understand the other person's needs, you've got to be able to climb inside him, see the world through his eyes, understand how he thinks, how he feels, what he cares about. Find out what he reads (this is another reason I subscribe to all those newspapers), what he eats, what he listens to. Find out where he went to college, what he majored in, what sports he might have played. Is he married? How many children does he have? What are their ages? Their names?

Learn about his politics, his personal philosophy, his outlook on the world, all with an understanding that you must never underestimate the degree to which another human being can take what you might believe to be an irrational or preposterous position and completely justify it in his own mind. Rather than simply dismiss the other party's position entering a negotiation as unrealistic, unfair, and unjustifiable, it is far more fruitful to consider that position from his viewpoint, to climb inside his head and understand how he could possibly justify his position to himself. Then *you* will be in a better position to respond to that justification and to begin the process of convincing him to shift his view.

2. Learn all you can about the other party.

It has become increasingly important in my profession to understand the emergence of a new breed of team executive that has begun to replace the "old-guard" owners and general managers. The old guard is typified by people like San Diego Chargers team president Bobby Beathard, Washington Redskins general manager Charley Casserly, Los Angeles Lakers general manager Jerry West, Atlanta Braves general manager John Schuerholz, Buffalo Bills vice-president John Butler, Indiana Pacers president Donnie Walsh, and owners like Dan Rooney in Pittsburgh, Ralph Wilson in Buffalo, and, in some ways, Al Davis in Oakland. These are people who have been around their particular sport all their lives. They have put their life's blood and sweat into the sport. They care mightily about such traditional concepts as team chemistry, dedication to the game, loyalty, hard work, and sacrifice. By and large, they are repulsed by the economics of modern professional sports. They remember when the highest paid player on a team received $16,000. The figures today are staggering to them. Even though they understand the economics, these executives still have an apocalyptic feeling about it all, a nagging sense that the world has gone to hell.

Part of that feeling comes from the fact that most of these men are long-term owners who vividly recall a time when they were barely scraping by, when a fixed cost was something that could put them into bankruptcy. In most cases, their sports team represents their entire business interest. They did not make their fortune in some other field and then come into professional sports. Sports is where they made their fortune. They began when the business was much smaller in scope, which leads them to be a little more parsimonious than their newer colleagues. Even though they have now entered an era of great profitability, at a gut level these men still do not trust it.

On the other side of the coin from these traditionalists is the emerging breed of what I call technocrats—business-oriented executives whose focus is almost exclusively on the bottom line. This new breed can be extremely creative and imaginative in the development of revenue sources. They can be quite visionary in projecting the business future of professional sports. Owners like Jerry Jones of the Dallas Cowboys, Ed DeBartolo of the San Francisco 49ers, Robert Kraft of the New England Patriots, Jerry Colangelo of the Arizona Diamondbacks, and Paul Allen of the Seattle Seahawks and Portland Trailblazers exemplify such businessmen. Executives Michael Huyghue of the Jacksonville Jaguars, John Shaw of the St. Louis Rams, Noah Croom of the Vancouver Grizzlies, Ed Wade of the Philadelphia Phillies and Ted Phillips of the Chicago Bears carry out the will of these owners. Unlike the old guard, who understood the game of football long before they became negotiators, these newer executives have cut their teeth in other industries and professions, with little or no prior involvement in this or any other sport. They may, in many cases, be fans, but they do not have the deep-rooted connection to the game that their predecessors did. Their training is generally in business or law. They are there to do their job, and their job is to control costs and ensure profitability. They purchased their teams at 1990s prices, which often included great debt service. They are relatively dispassionate about salaries, which they see as simply a labor cost. The fact that a specific player is paid a large amount of money does not particularly bother them. They do not bemoan the fact that an athlete who now makes eight million dollars a year would, in the old days, have made eight *thousand* dollars and been happy for it. They do not have the feeling that the sport is in imminent financial danger. Salaries do not threaten them, because they are realistic about the revenue sources that are coming in. They do not care nearly as much about the concepts of team chemistry or player unity or the delicate relationship between a veteran and a rookie. They accept the system as it exists, become experts in it, and simply try to exert as much control as they can.

The point is not whether I prefer one type of executive or the other. There are, in fact, many owners and executives who are hybrids, embodying qualities from both categories. The point is that I need to know which type of person I am dealing with to properly prepare for a negotiation. While, for example, it might be effective to point out to an old-guard owner such as Ralph Wilson the special bond he has developed over the years with a player such as Thurman Thomas or Bruce Smith, to remind him of the wars they have been through together and of the father-son feeling they have for each other, it would be a mistake to make such an emotional appeal to a new-breed executive. Emotion would matter little or not at all to this person. With him, I would focus instead on such bottom-line issues as leverage, alternatives, and costs.

Besides understanding these differences myself, it is important that I make my client aware of them prior to the beginning of the negotiation. Whenever I prepared to negotiate with George Young, who was the New York Giants' general manager for many years before leaving to work at the NFL, I let my client know about George's blue-collar roots in Baltimore, about the fact that he had been a schoolteacher and one of the few registered Democrats in professional sports, about the fact that he was very much at odds with the star-system way in which sports has evolved, and about the fact that he was a man so secure with his own beliefs and value system that he was impervious to many of the normal pressures that most general managers feel. I would explain that George had a great relationship with his bosses, Giants owners Wellington Mara and Bob Tisch. He had complete job security. He was respected by the writers as well, so he didn't have to worry that somehow he would be unfairly criticized by the press. Not that that would have mattered much to him: He was well aware of the transient and fleeting nature of fan and public opinion. Short-term public support or disapproval was never as important to him as doing what he thought was right. He always took the long view. He prided himself on not taking advantage of players, but he also would not be taken advantage of.

What this all added up to, I explained to my clients who played or were considering playing for the teams George Young ran, was that it was impossible to do a stunning breakthrough deal with him. He simply would not allow it. Nor would he allow the player to be the victim of a stunning management victory. What you would get with George Young, I explained, was a B+ result—never a D, but never an A.

These are the kinds of things it is necessary to know about an individual before you face him in a negotiation. Beyond getting a sense of his personal philosophy, it helps to understand what the particular pressures are on that person. Is he facing budgetary constraints? Is his career currently on the ascent, on the descent, or on a plateau? Will he personally be held responsible for the success or failure of this negotiation? What part does his particular department play in the grand scheme of his company? What is his motivation? What does *he* want or need out of this process? What might be going on in his personal life that might affect his attitude and behavior?

Some of these answers may come from simply asking the other party directly during the negotiation process. But it's best to learn as much as you can beforehand, by doing library research (in the case of visible or public figures), by studying résumés, and most of all, by talking to people—his colleagues, his employees, his friends, other people who have done business with him.

Through this kind of analysis, you can zero in specifically on the other party's negotiating style. What are his track record and history in other negotiations and discussions? What are his behavioral tendencies? Is he blustering? Overbearing? Officious? Meek? Obsequious? What moves took place in prior negotiations? How big a first offer did he make, and what relation did that offer have to the final agreement? When that person said, "This is it, take it or leave it," was that really the case, or did the negotiations continue after that?

The more such questions are answered, the better you will understand the other party, and the better prepared you will be to anticipate and respond to that party's attitude and behavior, as well as to the specifics of his negotiating position.

When I began discussions for the first time with Carolina Panthers general manager Bill Polian concerning Kerry Collins's rookie contract in 1995, I knew and understood that Polian was an old-line GM who cared very much about team chemistry, about tradition, about players proving themselves on the field before they are paid large amounts of money. I knew that there were certain principles on which Polian would not bend, such as his inviolable beliefs that a player must be on time to training camp, that there be no holdouts, that a player never violate the contract he has signed, and that a player behave himself off the field. I agreed with those principles.

Prior to joining the Panthers, Polian had been a member of the NFL's management council and was deeply involved in the creation of the salary cap, as well as of the league's most recent collective bargaining agreement with the players. Consequently, I understood that he was going to have a distinctive point of view about what the cap was meant to do or not meant to do, that he would likely feel an emotional stake in that system and a need to defend it—all of which turned out to be true.

Knowing all of these things, I was prepared for the specific challenges that did indeed arise during our discussions with the Panthers over Kerry's contract. I was not offended or intimidated when Polian reacted with emotion during our first meeting. I was not caught off guard when he dug in his heels over the issue of salary-cap limitations. We were prepared to accommodate his concerns about the cap by presenting a seven-year $23 million contract structured to allow the Panthers to meet those limitations. And we addressed Polian's belief in players' proving themselves on the field by building statistical standards into the contract that required Kerry to meet specified performance criteria in each of the agreement's seven years.

Problem solving. This is the essence of negotiation—creating solutions that solve not just your problems but the problems of the other party as well. A key to creating those solutions is the ability to put yourself at every moment into the psyche of this other human being and to be able to somehow fashion a way of fulfilling both sets of goals—yours and his.

Whether or not this kind of preparation addresses the issues that actually arise in the negotiation you enter, or whether the discussions wind up going in an unanticipated direction, the other party will still be impressed that you have done the amount of work you have, that you have given as much thought to the details as you have. If nothing else, he will be impressed by your determination and professionalism, and that can only help in terms of the discussions that ensue, no matter which direction they go.

· Learn all you can about the individual with whom you will be negotiating.
· Learn about his negotiating style.
· Identify the pressures he is facing.
· Identify his problems.
· Identify his needs.

WHO HAS THE POWER?

ONE FINAL POINT to consider in researching the opposing party is determining the extent of that individual's power. Is the final decision in his hands, or is he merely a go-between to a higher authority who will be making the ultimate decision? You need to understand the pressures weighing on the party you are facing—his sense of security and his possible concerns about the unseen boss who is looking over his shoulder. If that higher power has the final say, you need to know what *that* person needs: *He* is the one you are actually negotiating with.

There are some owners in sports who delegate as much authority as possible to their presidents or general managers. But no one other than the owner himself has *complete* power. When I am dealing with Bob Kraft or Jerry Jones, there is no higher authority. When they say a deal is done, it is done. Period.

In every other case, though, it depends on the situation. Bob Whitsitt, president of the Portland Trailblazers basketball team and the Seattle Seahawks football team, is a hybrid. While Bob does not own these teams, he operates with complete authority and autonomy in nearly every situation. With most franchises, however, an overall budget is approved, and it is the general manager's job to split that up and spend it any way he chooses. Executives like Ted Phillips with the Bears, Ozzie Newsome with the Baltimore Ravens, and Carl Peterson in Kansas City have been given complete discretion in that process by the owners of their teams.

If, however, a dramatic, high-level free agent negotiation or high-draft-pick negotiation involving money that goes above the preexisting budget is at issue, every one of these men will have to clear that signing with the owner. Even a team president and part owner like Carmen Policy with the Cleveland Browns, who has as much authority as it is possible for a person in his position to have, will, in the case of a big-dollar negotiation, have to get on the phone with the majority owner, Al Lerner, and run it by him.

In most business situations, anyone who is negotiating for someone else will, at one point or another, have to go to that person for final approval, no matter how much power and latitude they have been given. But there is a difference between the person who has to do that at the end of a deal and the person who walks in the door at the beginning with virtually no power or discretion at all.

I remember negotiating with an NFL assistant general manager several years ago. He sat down with a sheet of directives in front of him. The list detailed specific instructions concerning the team's position on the length of the contract, the size of the signing bonus, how and when the bonus would be paid, the yearly salaries, incentive clauses, and other items of discussion. Every time I would bring up a point, he would look down and say, "It's not on my sheet." I would mention an incentive, and he would say, "It's not on my sheet." I would bring up a term, and he would say, "Well, that's not what I have here."

This went on and on. I finally became so frustrated that I pointed toward the window. "If, for the sake of argument," I said, "I proposed to you that the sun rose every morning in the east and set in the west and that was not on your sheet, would you agree that it was true?"

To which he paused, looked down at his paper, and said, "It's not on my sheet."

Hand in hand with knowing who has the actual power is knowing how long the party with whom you are negotiating will be in his position. It may just be that the person with whom you are discussing the terms of a four-year contract will be gone from the company in two years. If part of your decision to accept that agreement is predicated on his—or any other key individual's—being in a particular position, it may be in your best interest to include a provision in the contract that negotiations be reopened if he or any of those parties leave during that time period.

Look ahead. Always look ahead.

· Understand the power of the person with whom you are negotiating.
· Keep in mind that the person in power may not be there the next time you negotiate.

MAKING A CASE

THE FINAL STEP in the research phase of preparation for a negotiation is assembling your case—putting together the specifics of the presentation you intend to make, the supporting evidence for your position.

It's not enough to walk into your employer's office and simply say, "I want a raise of $15,000 a year." You need to be able to justify *why* you are worth that much. The ideal negotiation is a process of communication between reasonable people. You can never remind yourself enough that the root of the word *reasonable* is *reason*. Not *anger.* Not *fear.* Not *power.* Not *desire.* But *reason.*

The presentation you assemble is the package of reasons that support and rationalize your position—the fruits of your research. Facts. Statistics. Logical arguments. Evidence. This is the ground you will stand on throughout the course of the impending negotiation, the encounter itself. The more solid the presentation you are able to assemble, the steadier and more confident you will remain no matter how tense and stormy the negotiating process might become.

Again, it is imperative that the facts and conclusions you present be accurate. Hyperbole, exaggeration, or outright falsehoods will undermine everything you intend to accomplish. If the other party cannot trust the validity of your information, then your presentation will be worse than useless. It will be counterproductive.

I prefer to display my presentations in a packet form—typically, in a bound thirty-to-forty-page booklet, carefully researched, clearly written, illustrated with full-color charts and graphs containing and communicating all relevant statistics and other information. It is important that this package be graphically approachable, attractive, and dramatic. More than just an assemblage of information, this document has to *tell a story.* That story is one of success—of my client, of the organization with which we are negotiating, and of their future together.

A good story, first of all, makes sense. It is logical. It is coherent. But beyond that, a good story is *compelling.* It is *convincing.* It provides a lens or a framework through which issues and facts are seen from a particular angle. This is your intent in a negotiation, to have the other side see the issue at hand from a particular angle, through a particular framework—namely, yours.

In preparing for our most recent negotiation with the 49ers over Steve Young's contract, the packet we put together opened with a simple statement: STEVE YOUNG IS THE QUARTERBACK OF THE DECADE. Under that heading came a concise summary paragraph:

> Whether measured by individual statistics, by honors and awards, or by team accomplishments, there is no quarterback in the league today who can match Steve Young for qualitative performance in the 1990s. Young is possibly the greatest quarterback ever to play in the NFL.

We then presented a list of Steve's honors, highlighting his numerous league MVP and Player of the Year awards. We included a chart showing his year-by-year passing statistics, which showed him consistently at the top of the league in almost every category. We displayed a diagram tracing Steve's position at the top of the NFL's career leaders in terms of passing ratings. We listed the numerous league and team records he holds. And we laid out charts comparing him statistically—and in every case favorably—over the past five seasons with each of the league's other quarterbacks who have played over that period of time (Brett Favre, John Elway, Troy Aikman, Dan Marino, Drew Bledsoe, Jeff George, Scott Mitchell, Neil O'Donnell). Finally, we included tables of figures charting the evolving quarterback market since Steve's last contract was signed.

The overwhelming conclusion of these pages of information—the end of Steve's "story"—was that the most accomplished NFL quarterback of this decade and perhaps in the history of the league should be the highest paid player at his position. The 49ers agreed, and the result was the $8.2-million-a-year contract Steve now has.

The nature of each presentation depends upon the story you want to tell. A person in a management position might want to argue that the key to success in the business world is who the manager is. That's the viewpoint he wants to share, the philosophy he wants to convey, the reality he wants to construct. To tell it effectively, he might present a series of examples in which talented managers within that industry have improved growth, cut costs, and increased productivity. Then he might show his company's achievements in these areas and tie those achievements to his particular responsibilities and performance.

Now, there are obviously categories of facts that exist that you would like to emphasize less than others, that might point to your weak spots more than your strengths. You cannot ignore these, or you will lose credibility. If I'm attempting to show how superior Ricky Watters is to other running backs in the NFL and we are preparing a presentation on him, matching him up against other backs in a long list of categories, I have got to include the categories where Ricky comes out behind. If he is prone to fumble, I have to include that fact in my presentation. The other party is certainly going to be aware of that fact. It's better for me to acknowledge it up front and address it in a way that does not detract from my overall argument than to simply ignore it and hope it will not come up.

Again, we are talking about converging realities here—yours and those of the other party. Determining whose reality will prevail depends on erecting and establishing a convincing, compelling reality in the first place. That is what this initial presentation does. It introduces your reality to the other party, who until this point might have little or no idea of what your reality looks like.

With this initial presentation, you are seizing the initiative in setting the boundaries for the discussion that will ensue. You are creating the framework of the "reality" that will be considered. The creative employee can come up with an innovative framework, a new way of being compensated, a fresh formula that defines his relationship to the company. If this new framework is presented logically and compellingly, he will have dictated or at least influenced the direction, the course, and even the particular terms of the discussion that ensues.

A number of years ago, we began constructing a reality that is now accepted in the NFL, and that was that there ought to be a premium value put on the position of quarterback. Quarterbacks were our primary clients, and so we developed a theory of a "quarterback premium," assembling as much evidence as possible to support this notion that the quarterback is more critical than any other player at any other position to the success of each team and so the quarterback should be paid more than those other players.

This has not always been an accepted fact. When I entered this business, the quarterback was not necessarily considered the most important player on an NFL team. Even today, an argument can conceivably be made for a running-back premium or for an offensive-tackle premium. One could argue that Barry Sanders has more to do with the success of the Detroit Lions than the team's quarterbacks.

But the fact is that we went out some years ago and made a concerted effort to create and to justify a particular reality, one that is now generally accepted as a guiding principle around the league, which is that quarterbacks are almost always paid more than everyone else. The highest-paid quarterback in the league today makes $9.5 million a year, while the highest-paid running back makes $6.6 million. That is a reality, one that we argued for and helped create many years ago.

That is what an effectively assembled presentation can do: It can take an amorphous set of facts in a setting where there are no prescribed rules and can arrange those facts in a logical way that supports a particular theory or principle. That theory, if it is not refuted by an equally compelling opposing argument, is ultimately accepted and becomes reality. *Your* reality, in other words, has prevailed.

Intelligent people—and you should always assume that the party you are going to face is intelligent—aren't impressed by mere requests or demands. They want reasons. They want rationale. Most important, they want to make up their own minds. They want to feel that *they* have controlled their decision, not you. So what you are trying to do with this initial presentation is not simply to convince the other party that your particular position is justified. What you want to do is to influence them and allow them to convince *themselves* that this makes sense.

They may not entirely agree with your position. In fact, you can count on that. They may refute some of your premises. But if you come in the door and begin by putting an impressive presentation in their hands, they will realize that they are dealing with a thinking person who has given this subject a lot of consideration. They will see that you are serious and that you respect them enough to assume that they are just as serious as you are.

Even if your figures or demands are aggressive, the likely reaction is that the other party will know that you are earnest about what you are asking for, that you are determined to get a deal done here, and that you will give as much time and energy and reflection to the discussions that ensue as you have to the presentation you prepared.

- Gather all facts, evidence, and arguments that justify your proposal.
- Arrange the material into a clear, convincing, *compelling* presentation.
- Anticipate and address every question the other party might have.
- Include your weaknesses; turn them into strengths.
- Use this presentation to *create your reality*.
- Depend on this presentation as your foundation of fact and reason throughout the course of the negotiation.

3

POSITIONING

LEVERAGE

THE SPRING OF 1993 was a watershed both for my business and for the National Football League. The NFL had just signed a new contract with the networks, more than doubling its television revenues per team, going from $17 million to $40 million. At the same time, it instituted something the league had not known until then—a system of free agency, which allowed veteran players to take advantage of competitive bidding for their services.

The advent of free agency exploded the NFL's marketplace. It changed everything about the way players and their representatives did business, because it gave us the single most important advantage one can have in a negotiating situation.

It gave us leverage.

Choices. Options. Alternatives. There is nothing that increases value more in this world than competition and demand for a product or a person.

There is a tendency to take someone for granted until losing them becomes a realistic possibility. The woman who feels that her boyfriend is neglecting her will see an amazing transformation in his behavior if another man becomes interested in her. An employee may well find himself looked at in a new light by his company if he receives an attractive job offer from another firm. In business or in almost any other aspect of life, nothing is as powerful as a competitor on an option point. There is nothing like having a choice to increase one's worth. There is nothing like having an alternative to improve your bargaining position.

So it is critical well before a negotiation ever takes place to do all you can to create as many options as possible—to maximize your leverage. This is what I did in my very first negotiation—that 1975 Steve Bartkowski contract with the Atlanta Falcons—and it is what I have tried to do in every negotiation since.

As I mentioned, Steve had an agent representing him before me. This fellow had been negotiating with the Falcons for a couple of months. It became immediately apparent to me that the chief problem was that this agent had been negotiating *only* with the Falcons. There existed at that time another professional football league besides the NFL, an organization called the World Football League. Compared to the NFL, in terms of size and resources, the WFL was a mere sliver of a shadow. The NFL virtually ignored its existence, as did Steve's previous agent. Here was a rival league, desperate to make an impact. What better way could it do that than sign away the first draft pick of the NFL, a big, blond, blue-eyed, strong-armed, charismatic quarterback from California? Understanding this, I immediately opened discussions with the Chicago Wind and the Shreveport Steamers, WFL teams that are today just vague memories for all but the most adamant football fans.

Then I brought our proposal to the Falcons.

How did I arrive at a specific figure?

I began with the research I had done on comparable player salaries, on the Atlanta Falcons operation in particular, and on the NFL in general. Then I factored in our rationale in terms of Steve's specific value to the Falcons: that quarterback is the key position on an NFL team, that Atlanta was a team in desperate need of a marquee player, that there was a shortage of quarterbacks on the market at that time, that this was the first player chosen in the draft, and that this particular player possessed qualities that could translate directly into more seat sales. I also included a consideration of the effect on the Falcons if they did *not* sign this player: even worse attendance than the previous year, a wasted draft pick, bad public relations, and a loss of faith among their fans.

Finally, most significantly, I introduced the concept of the other league, arguing that Steve's value to the WFL was even greater than what he would be worth to an NFL team because of the new league's need to establish itself.

The numbers for Namath ($410,000) and Simpson ($350,000) provided a benchmark, which Steve's previous representative had used in his discussions with the Falcons. At the point I took over the negotiation, the Falcons had increased their initial offer, $360,000 for five years, to $430,000 for four years. So Steve was already at the ceiling of where any player had ever been.

But the ceiling loses meaning in a situation like this. A basic principle in shaping an offer for any negotiation is that you should always take a more aggressive position than what you are actually looking to end up with. In this situation, with a player of such quality and desirability, with a team whose need for that player was so pronounced, and with the leverage introduced by another suitor whose needs were just as great, the pieces were in place for a "breakthrough" contract, one that represents a quantum leap from the past. This does not mean that you leave the realm of reason. What you are seeking is the outer limit of *justifiable* figures. They may be unprecedented, but they are still reasonable. They follow from facts and rationale. Each time one of my clients—from Steve Bartkowski to Warren Moon to Steve Young to Troy Aikman to Drew Bledsoe—has signed a "breakthrough" contract, the figures have been justified by the subsequent results, by the productivity, performance, and benefits provided by that player to the team. The resulting income and revenue have, in each of these "breakthrough" deals, justified the money that was paid.

The package I finally proposed to the Falcons in the Bartkowski negotiation was a four-year contract for a total of $750,000.

The Falcons balked, as I knew they would. They told me I had to be kidding. They did not take me seriously. They did not take the WFL seriously.

I responded by reminding them that the American Football League began in exactly the same way, with the same attitude from the NFL. No one imagined in the mid-1960s that the AFL's teams would ever be as valued as the NFL's. Just as the Joe Namaths of the world were pioneers then, I said, so could Steve Bartkowski become a trailblazer now.

The Falcons realized that this was true. It didn't matter that Steve had never seriously considered going to that league, that his heart was set on playing in the NFL. As we got into discussions with the World Football League, his perspective might have changed and he could have actually made the decision to sign with a team in that league. In either case, though, the fact that the Falcons *believed* he might go was all that mattered. It was *conceivable* that Steve Bartkowski might go to the WFL, and that was enough. Once the Falcons accepted that the WFL was a viable alternative for us, it entirely changed the playing field of that negotiation. By creating a convincing option, Steve and I were able to introduce leverage into our situation. With that, we were well on our way to forging a four-year $650,000 contract with the Falcons, establishing Steve as the highest-paid player by far in the history of professional football up to that time.

3. Convince the other party that you have an option.

This was by no means the first time leverage was a factor in an NFL negotiation. The AFL had introduced the element of competition years before. When Al Davis would come to a college player's room the night after the Rose Bowl and spread handfuls of dollar bills across the bed, that player was looking at leverage. This was one of the reasons NFL salaries began to rise during this time. Even though players had no alternative within the NFL but to go to the team that drafted them, the teams still began paying heavy bonuses, because the AFL was a real, viable alternative.

The continued existence of first the WFL, the United States Football League during my first decade in this business, and the creation of the Canadian Football League were leverage factors of varying degrees in almost every NFL negotiation I conducted during that time. None, however, came close to the scope and significance of Steve Young's landmark signing with the USFL's Los Angeles Express in 1984.

To understand that negotiation, one must understand the power of television. ABC had agreed to televise several USFL games during the spring of that year. For that coverage to expand, however, the league had to attract major stars and establish a presence in the nation's largest television markets. The top market, of course, was New York, where the New Jersey Generals found their major star in University of Georgia running back Herschel Walker, whom they aggressively pursued and signed.

That left Los Angeles, where a businessman named Bill Oldenberg owned the L.A. Express. Oldenberg was not yet in his fifties and already had made his fortune as the head of IMI (Investment Mortgage International), a company that put buyers and lenders together on major construction projects. Operating out of a plush, lavish office in San Francisco, he was a flashy, high-flying representative of the *Wall Street*/Gordon Gekko/fast-lane 1980s, with private jets and Daimler limousines, a Times Square–style electronic message board above his office door, and a gong that rang every time a million-dollar deal was made. He was not a tall man—he stood about five feet six inches—but he walked with a swagger that made him appear larger than he was.

Bill Oldenberg was accustomed to dominance in everything he did, and he intended to dominate with this football organization. He was able and prepared to pay whatever it took to buy what he needed. And what he needed in this case was a franchise quarterback.

Both Oldenberg and his general manager, Don Klosterman, understood what it would take to succeed in Los Angeles. They understood that this is a star-obsessed city that traditionally has loved flashy, nice-looking quarterbacks, from Bob Waterfield and Norm Van Brocklin to Roman Gabriel, Vince Ferragamo, and Pat Haden. They understood that this is a showtime city, a Kareem Abdul-Jabbar, Magic Johnson, Wilt Chamberlain, Jerry West, Elgin Baylor city that loves big, larger-than-life stars. It's a Sandy Koufax, Don Drysdale, Maury Wills city that enjoys exciting, dominant performances by gifted, colorful athletes. Most Southern Californians knew virtually nothing about hockey, but the presence of Wayne Gretzky compelled them to learn. And it is a trendy city, always on the lookout for the next new thing.

Onto this scene stepped Steve Young, a quarterback from Brigham Young University, a handsome, dark-haired, blue-eyed Mormon with all-American values, a stupendous athlete who played with reckless abandon, a quarterback who could run as well as he could throw. From the moment I first met Steve, I could see that he had an extremely high IQ, that he was a very passionate young man with a wicked sense of humor. It was clear to me that this relationship was going to be special after we spent the majority of our first dinner together debating the economic theories of Ronald Reagan—with Steve as an enthusiastic supporter and me as a skeptic. In the years since, he has become like a younger brother to me.

There was no doubt in the spring of 1984 that Steve was going to be the first pick in the NFL draft, which belonged to the Cincinnati Bengals. This fit nicely into Bill Oldenberg's plans. What more dramatic way to not only put his team on its feet but to throw a body block into the NFL and to establish the new league's credibility than by signing Steve Young?

And so Don Klosterman and I arranged to meet. Klosterman was an astute, savvy football executive, well connected in the worlds of politics, journalism, and show business. He had style and panache. He had a keen understanding of how to build a football team and how to tailor that team specifically for the market in Los Angeles. And he had essentially been given a blank check by Oldenberg to sign Steve Young.

We began the discussions on a morning in March, at the L.A. Express offices in El Segundo. By midafternoon we had adjourned to Klosterman's house in the Hollywood Hills with its incredible 180-degree view of Los Angeles.

Klosterman had prepared in every possible way. He had carefully researched Steve's interests and was prepared to send Steve to law school, as well as to establish a scholarship fund at BYU in Steve's name. He had hired Sid Gilman, the architect of the modern passing game, to be the Express's offensive coordinator, giving Steve the opportunity to work under the greatest teacher of quarterbacks in the history of the sport. John Hadl, a legendary quarterback himself, had been hired as head coach. They had already put together a splendid offensive line, including players like Gary Zimmerman, who would become a star in the NFL. And they had signed Gordon Hudson, who was Steve's tight end at BYU. There was no question that this organization meant business. They were picking the NFL's 1984 draft clean before it ever occurred.

Steve, however, was dead set against the USFL. He had grown up with a poster of Roger Staubach above his bed. The great quarterbacks of the NFL were his heroes. All he had ever dreamed of was to play quarterback in the National Football League. This made my job easier in terms of dealing with Klosterman. Rather than doing the convincing, we were the ones who had to be convinced.

Or at least we assumed that position. The fact was that Cincinnati already had a Pro Bowl quarterback in Ken Anderson, who looked like he was going to play for many more years. That meant it would take some time for Steve to get any practical experience if he went to the Bengals. What appealed to him most about the Express's offer was not the amount of money they were willing to spend but the coaching he would get with this team, along with the opportunity to immediately begin playing and developing on the field. The money truly did not turn Steve's head; it was the Sid Gilman/John Hadl factor that meant the most to him.

But it was money that Don Klosterman and I had to discuss. The benchmark I came in with was John Elway's contract from the season before, which was for $1 million a year. Much of that money, however, was deferred; in reality Elway was getting closer to $600,000 annually in present value terms. That was the figure I had in mind going in.

That number, however, was rapidly eclipsed as Klosterman kept increasing and increasing his offer. The number of dollars kept spiraling higher and higher. The annuity the team was offering got bigger and bigger. The signing bonus got bigger. The per-year salaries got bigger. Pretty quickly, we were at figures two and a half times what Elway had gotten.

And we kept going. I got progressively more excited as the dollars kept improving, though naturally I did not show it. I kept in touch throughout the day with Steve in Provo and with his father, Legrand "Grit" Young, in Connecticut. Grit was a tough corporate lawyer, obsessed with thoroughness. He was also a man whose stern demeanor entirely changed around his family and friends.

That day went by, and night fell. Klosterman and I had dinner looking out over his lamp-lit swimming pool and, beyond it, the glittering lights of Hollywood and the city below.

After dinner we continued. At one point, about two in the morning, we took a dip in the pool to get refreshed, then we went back to it. The essence of the deal was in place by now, but there were dozens and dozens of details to work through.

The sun started to rise, and we stayed at it. Finally, at roughly seven o'clock that morning, we were done. Our deal called for a $37 million annuity to be placed for Steve with money provided by the Express, along with a $5 million payment in bonus and salary—a total package of $42 million.

At that point I called Steve and Grit and said, "Look, if this all checks out, we've got to take this deal."

And so a few days later, with word of the deal already making headlines across the country, Steve and I flew up to San Francisco to meet with Klosterman and Oldenberg to finalize the contract. When we got there, Oldenberg ushered us into his office. The electronic sign flashed, WELCOME STEVE YOUNG, QUARTERBACK EXTRAORDINAIRE . . . WELCOME LEIGH STEINBERG, ATTORNEY PAR EXCELLENCE . . . He showed us his Ronald Reagan room, festooned with photographs of him and the president together. He was excited. He was ready and eager to sign this deal.

Unfortunately, his staff had evidently not done a very good job of preparing him for the fact that this was going to take a little bit of time. We needed to go over documents whose language and details were fairly complex. Apparently, no one had told Bill this—and no one had told *us* that this was Bill Oldenberg's birthday. He had plans to go out that night, to celebrate both his birthday and this signing.

Those plans did not work out. Bill's lawyers and I camped in a conference room, around a table covered with contracts. Hours went by. Steve was in another room, watching television and making telephone calls. Occasionally, Oldenberg would poke his head in the office to see how we were doing. Each time he checked in, he looked a little more agitated. At one point he burst into the room and said, "Why isn't this happening? Are you balking? What's going on? Why aren't you signing this?"

"We're just moving through the process," I said.

Time went on. Night fell. By nine o'clock, Oldenberg was beside himself.

"What are you fighting about now?" he asked at one point.

"Guarantees," we said.

"*Here,*" he shouted, pulling a fistful of hundred-dollar bills from his wallet and flinging them across the table. "Here's all the [blankety-blank] guarantees you'll ever need."

We kept going. Now it was one in the morning, and in came Oldenberg again. "Listen," he said. "If this doesn't get done in an hour, it's not getting done at all. That's it."

An hour passed, and in he came.

"That's it," he said. "*Steve,*" he called into the other room, "I want to see you in my office. You too, Leigh."

Oldenberg was absolutely livid at this point.

"I don't know what's taking so [blanking] long," he said. "Why are you *doing* this [blank]?" he asked me. Then he turned to Steve.

"Do you want to be my quarterback or don't you?"

"Well, I do," said Steve, who was nonplussed by this strange situation. "But the lawyers are doing what they need to do."

Suddenly, Oldenberg reached out his arm and swept a set of drinking glasses off a table. They exploded against the wall, sending shards of glass all over the carpet.

"I don't know if you're *man* enough to be my quarterback," he said. Then he began jabbing a finger into Steve's sternum.

Then he began punching Steve in the chest with his fist.

Boom, boom, boom.

It looked comical, this statuesque athlete towering over this much smaller man, who was flailing at him in anger. But it was also horrifying.

"Listen," Steve finally said. "You do that one more time, and I'm going to deck you."

I thought, They didn't teach me about *this* in law school. I could see a major problem here if the owner of this football team was knocked out by his quarterback.

Fortunately, Oldenberg backed off. He gripped a chair.

"I'm so [blanked] off I could *spit,*" he said, and he made a motion as if he were going to hurl the chair through a plate-glass window. Steve grabbed his arm and pulled him back.

"I just don't understand," Oldenberg said, letting go of the chair. "This is [blankety-blank]. I'm in real estate. These deals take two minutes to do, I don't care how big they are. You either do a deal or you don't do it. I just can't handle this. This is [blank]."

He drew a breath.

"You guys get the [blank] out of here."

I actually understood Oldenberg's feelings. When a person is not used to a process like this, with stakes as high as those involved in this deal, minutes can seem like hours. Anxiety and tension can become unbearable. Bill Oldenberg had expected this deal to be done by three-thirty in the afternoon, and now it was three-thirty the next morning and we were not done yet. He was bewildered.

And we were banished, escorted out of the building by a couple of security guards. We stepped out into the night. California Street, in the heart of downtown San Francisco, was empty, completely deserted. Not a soul in sight.

Steve and I just stared at each other. Klosterman was with us, and he looked shaky. There wasn't much to say. He gave us a ride back to my home in Berkeley, where we finally got to sleep about dawn.

That day the newspapers, television, everyone in the nation with even a remote interest in professional football, was waiting for the big announcement that this deal had been signed. When nothing came out, speculation began swirling. The phone started ringing with lobbyists on both the USFL's side of the fence and the NFL's, trying to sway Steve in their direction. Howard Cosell called, pushing for the

USFL, since ABC had bought those rights. Joe Namath called, also on behalf of ABC and the new league. Roger Staubach weighed in for the NFL. The phone did not stop ringing that entire day.

By the next morning, a Sunday, Oldenberg had calmed down. Apologies were made. The situation on both sides was explained, and that Monday, finally, the deal came together and was signed.

Steve Young played for two years in the USFL before the league folded after the 1985 season. Those two years gave him the chance to play and to develop, which he had hoped for, and when he left to join the NFL, he was an independently wealthy man.

As for Bill Oldenberg and the other USFL owners whose hopes had been so high, I believe their premise was correct. Had the league been able to hang on until the expansion of cable television, they would have succeeded. Today, products that have one tenth of the allure of professional football are drawing large network contracts. Had the USFL been able to achieve that outlet, exposure, and source of income, it would have seriously challenged the NFL. By now its key franchises would probably have been absorbed into the NFL, just as the old AFL was.

But they became frightened by the red ink. They balked, and they backed out. I don't think, however, that this was the last we will see of a rival league rising to challenge the NFL.

After the demise of the USFL in 1985, the absence of an alternative to the NFL dramatically decreased players' leverage in bargaining situations. Not that we weren't able to continue negotiating healthy contracts for our clients during that time. But with the arrival in 1993 of free agency, which reintroduced the element of competition—this time among the NFL teams themselves—the factor of leverage became part of the league's negotiating process in a way it had never been before.

In any business situation where there is true free agency and there are a number of interested buyers for an individual's services, it is the dynamic of competition among those parties that will dictate and drive the process and the price. Consider the bidder for a painting at an art auction. He may find the painting listed in a blue book and see that it is perceived to have a value of $10,000. But if someone else wants that painting that day as much as he does, then the blue-book value becomes irrelevant. It is the bidding process between those parties that matters. Wherever the bidding stops—whether at $25,000 or at $50,000—*that* becomes the painting's value. That becomes reality.

This was the dynamic introduced by the advent of free agency in the NFL. It was this factor, more than any other, that resulted in the opportunity for me to negotiate $325 million in contracts for my clients in the spring of 1993—an unheard-of total up to that point. Troy Aikman, Steve Young, Thurman Thomas, Drew Bledsoe, Derrick Thomas, Tim McDonald—they all benefited that year from the new negotiating climate.

It was Tim, in fact, who inspired a phrase that spring that would become part of America's 1990s cultural lexicon. Cameron Crowe, the film director, had called me early that year. He was doing research for a movie he was planning to make about a sports attorney, and he wanted to immerse himself in my world. I was familiar with his work as a director and as a journalist. I had loved his film *Fast Times at Ridgemont High,* and I had been struck by the compelling pieces on the rock music scene he had written for *Rolling Stone.* I told him I would be happy to act as a "guide" to my profession, and so began a three-year process of our spending a good amount of time together. He joined me at the NFL draft, at league meetings, at NFL games, and on-campus scouting visits. He spent hours in my office, watching me on the telephone and in meetings. He went with me to the 1994 Super Bowl. In 1996, we took Cuba Gooding, Jr., to the Super Bowl in Phoenix and asked him to pretend for several days that he was a football player and my client. In a club one night I remarked to him that his role was so entertaining that he could win an Oscar for Best Supporting Actor.

When shooting began, I spent time on the set, working with Cuba and Tom Cruise on their characters. I showed Jerry O'Connell, who played the quarterback in the film, how to throw a football like a professional.

Cameron and his crew came to my office as well. They photographed everything from my wardrobe to my legal pads to my telephones and my wallet. They used photographs on my wall, where I appear with Drew Bledsoe and Troy Aikman, and superimposed Tom Cruise's face on mine—these shots were used in the beginning of the film. Even awards I received—plaques and certificates for public service—appear in the film in Tom's condominium apartment, with the name Jerry Maguire superimposed on them.

Numerous bits and pieces of the time Cameron spent with me worked their way into the film, including a moment that occurred early in the process, at the 1993 NFL owners meeting, which was held at the Palm Desert Marriott in California. As always, the team executives were all there, along with dozens of coaches, sports writers, and player representatives like myself. No one had ever brought players to this gathering before, but now we had free agents to move around. That was why I brought Tim, who was then a strong safety with the Arizona Cardinals. Besides being an exceptional athlete, Tim McDonald is an impressive person. I wanted the owners to see that. I wanted them to meet him. I wanted them to *want* him.

Cameron watched Tim and me make our way through that scene, joining the swirl of people moving in and out of meetings, hanging out at the restaurant, the bar, all over the hotel complex. Tim was naturally a bit nervous at first upon entering this setting, but as the day passed, he grew more comfortable and confident. Cameron noticed this initial vulnerability of a professional athlete in an alien environment, and he was touched by it.

That afternoon, Cameron joined Tim and a friend up in Tim's hotel room. A broadcast of *CNN Moneyline* was playing on the television as Tim talked to Cameron. "You know," said Tim, "I just want what I deserve. I have a wife. I have a family. At this point in my career, I've put in my time, and I feel like, 'Where's the money? Where's the money?' "

He said it just twice. *Where's the money?* A simple phrase. But it struck Cameron. To him, those three words, which might normally sound greedy or mercenary, seemed poignant in this context. Cameron saw a man talking about providing for and rewarding the wife and family who had supported him and helped him get to where he was in his life. That didn't sound greedy to Cameron. It sounded noble.

Out of that small observation came something much bigger. When the time came to write his film, Crowe turned the phrase into a modern war cry. And to this day, I can't walk through an airport without someone shouting, *"Show me the money!"*

· The single most important advantage in a negotiation is leverage.
· The more options you can create, the greater your leverage will be.
· Convince the other party you have an option, even if you do not.

IRREPLACEABILITY

MOST PEOPLE DO not have the leverage enjoyed by an NFL free agent. They do not have the luxury of several parties bidding for their services.

Not all professional football players enjoy such leverage, either. A rookie draft pick, for instance, is in much the same situation as an employee with no alternatives but to work for the one company that has hired him. When Dallas Cowboys owner Jerry Jones offered Troy Aikman $10 million as the Cowboys' top draft pick in 1989 and we wanted $11.5 million, it was not as if Troy had the choice of saying, "The heck with this," and going back to UCLA to develop a new theory of superconductivity or going to play cello in the Los Angeles Philharmonic. Playing professional football was Troy's only viable option. His prospective employer, Jerry Jones, knew this.

Even in that situation, however, there was room for positioning, for the creation of a different kind of leverage. If Troy could put himself in the position of being so needed by the Cowboys that the possibility of losing him became as frightening to that organization as was the prospect of not playing football was to Troy, then we would have achieved a measure of leverage—which was precisely what happened.

The Cowboys were in a state of chaotic flux at that time, a fact of which we were well aware. They had a new owner—Jerry Jones— who was considered an outsider, a hillbilly from Arkansas who had had the gall to come in and fire an icon—head coach Tom Landry— and replace him with another outsider, Jimmy Johnson. I learned quickly, as have most people who have dealt with him, that image and reality clash with a man like Jerry Jones. He is without a doubt one of the most brilliant, visionary, and creative executives I have ever dealt with in sports, a man filled with charisma. But he was far from popular when he arrived in Dallas. The team's record had been dismal the year before, and it looked as if things were only going to get worse.

The single ray of hope in that tumultuous situation was the arrival of this rookie quarterback. The prior management—Landry and Tex Schramm and Gil Brandt—had created tremendous excitement and hoopla over this young kid after his performance in his final collegiate game, in the Cotton Bowl, right there in Dallas. Besides his football talent, Troy had other qualities that the Cowboys knew they could market as well—good looks, a winning personality . . . and it didn't hurt at all that he liked country music.

When Troy and I agreed to work together that year, we began a relationship that has only deepened with time. Troy is a man's man, rugged and tough, but with a warm, sensitive side. He knows how to shoulder responsibility. At the end of his first year, when the team went 1 and 15 and he was subjected to brutal physical punishment on the field, I asked him what course of action he wanted to take. Did he want to be traded? He said, "No, I want the season to begin again so we can do it all over and do it right. I just want them to give me the ball, and I'll go out and win."

It was that character trait that I wanted the city of Dallas to see when I began to negotiate Troy's rookie contract that spring of 1989. My priority when Jerry Jones took over was to perpetuate what the local press had come to call Aik-mania. We needed the team and the city to need Troy, and so we made him as much of a presence as we possibly could. Troy Aikman became a Dallas Cowboy long before his contract was actually signed. That made it harder for the Cowboys to consider living without him. And *that* made the team more amenable to the terms we were proposing. As far as the Dallas Cowboys management was concerned, Troy Aikman had become essential to the team's future. He had become irreplaceable.

This concept of irreplaceability is fundamental to the process of positioning for a negotiation. We live in a world that is increasingly modular, a network of parts and people and services that are considered easily interchangeable. The challenge to any employee in this climate is to separate himself from that modular mode, to make himself unique, necessary, valuable, and not easily replaced.

The office manager who is totally tuned in to her boss and makes his life infinitely easier in a multitude of different situations, who has over a long period of time developed a deep knowledge of his needs, is someone who has leverage, whether she knows it or not. That executive cannot afford to lose her, whether *he* knows it or not. He will certainly learn how much he needs her if he is faced with the possibility of losing her, which is something the office manager needs to realize, especially if she feels she is not being properly compensated. Her irreplaceability is a powerful weapon for a negotiation.

Perhaps you are an employee who feels undervalued, even expendable. You have no other job options besides your current position. In six months, you are due for an assessment by your employer. Rather than spending those six months fretting or complaining or worrying about your low pay and the insecurity of your position, you need to focus on every possible way that you can increase your value to your employer. You need to do all you can to make yourself needed, to make yourself special, to make yourself irreplaceable. Then you will walk into that negotiation with some leverage. Then you will be operating from a position of strength rather than weakness—a far better position than the one you feel you are in right now.

I lay this all out in the presentation I make whenever I meet with an NFL rookie who has become my client. I explain that he does not have a lot of power. Whichever team drafts him is not going to fold up its tent if it doesn't sign him. The team will go on. He, on the other hand, can play football for them or not play at all. That is why it is important for that player, as soon as he is drafted, to connect himself to the organization that chose him, to the coaches, and to the community. I explain in detail why it is important to win over not just a team but a city, why it is important for that player to establish himself as an appealing human being, a positive role model. I carefully explain that my negotiations are a two-track process: one track is me negotiating; the other is the player acting in every way as if he already has a job—

which, as far as I am concerned, he does. His job, even as I am negotiating his contract, is to work his way into the hearts of his coaches
and teammates and win the attention and affection of the community
by showing what kind of person he is, both on and off the field.

I point out to my clients that by joining the NFL, they are entering the *entertainment* business. They are no longer just quarterbacks or
strong safeties or defensive ends, as they were in high school or college; they are now *corporate assets,* whose value extends far beyond the
boundaries of the football field. Professional sports are no longer just
about the game and the score. The right player, with not only the
right talent but the right personality, gives a team the potential to
build an entire franchise around him, generating excitement and
community support, selling tickets, marketing merchandise, landing
lucrative television contracts, and cross-marketing the team, its players, and its products into a multitude of other outlets—all adding up
to tens of millions of dollars for the organization and ample compensation for the player.

None of this will eventuate, however, if there is a distance—or,
worse, if there is animosity—between the player and the team. This is
why I am adamantly opposed to player holdouts. Nothing can hurt a
negotiating environment more than an athlete not reporting to training camp. Playing hardball in any negotiation is a last resort. Your intention should always be to do everything possible to keep the
channels of communication open and to maintain a climate of cooperation, not conflict. Once the negotiation becomes a face-off, a test
of wills, it becomes perilously close to breaking down.

It is crucial to always, *always* remember that a negotiation is not
personal. It is business. A negotiator may work within the *context* of a
personal relationship with the other party, but the discussion itself
must never become personal. When I am negotiating with Jerry Jones
over Troy Aikman's contract, I do not approach it as if it is Jerry who
is paying Troy. It is the *Dallas Cowboys* who are paying my client, and
that is the level at which both Jerry and I keep the discussion. This is
a subtle distinction, but it is absolutely essential to effective negotiation. When the discussion becomes a face-off between individual
egos and wills, the result is almost always catastrophic.

I watched this happen not long ago with a client of mine named Kevin Greene. Kevin is a premier sack artist, a throwback to the days of leather helmets. At the end of the 1994 season, the Pittsburgh Steelers, who had just gone to the Super Bowl, decided to reshape their 3-4 defense. A key player in that defense had been Kevin, whose linebacker skills were perfectly suited to the Steelers' system. When the team decided to make the change, Kevin, who had always thought he would play out his career in Pittsburgh, became expendable. The Steelers would have re-signed him at that point, but for figures far lower than what he had been earning before.

Kevin was devastated. And his problems became compounded by the fact that there were very few teams in the league that used the system the Steelers had just scrapped, a system that played to Kevin's strengths. One of those teams was the Carolina Panthers. Because the market was so limited, the Panthers' offer, though better than the Steelers', was still well below what Kevin thought he deserved. He had been as productive as defensive linemen and linebackers around the league who were making $3 million a year, but the best Carolina offered him was half that amount. Still, there was no one to offer more.

So Kevin grudgingly signed with Carolina for the figures offered. Then he went out and had a dream season, helping to lead the second-year Panthers to the NFC championship game and being voted into the Pro Bowl. At that point, Kevin felt even more undersalaried than before. He believed he deserved to have his existing contract redone. But in Bill Polian he was up against a general manager who believed just as strongly that a contract is a contract. The Panthers refused to renegotiate. And Kevin vowed not to play again until they did.

Kevin Greene and the Panthers seemed to be a marriage made in heaven. But completely unthinkable results can occur when parties become deadlocked in a negotiation. Spring turned to summer, both parties became increasingly macho and hostile, and Kevin wound up holding out from training camp. That ended any chance of renegotiation as far as Bill Polian was concerned. The Panthers wound up waiving Kevin, and both sides ended up suffering. Carolina lost the heart and soul of its defense, and Kevin went to the San Francisco

49ers, where he was frustrated in a new role as a situation player coming off the bench on passing downs. He still had a good number of sacks, but he was disenchanted.

As a footnote to this story, in a great display of how curious life can be, Kevin Greene re-signed with the Panthers in early 1998.

Maybe Kevin's story would have been different if he had not held out from the Panthers' camp. Maybe not. But because he did, and because neither party would give in or back down, Kevin Greene eventually became, in the eyes of the Carolina Panthers, replaceable. This is something no one wants to become. Irreplaceability is a principle that applies to any employee in any business. A key element in setting the stage for any negotiation is to make yourself so wanted, so connected to the company, so *needed,* that the employer, far from having to be convinced of your value, will be put in the position of doing all that is possible to keep you with the organization. Make your boss look better. Tie your performance to his. Create a vested interest on his part in your success both now and in the future. Allow him to take credit for your success if he so chooses. The point is to do all you can to make your needs and his intertwined, to develop a professional relationship in which anything that helps one of you helps the other—and, conversely, anything that hurts one hurts the other.

Creating this interdependability will give you leverage once the time to negotiate arrives. In those negotiations for Steve Bartkowski in 1975, it wasn't just the threat of the USFL that strengthened our position. Steve developed a love affair with Atlanta even as my discussions with the Falcons management were under way. The press and the public fell head over heels for this polite, articulate, charismatic young man with movie-star looks. They took to calling him Peachtree Bart and the Golden Pole before he was formally a member of the team. He was touted as the salvation of the franchise.

When that deal was finally completed, Steve and I were shocked by the force of public response in the city of Atlanta. Far from resenting or questioning the large amount of money the team was paying this new player, the Falcons fans treated Steve like a conquering hero. When we arrived in Atlanta for the signing, there was a police line waiting as we got off the plane. Spotlights were shooting back and forth across the sky. TV crews were everywhere. The local NBC affiliate interrupted the Johnny Carson show to announce that Steve Bartkowski and his agent had just arrived. Steve and I looked at each other, shook our heads, and said, "We're not in Berkeley anymore."

- To maximize your leverage, make yourself irreplaceable.
- Prepare for an employment or salary negotiation by connecting yourself to the company in as many ways as possible.
- Create a vested interest between you and the company; tie your needs to one another.
- Proceed as if you are already a part of the company, even if you are not.

TERMS

BESIDES BEING PREPARED to pay or be paid a specific price for a product or services, a person entering a negotiation should also have an understanding of the way in which he would like that money—or other form of compensation—to be paid. Identifying and shaping the specific terms, the detailed points that you would like included in an agreement you are seeking—and being prepared to offer a convincing rationale for each of those terms—is as important as any other stage of preparation for a negotiation.

Anticipating the terms the *other* party will likely ask for and preparing a response to that party's position are just as important. Once again, this has to be done before the negotiations begin.

In my business, where each particular negotiation is different in terms of the multitude of circumstances that dictate the player's situation and the team's, there are nonetheless some basic issues we consider with every contract we prepare.

The first issue is the contract's length. NFL teams generally prefer a longer contract than the player, because while each contract puts a maximum limit on how much the player will be paid, there is rarely a minimum in terms of guaranteed money if that player is seriously injured or cut. The best protection against those possibilities is a large signing bonus, money that is paid up front, dollars that are immediately put in the player's pocket. Most NFL contracts are package deals, combining a signing bonus with an annual salary for a specified number of years. One of my bedrock principles is to do all I can to maximize that bonus, to have my client paid as much as possible as soon as possible, to put money in his pocket *now*, so he can build security against an uncertain future.

In baseball and basketball, where contracts are guaranteed and *do* provide security, this dynamic shifts and considerations are often completely opposite to those of an NFL negotiation. In these sports, a player may well want the *longest* contract possible. But the NFL is different. Most teams prefer to link the amount of the signing bonus to the length of the contract—the longer the contract, the larger the bonus. Again, except for a veteran player, who might have already enjoyed his best years and whose priority has become security during the final stage of his career, we generally do not want a long contract. So one of our challenges is to combine the largest signing bonus we can get with the minimum commitment in terms of number of years.

Incentives are another consideration. In a profession as performance driven as football, it is very reasonable to propose contract terms that are dependent on a player's ability to produce results. If our client is not a starter, for example, we might not be in position to push for as much up-front money as we would like, but we can negotiate for bonus payments to be made based on his playing time and performance. He may take a smaller salary, but we will include terms that pay him extra money if he appears in, say, 25 percent of the plays in a particular game. Or we might include a clause that pays him $25,000 for each game he starts. Kordell Stewart made almost a million dollars from his incentive clauses in 1997.

For a client who is a starter, we might push for incentives as well, ranging from bonuses based on season-total statistics (for a quarterback, those statistics might include categories such as completion percentage, number of completions, total yardage, number of touchdown passes, and overall quarterback rating) to postseason rewards (a graduated scale of bonus incentives if the team makes it into a wild-card game or wins its division championship or wins the conference title, or makes it to the Super Bowl, or wins the Super Bowl) to individual honors (bonuses paid for being named All-Conference, or All-Pro, or MVP). Typically, the more unattainable the incentive appears to be, the more money a team will offer. In a quarterback contract, for example, being MVP of the Super Bowl might be worth $750,000, whereas being named All-Conference might be $25,000.

One warning about incentive clauses: They should never take the place of guaranteed money, as in signing bonuses, nor should they replace salaries or other bonuses. They should be more like cherries on the top of the sundae, clauses that appear only after the most important parts of a package have been negotiated to your satisfaction.

That said, I like to include charitable incentives in our contracts as well, in which, say, after every win, both the team and the player donate a certain amount of money to a particular cause. When San Diego State's Dan McGwire signed with the Seattle Seahawks in 1991, they agreed to donate $10,000 to his high school in Claremont, California.

Another crucial issue to consider in any contract involving money is the question of how that money will be paid out. In my business, the issue of deferred payments is a constant point of discussion. Teams would like bonus payments to be deferred forever, because the value of those payments is destroyed by inflation.

A critical consideration in any discussion of deferred money is the concept of present and future value. I typically take every dollar owed and discount it by the prime interest rate for each year that it is not paid. In that way, I can ensure that an agreement made in 1998 dollars, paid in annual installments over five years, will still have the same value in 2003, when the final payment is made, as it does today, when the first payment is made.

A contract's value is not measured by the total amount of money it pays but by the number of after-tax, spendable dollars it puts in your pocket.

· Specify the terms of your proposal before the negotiation begins.
· Anticipate the terms the other party might propose.

· Remember that the manner in which money is paid is equally important to the amount being paid.
· Focus on dollar *value,* not on dollar amounts.
· There is danger in deferment; push to be paid as much as possible as soon as possible.

TIMING

IN THE SAME way that the terms of a negotiation are critical, so is the timing. Knowing *when* to launch discussions is as important as knowing how. Thorough research and an ability to be constantly aware of shifting circumstances in the market in general and in the particular company or party with whom you plan to negotiate will enable you to make the right move *at the right time.*

Knowing, for example, that an employee in a comparable position to yours is about to break through and sign a large compensation package could be a critical factor in deciding to wait until after that deal is done to begin your own negotiation. Knowing that your company is planning to announce record annual sales at the end of the year might be a reason to hold off your salary discussions until after that announcement. Knowing, on the other hand, that the sales picture at the end of the year is going to be decidedly negative, that there might even be layoffs or, possibly, a merger with another company might be good reason to go ahead and begin your negotiation as soon as possible, both to receive maximum compensation and to ensure your own security.

This was the case with Thurman Thomas's contract during that spring of 1993, the first year of free agency. Thurman had been a second-round draft choice of the Buffalo Bills in 1990 and had established himself during his first three seasons as one of the NFL's top three running backs, along with Barry Sanders and Emmitt Smith. Thurman's level of compensation, however—a $1 million average annual salary—did not match his performance. He had one year left on that 1990 contract. The Bills could have chosen to force him to play out that season and then, under the new free agency rules, could have designated him as their "franchise player," whereby Thurman would be prevented from negotiating with any other teams and would be forced to sign a new contract with the Bills, a contract which, under those free agency rules, would pay him an average of the salaries of the five highest paid players at his position.

Those players, including Sanders and Smith, were still earning pre-1993 contracts ranging between $1.1 million and $1.6 million. Among those five running backs, only Smith's contract was up for renegotiation that spring. So the most Thurman would be paid as the Bills' "franchise player" would have been around $1.1 million.

To the Bills' credit, they were willing to discuss a new deal that spring. They acknowledged the enormity of Thurman's contributions to the team, both on the field and off, and agreed that he should receive the compensation he deserved, which was clearly more than he was currently being paid.

The issue for us was whether we should wait for Emmitt Smith to make his new deal with the Cowboys before beginning our discussions or whether we should go first and set the market price ourselves. Among the many things we considered was the fact that Thurman, unlike Smith, still had a year left on his contract—the Bills could argue that because of that, Emmitt should be paid more than Thurman. We finally decided to go first, to set the price ourselves rather than wait to see what Smith might be paid.

That turned out to be the right move. I spent weeks in discussions over the telephone with Bills general manager John Butler and with the team's owner, Ralph Wilson. I had never been to Buffalo before, but I went that summer, and I got to know Ralph Wilson in a way that has bonded us to this day. The casual atmosphere of training camp on a sleepy college campus, with players coming and going in shorts and flip-flops, provided a relaxed backdrop for Ralph and me to get to know each other in a way we never would have in an office. I found him to be charming, with a great sense of humor. He was one of the original pioneers in the AFL, and he has kept his team to this day in a difficult market. When I later led an effort to save the Los Angeles Rams, Ralph was a valuable ally. He shared a lot of wisdom about what it takes for a team to retain its fans.

The fact that I was physically there at the Bills' camp that summer of 1993 meant a great deal to Ralph Wilson. The fact that I had made the effort to come and that I had taken the time to stay is, I have no doubt, what enabled us to come to an agreement on Thurman's contract. There are some people who speculate that each time I travel during negotiation season, I make a deal. That is not always true, but it is true about 90 percent of the time. Often there is no factor more powerful in a negotiation than simply showing up in person.

Another factor in getting Thurman's deal done that summer was that I made sure Thurman took part in training camp, even without a new contract. That made Ralph Wilson much more amenable to considering our argument, which was that Thurman had a quarterback-type of effect on the Bills' high-scoring offense and therefore deserved a quarterback-type of salary. I pointed out to Ralph Wilson that despite his pessimism about the economic future of the Bills' particular market, the economic future of the overall NFL was exceedingly bright, thanks to the league's new television contract—a contract that became even more overwhelmingly lucrative earlier this year. The result of that negotiation was a new four-year contract for Thurman that paid him an average salary of $3.4 million a year—making him the highest paid running back in the NFL.

The operative principle in Thurman's situation, and in every negotiating situation I enter, is that an awareness of the marketplace and an understanding of which comparable deals are in the process of taking place around you will dictate how and when you decide to begin your particular discussions. There is no substitute for the value of being plugged into your profession, of having a network of relationships and friendships within your industry through which to monitor developments and events that may affect many aspects of an impending negotiation, including when is the best time to make a deal and when is the best time for you to deliver your best performance.

We approach our clients' contracts not only by assessing where each player is at the moment but also by looking ahead at where we expect him to be in the future. Then we do our best in the negotiation to shape the contract's length in terms of those expectations, trying to time that player's climb in performance with the number of years on the contract. Ideally, the peak of his climb will coincide with the end of that contract.

A quarterback who has just taken his team to the Super Bowl and who has been named the league's MVP would love to see the end of that season coincide with the end of his existing contract. That would be the very definition of leverage.

Great football players tend to have career performances in the season before they negotiate. Todd Steussie had been a very good offensive lineman for three years with Minnesota, but last season, as he came up for free agency, he stepped up a level and made the Pro Bowl, which had a dramatic impact on our negotiating session with the Vikings. The result was a package that pays Todd an average salary of $4.4 million a year, putting him at the top of the league among players at his position.

The fact that Desmond Howard was the MVP of the 1997 Super Bowl for Green Bay made a huge difference in our free-agent negotiations for him several months later. Had Desmond's performance in that one game not been close to the end of his contract, who knows if we would have been able to get the deal for him that we did— tripling his salary, from less than $500,000 a year to $1.5 million.

Kerri Strug, the gold-medal gymnast from the 1996 Olympic Games, had a performance in Atlanta that electrified the world. With a billion viewers watching and with an especially painful injury to her leg that should have made competing impossible, she displayed enormous courage by attempting and sticking a vault that won the gold medal for the U.S. team. Making deals for her in the afterglow of that moment was very easy for me to do.

The concept of "hotness" can have a huge effect on these situations. In a way, it makes little sense that near the end of a contract which has run for, say, five years, a player's performance in a single game or two can be weighted so heavily compared to his overall performance during those previous five seasons. But the fact is that this often occurs. If Bruce Smith gets four sacks in an afternoon, that one performance may have the effect of emotionally firing up his general manager to pay him more money. Conversely, if Bruce goes out the next week and struggles all day and winds up with no sacks, the GM's enthusiasm of the previous week may disappear.

Should a long-term entity such as a multiyear contract be affected so dramatically by so short-term a factor as what happens in a particular afternoon from week to week? It really should not. But it does. Because people are emotional. Perceptions are filtered through emotions. And the process of negotiation is centered around perception. A saleswoman who has been remarkably productive over the course of the past two years but who has problems during the month just prior to a salary discussion with her boss can find herself having to argue out of a perceptual hole created by her recent performance. She may have to explain why she is lacking or fading lately. Never mind that she may have racked up a long list of sales records and awards during the prior two years. When the subject is personal services and performance—in any industry—the mentality is often, What have you done for me *lately*?

It would be wise, therefore, if you know that a negotiation is approaching, to plan ahead and arrange your circumstances to allow you to score some big points at or near the time of those discussions.

- Knowing *when* to negotiate is as important as knowing how.
- Be aware of circumstances within your company or in the marketplace at large that might affect your negotiation.
- Know the status of recent, ongoing, or upcoming negotiations that are comparable to yours.
- Use your knowledge of comparable negotiations to decide when you should begin your own.
- Try to negotiate at a point of peak performance.
- Plan ahead to predict where that point might come next.

BOOTSTRAPPING

IN MY BUSINESS, each signing builds on the ones that came before it. The parameters of the market are defined by the deals that have

most recently been made—the comparables. Because I often represent more than one player in negotiation at the same position at the
same time with different teams, I have the opportunity to arrange and
orchestrate those deals in a process called bootstrapping.

If I am representing several quarterbacks in negotiation at the same
time, for example, I arrange them from weakest to strongest. Then I
begin by negotiating the weakest one first. This allows us to set the
scale for the ones that will follow. Based on the outcome of that negotiation, I argue the next, then the next, working my way up to the
player with the strongest position, with each deal acting as a stepping-
stone for the subsequent one.

A prime example of this process was in 1989, when I negotiated a
series of veteran quarterback contracts for Tony Eason with the New
England Patriots, Ken O'Brien with the New York Jets, Warren
Moon with the Houston Oilers, and Wade Wilson with the Minnesota Vikings, as well as Troy Aikman's rookie contract with the Dallas Cowboys.

I did the Tony Eason deal first. Tony was making roughly $600,000
a year at the time. He had been injured for most of the season before,
and that became the focus of my discussions with the Patriots' owner,
Victor Kiam. Rather than viewing Tony's injury as a mark against
him, as a liability, which was Victor's position, I argued that the injury was a measure of Tony's commitment, that it had come in the
line of duty, while he was playing the game with reckless abandon. I
maintained that, far from being penalized for that, Tony should be rewarded. I asked Victor to imagine he owned a construction business
and that one of his employees, a very talented ditchdigger, was injured on the job. When that ditchdigger regained his health and was
once again a very talented ditchdigger, wouldn't he be entitled to fair
market value for those talents? Tony Eason was healthy now, I pointed
out, ready to take his team forward the next season at 100 percent.
Shouldn't *he* be entitled to fair market value? That was the argument
that carried the day—the ditchdigger argument. Victor and I ultimately agreed on a new contract for Tony that averaged $1.3 million
in annual salary.

Then I turned to Ken O'Brien and the Jets. I pointed out to Jets president Steve Gutman that Tony Eason had been hurt the year before with the Patriots and that Ken O'Brien had been healthy. Ken had played the entire year injury-free. Didn't he therefore deserve more than a player who missed a number of games because he was hurt? We wound up with a package average of $1.425 million for Ken.

That brought us to Warren Moon, whose position was the strongest of the four veterans'. We said to the Oilers, "Here's a guy who has taken you to the play-offs, who's been in the Pro Bowl a number of years, and who still has a long future ahead of him." Based on those facts, and using the benchmarks of other quarterback contracts that had already been signed, we were able to get $2 million a year for Warren, which made him the highest-salaried quarterback in the NFL at that time.

That positioned us to approach Dallas. Our argument there was that when a quarterback was picked at the top of the draft, as Troy had been, he traditionally received a package average close to that of the highest-paid quarterback already playing in the league. Using that principle, and applying the figure we had just gotten for Warren Moon, we were able to sign a rookie record six-year $11.2 million deal for Troy that averaged just under what Warren was earning per year.

That brought us to Wade Wilson and Minnesota, which at that time was the most difficult team in the NFL to negotiate with. This was why I had saved this deal for last. The Vikings' general manager and part owner at the time, Mike Lynn, was a real purist, notorious for paying his players the least of anyone in the league. He was very effective at establishing *his* own reality. The Vikings were paying Wade $250,000 a year at the time, $150,000 of which was deferred, so Wade was actually making only $100,000 a season.

Wade had just gone to the Pro Bowl the year before. That fact became the basis of our argument, along with the contracts already signed by Eason, O'Brien, Moon, and Aikman. In the midst of those discussions, Mike Lynn had me out to his estate on Lake Minnetonka.

We went out on the lake that warm, gorgeous spring afternoon, and Lynn spent the entire boat ride trying to convince me that the weather was like this almost year-round. Understand that we were talking about Minnesota. "Mike," I said. "If I concede that as a fact, then you're right—Wade Wilson *should* be making $100,000 a year." We wound up getting $1.1 million for Wade, which, within the pay scale of the Minnesota Vikings, was extraordinary.

This same process—using one deal to set up another—applied to the Ki-Jana Carter contract with Cincinnati in 1995. Along with Ki-Jana, we also represented Kerry Collins that year, who was the Carolina Panthers' first draft pick and the fifth pick overall. Since Ki-Jana was the first overall pick, we did Kerry's deal first. The $7 million signing bonus we were able to secure for Kerry was a direct stepping-stone to the $7.125 million bonus we were able to get four days later for Ki-Jana.

Not all bootstrapped deals happen four days apart. Or four weeks. Or four months. But they illustrate an underlying truth of negotiation, which is that one deal *always* sets up another.

· Keep in mind that one negotiation always sets up another.
· If you are involved in several negotiations at once, arrange them in order from weakest to strongest.
· Build each deal on the one that came before it.

LOGISTICS

A FINAL STAGE of preparation for the actual negotiating encounter involves logistical questions:

Is this deal going to be done in one day, in one continuous session, or will it require multiple sessions over a longer period of time?

Will the discussions take place in person or over the telephone or by some other means?

Will they be one-on-one, or will a number of people be involved?

Where will the discussions take place?

The answers to these questions will help you make the preparations necessary to maximize your comfort level in the actual encounter. This is critical. Any physical discomfort, any emotional distractions, anything at all that you might carry into the encounter that will keep you from being absolutely focused on the process at hand must be removed before you begin.

You are preparing, in a sense, to enter a war zone. A deep reservoir of energy will be required, as well as limitless stores of patience. The ability to remain acutely aware of ongoing circumstances at a variety of levels, to be able to read the situation as it unfolds at every moment, will be critical. You are going to feel pressure. You do not want to increase that pressure by bringing outside anxieties and concerns in with you. You may or may not be in control of the environment you are about to enter, but you must do all you can to be in complete control of yourself.

It's important to know whether you are more comfortable negotiating on your own turf or at someone else's office or place of employment or at a neutral site. Understanding your strengths and weaknesses in each of those situations will help you prepare accordingly—or to respond appropriately when it is impossible to prepare, as was the case in a negotiation I did in Kansas City in 1991.

I had flown to meet with Chiefs general manager Carl Peterson to discuss Derrick Thomas's contract. Because Peterson wanted no one—least of all the press and the public—to know that this discussion was taking place, I found when I arrived that he had arranged for us to meet in probably the most secretive, most bizarre, and, for me, the most uncomfortable negotiation setting I have ever experienced.

Lamar Hunt, the team's owner, had converted an underground storage complex in the Kansas City area—essentially, a series of subterranean caves—into a private industrial park of sorts, including some executive offices. This was where I was taken to meet with Peterson. The "office" in which we met had no windows, of course. Neither did it have a clock. The air was stale. I noticed rock outcroppings along one wall.

Understand that I am someone who enjoys space, light, the outdoors. Part of that comes from growing up in Southern California.

Part comes from the fact that for as long as I can remember, I have had a mild touch of claustrophobia. I crave openness. My office in Newport Beach looks out on the Pacific Ocean. The walls are floor-to-ceiling glass. My office in Berkeley has a view of the Golden Gate Bridge. I like that sense of spaciousness, of the whole world spread out around me. My idea of torture is having to sit in the middle of a five-seat row on an airplane. I can't imagine being submerged in a submarine.

So here I was, walking with Carl Peterson into this completely artificial reality, a room with no view, with no fresh air, with no sense of time (I don't wear a watch, which I will explain later). It would have been easy in such a situation to feel trapped, to be emotionally and psychologically disarmed by the setting. I wasn't expecting it. But I adapted. I gathered myself, trained my mind entirely on the issues at hand, and was able to overcome the setting, the sense that those stone walls were closing in around me.

Erasing all outside distractions—this is a critical step in preparing for a negotiation. Some situations, such as being stuck in an underground bunker, are hard to anticipate. You simply have to gather your resources and respond. But in most cases you have a good idea of what to expect, and thorough preparation then becomes largely a matter of logistics.

Typically, I begin and end a negotiation in person, usually on the other party's turf. In between, much of the process occurs over the telephone, by fax, and by other electronic means, though there often arises a need for more face-to-face meetings, again almost always requiring me to travel to meet the other party on his home ground.

Naturally, I feel most in control when I am in my own office, dealing with an owner or general manager on the telephone. I have immediate access to our computers, to our records and files, to every detail of every contract we have ever done. A question can arise during my conversation, I can toss a note off to one of the other attorneys in our firm, and in an instant he'll be back with the salient detail. We have an entire staff ready to crunch numbers, compile statistics, and research a particular question so that rather than destroy the momentum of the moment by having to break off and go find what we need, I can continue the conversation while a particular question is being answered by one of my partners.

If you are conducting a discussion in person, there can be an advantage in being the "visitor"—in meeting the other party on his turf. Enjoying the familiar comfort of his own setting, the other party may become more relaxed. An individual who might be suspicious, edgy, and truculent in the outside world may loosen up in his own environment. He may also appreciate the fact that you have taken the time and made the effort to travel to meet him; it might prompt him to be more amenable to getting a deal done more swiftly and not dragging things out. If things do drag out or if problems arise that you feel necessitate taking a break, it might be easier as the visitor for you to suggest a recess than if you are the "host" and in essence have to order someone out of your office.

Typically, however, the disadvantages of negotiating on the other party's turf outweigh any advantages. The host will have his resources and support staff in place; you will have to bring your resources with you. The host will control the environment: The temperature, the lighting, the seating, the timing in terms of interruptions are all in his hands, not yours. If your travel involves going to another city, the host will have the comforts of home, family, and a familiar setting to turn to between sessions; you will have a hotel room, far from your family, in a city filled with strangers. This is not to mention the stress of traveling itself—standing in line at the airport, the delayed flight, the lack of comfort on the airplane, the hassle of retrieving your baggage, the headache of getting to your hotel from the airport, the adaptations you must make in a multitude of personal routines, from eating to exercise.

All this stress, all these inconveniences and discomforts, can create the temptation to get the deal done more rapidly than perhaps you should. Consciously or unconsciously, you may be prompted to jump at an early offer, to settle, to compromise more than you otherwise might, simply so you can go home and sleep in your own bed.

This makes little sense. After spending so much time and effort on the details of research, preparation, and planning your negotiating position, to come to the actual encounter and give up ground simply because of logistics is more than a shame. It absolutely should not happen. Again, in the same way that planning, preparation, and acute attention to detail are critical in shaping an argument, so are they the key to removing extraneous pressures and distractions that might arise during the discussions themselves.

That preparation should begin with communication and understanding among you and your family, if you are married. Before leaving home, it's important to take care of as many pressing family issues as possible so that you won't be preoccupied with those issues while you are away. It's also important to plan on a long enough period of time away; it will enable you to respond to delays or extensions during the negotiation process without feeling squeezed by the need to return home at a designated time. A phone call from an unhappy spouse who feels neglected back home or a call from your children who are in tears because they miss you can have a debilitating effect on your performance in the negotiation.

One of the most difficult times in my life in terms of balancing my work and home life was the summer my wife, Lucy, and I got married, in 1985. We were on our honeymoon in Maui that June when I received an urgent phone call from my office in Berkeley. A fellow I had been practicing law with had chosen this time to leave our practice and to try taking as many of our clients as possible with him.

That news did not make for the most restful honeymoon. On top of that crisis, it was also the year the USFL died, which opened the door for the NFL to bring the hammer down on what it perceived as a ridiculous rise in rookie contract figures during the previous two seasons because of the competition. An NFL rookie cannot report to training camp until he has signed his contract. Because of that, a team always has the power to freeze a rookie out and delay the beginning of his career by taking a very tough stand in his negotiation. That power was diminished when the rookies had the option of going to the USFL. With the death of that league, however, the owners seized this leverage with a vengeance. The teams circled the wagons, took a united industry stand, and, for lack of a gentler term, colluded with each other to keep the size of rookie contracts down.

This prompted an organized attempt by the agents to respond. We actually held a meeting in Chicago—the first and only time such a gathering of sports agents has ever occurred. Ours is not a profession known for its conciliation, cooperation, or support for one another. It is hard to find a sports agent who will have something good to say about another agent. For some reason, while a talented surgeon can appreciate the work of another gifted surgeon, and while a film director can extol the artistry of another director, sports agents seem pathologically unable to recognize or acknowledge even the smallest level of skill or commitment in any individual besides themselves. This is a sad state of affairs, because there is so much we have to offer one another in terms of advice and information. No one better understands the numerous difficulties and frustrations faced by an agent in the areas of recruiting, negotiating, and client maintenance than another agent. And yet the only energy spent on one another is to trash and attack.

I have always considered such bad-mouthing a waste of time. My partners and I prefer to spend our energy talking to potential clients about our practice and what makes it unique. To indulge in self-serving disparagements of other agents simply makes no sense.

A recent development that concerns me even more than the standard savaging of agents by other agents is the rise of a racial slant among some of the people who have entered this profession lately. There are now some agents, along with people calling themselves agents, who claim that only an African-American representative should deal with an African-American athlete. Martin Luther King, Jr., and all the other brave civil rights pioneers who fought so hard for a multiracial society and died in the process, would roll over in their graves if they saw this. For twenty-three years I have been privileged to represent countless numbers of proud African-American clients. I have also met and worked with a number of outstanding African-American agents. Our own office is staffed by a multiracial mix of attorneys and other staff. To introduce racial and ethnic divisiveness into a sector of our society— professional sports—that has always been ahead of the rest of America in terms of interracial unity is reprehensibly destructive.

The June 1985 meeting in Chicago, which took place at the O'Hare Hilton, was the one instance in which the people in our profession were able to put aside their differences and address a true crisis. At that meeting, a list of first-round players was posted and a united strategy was expressed in which we agreed to share information with one another and to buttress each other's determination to respond to the owners' attempts to control the market. That unity, however, did not last long. Within two months, it was back to pillaging one another in the fight for new clients.

It was against that backdrop that my marriage to Lucy began. On top of that, we had not settled on a place to live. My parents were gone that summer, on an extended trip to Europe, so we were living in their house, which was also where I had my office at the time. With the departure of that lawyer, it was left to me and Jeff Moorad, a bright young attorney who had just joined me several months earlier, to salvage our business—to keep our clients and to prepare to deal with dug-in owners over contracts for our clients, who included four of the top twelve picks in that year's draft. Fortunately for me, Jeff turned out to be a quick study. His growth curve was accelerated greatly in this crisis.

The owners were not eager to talk with Jeff and me. We had taken positions based on the previous year's crop of rookies and what ought to be a natural appreciation in salaries for this year's players. But the teams maintained that those 1984 numbers had been artificially inflated by the influence of the USFL. Now, they indicated, it might even be time to roll those numbers *back*. The owners were happy to let the pressure build on us, which it did.

One of the compacts I attempt to make with rookies, and especially with their parents, is to have the players—their sons—be on time to training camp. I have always said that it doesn't take a genius to hold a player out of training camp, in the same way that it doesn't take a genius to accept too little in compensation. The trick and artistry in negotiating for rookies involve allowing the player to come to the city, develop a relationship with the fans, make friends with the coaches, go through a good deal of training prior to camp, elevate his position, get ready to start the first year, and have the first public experience of the team with the player be one where everyone is sitting together at a press conference table with a signed contract.

As the middle of July approached and training camps were getting set to open, nothing was happening. Jeff and I were on the phone night and day. When we weren't on the phone, we were deep in discussions, struggling to figure out a strategy. The tension was compounded by continual calls from players and their parents wanting to know what was developing. We had very little progress to report. We had taken positions, the teams had taken positions, and there was no negotiating taking place. The anxiety in our office—which was in Lucy's and my house—was extreme. These were not ideal circumstances in which to begin a marriage.

Finally, in the middle of the month, I decided to go on the road and put an end to this. Often, in any business, especially if the bulk of a negotiation is being done over the telephone, there comes a time when it is necessary to grab the bull by the horns, to make a dramatic move and break a deadlock. In many cases, that move may be something as simple and direct as getting in a car, or boarding an airplane, and going to meet the other party face-to-face.

This was what I did in July 1985. First I went to San Diego, where I was able to make a deal with the Chargers for Jim Lachey, an offensive tackle from Ohio State who was the twelfth pick in the first round. Then it was on to Tampa, where I negotiated the contract of Ron Holmes—a defensive end from the University of Washington who was the eighth pick in the first round—with Hugh Culverhouse. Hugh was a silver-haired, leonine figure. As I faced him across a long table on that particular afternoon, the sky outside the plate-glass windows behind him began to grow dark. Tampa is the lightning capital of the world, and sure enough, tendrils of electricity began flashing around Culverhouse's head. I felt as if I were facing Moses.

We were able to do that deal that day. When we finished, I told Culverhouse I had two draftees left to sign, Duane Bickett, a linebacker from USC who had been drafted by the Colts as the fifth pick in the first round, and Ken Ruettgers, a USC offensive tackle who had been selected by Green Bay. I couldn't figure out which one to do next. Did he have any suggestions?

"Wait a second," he said, and he left the room. I could hear him on the phone with someone. A couple of minutes later he came back.

"If I were you," he said, "I'd go to Indianapolis."

So much for the owners denying collusion.

So I headed to Indianapolis, where I had my first experience with Jim Irsay, the son of owner Robert Irsay. The Colts had just moved from Baltimore. Jim, who was twenty-six at that time, met me in the team's temporary headquarters, which were housed in an elementary school. We had instant rapport. He was a soulmate, who loved rock music and cutting-edge culture. We met in the principal's office, where we sat on a couple of child-size plastic chairs and worked out a deal for Duane Bickett.

Now, finally, it was on to Green Bay. By the time I arrived there, I was exhausted, absolutely worn-out. I had not had time to prepare for this trip, and I had run out of clean clothes. When I picked up the local newspaper, there was a quote from Forrest Gregg, the Packers' head coach, saying, "Oh, another agent's in town. Maybe I should invite him over to the house for supper. We'll serve him rat poison."

That was not a good day for me. But I was able to pull it together, meet with Packers general manager, Chuck Hutchinson, and do the deal for Ken Ruettgers, the seventh pick in the first round. I was beat, but I was done. I immediately found a phone in the Packer complex and called my wife.

"Lucy," I said. "I've got good news. I just finished Ken Ruettgers. I'm on my way home."

"Well," she said, "I won't be here when you get back. Next time, marry Chuck Hutchinson."

And she hung up.

Thirteen years and three kids later, Lucy and I are still together, partly due to the fact that I have not allowed things to get out of hand as they did that summer. There is no way to overstate the importance of keeping a balance between your home and your work life. The happiness and fulfillment you feel in one depends greatly on the happiness and fulfillment you feel in the other. The freedom and flexibility you will need to respond to business emergencies and crises that might take you away from your home and family are best achieved by developing a healthy level of communication and awareness with your spouse and children when you are with them. Your family will be better able to prepare for and give you time away if you make a point of giving them yourself and your time when you are home. I do not bring my business home with me. My children will only be this young ever so briefly, and I don't want to miss these moments. When I'm home, my job is to be a dad and a husband, to watch my boys play soccer and my daughter dance, to let them wear me out on the living room rug at night and read books to them at bedtime.

Balance is the key to most things in life. And preparation. The simple packing that I did *not* do for that 1985 odyssey is exactly the kind of small detail that can make a difference in a negotiation where you have to go on the road. Anticipating your particular needs for a trip and covering all contingencies are critical to removing all possible distractions. Give yourself flight options, in case there is trouble with the particular flight you have booked. Reserve a flight that allows you to arrive at your destination with time to rest properly before the negotiation begins. Arrange for alternative return flights in case the process lasts longer than you expect. If the food on the plane is going to pose a problem, call ahead for a special alternative selection.

Stay in a hotel that offers a fax machine in the room. If possible, arrange to have a telephone with multiple lines. Carry a cellular phone—or even two. The situation may arise where you are on one line and you desperately need to speak to a second, or even third, caller at the same time. If missing those other calls might change the entire course of the negotiation, you want to remove that possibility.

Speaking of the hotel, make your reservation for more nights than you expect to need, again in case unforeseen circumstances arise. You don't want a negotiation to run longer than anticipated and be saddled with concerns about where you are going to sleep that evening.

Work out all ground transportation beforehand. If you are driving, don't make the mistake of parking in a lot with a closing time. One of the worst feelings in the world is to come to the end of an exhausting negotiating session that has run late into the evening and realize that the lot is now locked up, with your car parked inside.

The point is to think ahead and be prepared for every possible eventuality, removing all conceivable distractions so you will be free to focus on the process.

- Choose a negotiation location with which you are most comfortable.
- If you cannot choose the location, make all preparations possible to minimize your stress and maximize your comfort level.
- Remove all possible distractions beforehand.
- Prepare for every conceivable need.
- Be prepared to adjust to discomfort and circumstances beyond your control.

THE TELEPHONE

WHILE THE TRADITIONAL thinking about negotiation is that it is a face-to-face process, *mano a mano,* two parties squaring off across a conference table, the reality is that in today's business world, a large part of negotiation is done long-distance, electronically. The classic smoke-filled room is becoming a thing of the past, replaced by telephones, personal computers, fax machines, car phones, airplane phones, and other communications technology undreamed of twenty years ago.

Troy Aikman's rookie contract with the Dallas Cowboys was an example of this combination of face-to-face discussions and long-distance technology. The foundations of the negotiation were laid prior to the draft, in early April in Dallas, where Troy and I met with Cowboys owner Jerry Jones, head coach Jimmy Johnson, Jerry's son, Steven, and Jerry's oil-business partner, Mike McCoy.

We started our discussion at five o'clock in the afternoon at the Cowboys' offices in Valley Ranch, Texas. Jerry Jones had just come back from visiting with President Bush and was fired up. As the hours rolled along, we became progressively hungrier. Finally, Jimmy Johnson served us dinner—a bowl of microwave popcorn, which he fixed there in the office.

This was a get-to-know-you meeting. A lot of the conversation was about hunting and fishing. Everyone in that room, with the exception of me, was from Arkansas, Texas, or Oklahoma. I soon felt that I was the one with the heavy accent.

We adjourned just before midnight for a late meal at a fifties-style diner inside the hotel where Troy and I were staying. After the meal, Jimmy, Jerry, and I moved to the lobby, where we sat and talked football almost all evening. With every hour that passed, the collection of empty beer bottles on the table in front of us grew larger.

Around 3:30 A.M., Jimmy finally got tired. Jerry and I went on with a discussion of basic NFL economics until seven that morning. After a short break, he and I picked up again at 8 A.M. and went on into the afternoon.

When I finally left Dallas that day and flew back home, we were far from finished. But the groundwork had been laid. From that point on, it was a matter of continuing to reinforce our case, and most of that process took place between my office in Berkeley and the Cowboys' executive offices in Valley Ranch, Texas. We sent more than fifty exhibits to the Cowboys by fax—displays of Troy's achievements, his abilities and potential compared to other quarterbacks' in that year's draft and to those of quarterbacks already playing in the NFL. We were on the phone constantly. When it came to finally closing the deal, we hooked up through an advanced communications system called Bright Link television. Troy, Jeff, and I sat in a room in Thousand Oaks, California, watching Jerry Jones, Jimmy Johnson, and Mike McCoy on a wide-screen television as they sat in their office watching us. We completed the contract via that two-way video communication.

I don't use something like Bright Link every day, but I virtually live on the telephone. Between talking to my clients and their families, speaking with the press, dealing with a vast network of people within professional sports in order to keep up with the constant flow of information and events, and, during signing season, conducting one negotiation after another, I can easily make a hundred telephone calls in a day.

Negotiating on the telephone could easily justify an entire chapter on its own. The vast majority of my contract-negotiation discussions are done over the telephone. Spending that much time on the phone requires an awareness and a sensitivity to the nuances of non-visual communication. All the cues of body language that are so telling in an actual encounter—facial expressions, hand gestures, the head turning a certain way, a roll of the eyes, reddening of the face, someone clearly dying to express a thought, someone expressing nervousness, someone expressing aggression—the nonverbal cues that allow us to "read" another person, are not there in a telephone conversation. Neither are the cues that allow that other person to read us.

It's easy to forget this, to speak as if the person is there in that room with you. You may be glaring at the clock, strongly affected by the time, and you may assume that the other party is aware of your feelings. There may be five other people in the room with you, creating an onslaught of ancillary stimuli, and you may forget that the person at the other end of the line is entirely unaware of this. Although those stimuli are part of your reality, they are not part of his, and you have to remember that. You must be disciplined enough at all times to separate your environment from the environment of the person at the other end of the line and not project the circumstances surrounding you onto him. All he has is your voice.

That can, of course, work to your advantage. Some people feel much more comfortable and in control on the telephone than they do in person. They may feel that they give themselves away too easily in person. Their emotions are too visible, their fears or insecurities too apparent. They may feel much more protected, much more comfortable and in control of the situation over the telephone. Knowing this about themselves, they should arrange to minimize the time spent in face-to-face negotiation and maximize the time spent conducting their discussions on the telephone.

A final note about awareness on the telephone: If you are traveling and using a portable or public telephone to conduct business, be aware of eavesdroppers. This may sound like a fine point, but it is a lesson I have learned the hard way more than once.

During the negotiations over that Troy Aikman rookie contract, I had a particularly intense car phone conversation with Jerry Jones. I was stuck in the infamous Los Angeles rush hour traffic on the San Diego Freeway, and Jerry was stuck at his offer of $10 million.

"Jerry," I told him, "we've got to have eleven and a half."

"Son," he said, "that dog won't hunt."

"Jerry," I said, "this is fair."

"Son," he answered, "we passed *fair* about eight million dollars ago."

Back and forth it went, until suddenly a third voice came on the line, a stranger who had crossed cell-phone signals with us.

"Listen, buddy," the voice said, addressing me with a Texas drawl, "if you don't want the ten million, *I* do. Take the deal."

A similar thing happened during the Kordell Stewart deal in 1997. Kordell's rookie contract was still in effect, but the Steelers were planning to make him their starter for that season, and we were negotiating a new contract accordingly—none of which was publicly known. The subject of who the Steelers' starting quarterback would be was a topic of intense speculation in the city of Pittsburgh. The decision that it would be Kordell was a secret that Steelers coach Bill Cowher had carefully kept to himself. Just as secret was this new contract for Kordell, which the Steelers were prepared to sign. Pittsburgh owner Art Rooney had been greatly concerned about the confidentiality of this negotiation, and I had been extremely careful to keep that confidentiality.

Now, finally, I was on a flight to Pittsburgh to close this deal. While en route, I called back to my Newport Beach office to check on several matters, including some details on the Stewart contract. Before I began speaking, I looked around the first-class cabin. There was no one I knew or recognized. There was no one wearing NFL team colors or carrying a briefcase or duffle bag with team insignia, as most people involved in the world of football do. I felt free to speak, and went ahead with the discussion.

No sooner did I arrive in Pittsburgh, pick up my luggage, and climb in a car sent by the Steelers to take me to Three Rivers Stadium than an announcement came over the sports talk show the driver had tuned on the radio:

"Agent Leigh Steinberg arrived today to do a brand-new contract for Kordell Stewart . . ."

I was stunned. I learned later that someone in that first-class cabin had indeed overheard me. Knowing that this was a hot news item, the person had rushed to a pay phone as soon as we landed and called the radio station. Just like that, my arrival made headlines.

The Steelers were understanding, and we went ahead and signed the contract. But I learned once again that nothing, but *nothing,* can ever be assumed or taken for granted. Including privacy.

- When you are on the telephone, remind yourself that the other party can only hear your voice; he has no other clue about the circumstances or conditions at your end of the line.
- If you feel more comfortable on the telephone than in person, arrange the negotiation accordingly, to maximize your discussions on the phone.
- When using telephones in public places, be aware of possible eavesdroppers.

PERSONAL APPEARANCE

IN THE SAME way that you want to remove anything that might distract you during the course of a negotiation, so should you be aware of anything that might distract the other party—most notably, your clothing and personal appearance. Ideally, the other party should notice nothing but the words coming out of your mouth. That is what you want him to focus on.

Facial hair, visible tattoos, earrings, ostentatious suits, short skirts, tight blouses—there is nothing wrong with any of these things in and of themselves. There is nothing wrong with making a personal statement through your appearance. But whether you want to make that statement in a business setting is another question.

I would suggest that you do not. Anything and everything you bring into a negotiation—from the information and argument you have assembled to your attitude and demeanor to the clothing you wear—

should contribute to achieving the intended result. Anything that detracts from that goal should be put aside.

My partner Jeffrey Moorad has a beard, and it presents no problem for him. It does not detract in the least from his effectiveness as a negotiator. That is because he is a polished, comfortable, and extremely capable professional. The beard is simply a part of who he is. Wearing that beard is a judgment call, and Jeff's judgment is very good.

For you and for me, such a decision is a judgment call as well—a decision that depends on our own assessment of each business situation we enter. I have lived my entire life in the casual, relaxed atmosphere of Southern California. I'm most comfortable barefoot, in a pair of shorts and a T-shirt. In fact, that's the way I often come to the office, when I know I'll be doing business on the telephone that day and my appearance will make no difference. Even this innocent assumption can occasionally be dangerous, as I learned not long ago, when a writer from a national magazine came to do a story about *Jerry Maguire,* spent some time with me at my office, and went back and wrote a story about these eccentric Californians who don't wear shoes.

Generally, though, what I wear to work makes no difference. In negotiations, I'm usually meeting with people I have known for years. But for younger lawyers, especially in face-to-face meetings, clothing can make a difference. For a person in his early twenties or thirties, the presumption of lack of experience or seriousness by an older person can be a disadvantage. Older businessmen or businesswomen can tend to take a younger person less seriously than someone their own age. So the youthful person may need to work harder to get an older party to focus on his words and not his age. Wearing a suit or some other form of professional attire can add credence to their presentation.

The key in any face-to-face negotiation is to have the other party concentrate on the message you are trying to deliver without becoming distracted by anything else, including your appearance. I would suggest removing anything at all that might send some sort of signal that interferes with the process. I don't wear a $20,000 wristwatch.

Not only is that not my personality, but I don't want the other person studying that watch, trying to deduce what it might or might not say about me. The fact is that I don't wear any jewelry at all. I don't wear a designer suit intended to display my power with its price tag. Some people make a point of displaying their power through their appearance. That is part of their approach, part of their conscious negotiating style. Subtly (or not so subtly), their strategy is to throw down the gauntlet in terms of their wealth and prestige.

Whether I'm up against the stereotype of a fast-talking, slick-dressing agent or preparing to walk into a negotiation with someone who has known me for years, the point remains that my singular focus is to achieve my intended goal in that particular negotiation. This means I want the other party to concentrate on the meaning of the words coming out of my mouth and nothing else. Anything that might interfere with that purpose—a loud tie, a ponytail, or a tattoo—is best left behind or covered up.

- A business setting is no place to make a personal fashion statement.
- Anything you wear that would distract the other party from the business at hand should be removed.

PARTNERS

NO MATTER HOW independent or self-sufficient you are, it always helps to know that you are not on your own. If you are negotiating by yourself, it helps immensely to have some sort of support structure, some partners, colleagues, or friends whom you can depend on to act as a sounding board, for both strategic and factual advice and emotional support. I have always felt that the best negotiation concepts are forged through a very heady process of having a series of people bouncing the issues back and forth, providing different perspectives on every conceivable problem and solution.

Whether I am planning and shaping a negotiation or actually conducting one over the telephone, I am surrounded by my staff and partners, all of us working together as a team, each aware of his particular strengths and responsibilities. When I travel for a face-to-face encounter, I am typically alone, although I stay in almost constant communication with the team back at my office; all of them are prepared to provide me with whatever information or advice I might ask for.

There are times when I bring a partner with me to a negotiation encounter, when we participate as a team. The dynamics when negotiating with a partner are entirely different from those when working by yourself, and it's important to be aware of those dynamics.

The difference between negotiating one-on-one and negotiating with a partner is akin to the difference between playing doubles and singles in tennis. With singles, the entire game is in your head and your hands alone. Every move, every shot, every ploy is yours alone to choose and execute. When you have a partner, however, the weight of each decision and its ramifications is more than doubled; it is exponentially multiplied. The need for both partners to understand, anticipate, and react in tandem to each shot is paramount. Any trace of disunity or confusion can be disastrous. There must be total communication between you, as well as complete commitment to the same game plan.

The same coordination is necessary in negotiation. A response that catches your partner off guard, an unexpected suggestion, the slightest hint of disagreement between the two of you will be seized upon by the other party. Any crack in your team's facade will be exploited by the other side, so it is essential that two people going into a negotiation together be completely prepared to enhance and back each other up.

This is not easy for bright individuals who are accustomed to having complete control and used to making decisions by themselves. Working with a partner means giving up that control—not an easy thing to do for some people, but absolutely necessary if you are going in to a negotiating situation together. Just as ego can be the most destructive element in a discussion between strong-willed opposing parties, so can the presence of ego be poisonous between two parties on the same side of the table.

My partners Jeff Moorad and David Dunn and I negotiate very well in tandem with one another. We've been together for so long that we not only think as one in terms of planning and preparing strategy beforehand, but we respond the same way to the things we see and hear during negotiations. We have the same sense of timing. And we are thinking of the same way in which we will respond. We are thinking of the same next move.

When working together, my partners and I will often divide up the different tasks in a negotiation. I may focus on the high-concept part of the deal while Jeff or David handles the nuts-and-bolts part of the process. When I'm by myself, I handle those details as well, but when we're together, my emphasis might be on the presentation, establishing the concept from which the numbers will flow, and Jeff or David might take care of the actual figures.

Sometimes there is an orchestration to the team process. One partner's skills might make him the better choice to open and close the discussion, while the other might better handle the nitty-gritty details that make up the guts of the process. David Dunn, for example, has a very comforting presence, an easygoing personality that puts others at ease. So he is naturally effective in certain phases.

Then, of course, there is the tough-cop/nice-cop strategy, where one partner plays hardball in the discussion while the other mollifies. Keep in mind, though, that you shouldn't have to play these roles at all if you are engaged in a frank, honest, ethical discussion.

One of the greatest advantages of having multiple people involved in the process is the team's ability to keep the momentum going. There is a rhythm to every discussion or series of discussions. There are times when you want to slow things down, and there are times when you want to speed them up. Typically, the former is when things are not going well; typically, the latter is when they are. If a negotiation has really hit its stride in terms of the direction you want it to be heading, if the spirit and the momentum of the discussion are heading straight toward the deal you desire, then the last thing in the world that you want is to interrupt that mood, to stop that momentum by taking a break.

All sorts of things can occur during such a break, and few of them are good. The other party may begin to have second thoughts. Questions might arise about whether things are moving too fast, about whether someone is being railroaded. A break gives the other party an opportunity to call a colleague, to ask his opinion, and that colleague might tell him he's crazy, that the terms he's thinking about accepting are ridiculous. Worse, he could call his boss and hear the same thing.

During a negotiation, there are often outside parties, people involved with but removed from the actual discussions, who have strong opinions about the strategy and decisions that are being made—opinions that almost always differ from the negotiator's. Almost invariably, whenever I take a break to confer with my partners during a deal I am doing alone, they tell me I'm not being tough enough, I'm making a major mistake, I'm giving up the store, I must have taken leave of my senses.

This is a very common syndrome. People not directly involved in the discussions are almost always certain that whatever deal the negotiator is making is much worse than the one he should make. These third parties have the luxury of distance. They are not involved in the give-and-take of interaction. Their perspective is more clinical, more detached. Their opinions are predicated strictly on research and advocacy arguments, on the exhaustive preparation done before the actual discussions began.

The problem is that this attitude confuses advocacy with the art of what's possible. When we prepare our presentation, we are arguing the strongest conceivable position. We are taking the greatest strengths of our client. We are projecting the largest expansion of the marketplace. We are assuming the most favorable interpretations in terms of comparables. These are all logical, rational positions. But what seems overwhelmingly logical to a researcher sitting at his desk with his charts and computer may become impossible in the real world, in an encounter between human beings.

Remember that the third party is not present in this situation, reading the chemistry as you are. On the one hand, you may find yourself agreeing to terms because you are tired and sick of the process, or you may have become intimidated or started to believe the arguments of the other party. In such a case, an outside perspective can be helpful in getting you to refocus and take a more productive stance. On the other hand, if you are sure that your approach and the result it will yield are sound, you must not allow a third party to destabilize you. You, and not that third party, have the responsibility for consummating the deal.

Keep in mind that third parties will always assert at the end of any negotiation that they could have achieved a better result. This comes with the territory. When a husband comes home and conveys to his wife the details of a negotiation session he just had with his boss on the subject of his raise, the wife may say, "How could you have been so weak? That figure is insulting. Do you always have to let them take advantage of you that way?" When the businessman comes back to his office after having made a deal with one of the suppliers, his boss may say, "I can't believe you agreed to pay that much money. I send you out to do a job, and you let them take you to the cleaners." You have to filter these judgments through your own sense of the experience you just went through—an experience none of these other people shared.

Something important to understand about the reactions of third parties is that they often depend on expectations. How you prepare your colleagues and your clients for a negotiation you plan to conduct will in large part determine their response when it is concluded. The negotiator who rashly or brashly promises to get figure X in an impending negotiation will have more to explain and answer for when he returns with the lower figure Y than the individual who has stated more realistic expectations.

An advantage of having a partner present during a discussion is that when the momentum is in your favor, you don't have to interrupt the flow in order to have some figures calculated or to get a particular point in a proposal checked. You don't need to stop the discussion to run those numbers or to call your office. Your partner can take care of it on the spot while you continue moving things forward.

One final note on the presence of a partner is about the dynamics of a two-against-one situation—when you are the one. It's easy to feel overwhelmed when you are outnumbered. Years ago, I did a contract with the San Francisco 49ers for a linebacker named Gordy

Ceresino from Stanford. Both John McVey and John Ralston represented San Francisco's front office in the discussions. Every time one of them would make a point, the other would nod his head and say, "That's right, John. I certainly agree. *Everyone* would agree." They were "Johnning" me to death. I had to remind myself that I was not facing two people; I was facing one position. Eventually, I was able to get them to stop by reminding them of that same fact.

It is important to remember, and to remain aware, that no matter how many people are on each side of the table, it is still one position against another. The fact that there might be seven people facing you does not mean they have seven votes to your one. And it does not mean you have to allow them to express their opinion seven times. Don't allow yourself to be intimidated by their number. Your ground is the same size as theirs, no matter how many of you are standing on each side.

- Surround yourself with as much support as possible, both before and during a negotiation.
- If you negotiate with a partner, make certain that you are committed to the same approach.
- If working with a partner, identify your individual strengths and prepare your roles accordingly.
- Set your egos aside; you must act in concert, not as individuals battling for control.
- Never question or contradict your partner; one trace of discord or disunity can be disastrous.
- Use your partner to help keep the momentum of a good deal moving.
- Don't be intimidated if you are outnumbered.

SETTING LIMITS

WHENEVER THE NFL passes a new rule, my partners and I immediately study it, turning it inside out in order to create new techniques and options that allow us to continue to maximize our position in every negotiation we enter.

No matter how many options we are able to create, however, we realize that it is unlikely that we are going to get everything we want. As the discussions progress, both sides will probably have to give ground. The question then arises as to how much ground you are willing to give. This answer, like so many others, must be decided before the negotiation begins.

4. Set your limits before the negotiation begins.

This is imperative in any negotiating situation: Limits must be set in advance for what you are and are not willing to accept or concede. Prior to your first meeting with the other party, you must be clear with yourself (and your client, if you are representing someone else) about the boundaries of your position. You must identify the points where you are flexible and the points where you are not. Whether that point is the highest price you are willing to pay for a house or the lowest salary you are willing to accept from a new employer or the maximum number of friends you will allow your daughter to invite to her birthday party—whatever the issue being discussed—you must know your limits before the negotiating begins.

And you need to be prepared for the worst-case scenario, which is that you and the other party will fail to find a resolution within the limits you have set, that one or both of you may have no choice but to walk away from this deal.

Can you live with that?

This is probably the single most critical question a person preparing to enter a negotiation must answer: Are you prepared to lose this job? Are you willing to give up your dream of that perfect house? Can you conceive of life on your own, without your partner or spouse?

The cold, hard fact may be that you cannot live without that job, at least not right now. You may *not* be able to leave your spouse, at least not right now. That may be the reality. But in the face of that reality, it is the *willingness* to walk away from the deal you are trying to make that will give you the strength and confidence, the emotional leverage, you will need as you enter the negotiation.

I am talking here about the ability to be in a state of *denial* about the ultimate catastrophe of an unsuccessful negotiation. I am talking about the ability to stare into the face of apocalyptic doom and not back down, not allow fear to undermine your confidence and the strength of the case you are trying to make. This is a subtle point, but one on which the entire outcome of a negotiation may hinge.

Every day of my life, I negotiate in circumstances in which we will ultimately accept the last best offer we receive. When I am discussing Warrick Dunn's rookie contract with the Tampa Bay Buccaneers and we want $4 million to sign and the Bucs say they are not doing the deal for more than $3 million, it's not as if Warrick has the choice of walking away and doing something else for a living. And yet we have to continue pushing toward the Bucs' last best offer *as if* Warrick can walk away. When I'm discussing Jake Plummer's rookie contract with the Arizona Cardinals, it's not as if Jake has a choice of walking away and doing something else for a living. And yet we have to pursue the Cardinals' last best offer *as if* Jake can walk away.

This is an absolutely necessary mind-set. It may be a fact that this is the only job possibility that you have and that you cannot afford to lose it. But you need to be able to *ignore* that fact. In the face of financial ruination, in the face of losing your dearest dream, in the face of devastating emotional loss, you must have the capacity to argue your position—the position that you have painstakingly created through exhaustive preparation—*as if* you have the ability to walk away.

You simply cannot allow the negotiation to be the playing field of your own fear, your own lack of options, the feeling that you are stuck or trapped . . . *even if you are.* Effective negotiation requires a conscious decision to ignore the reality of your needs and dependencies, to ignore your own deepest and darkest fears, and to continue to fight for what you believe is fair.

If you are unable to find that underpinning of emotional independence, if you enter the process in a position of subordination, need, and fear, then you are not ready to negotiate.

- Set your limits *before* the negotiation begins.
- Do not compromise those limits, even if an agreement seems unreachable.
- Prepare for a negotiation *as if* you have the option of walking away.
- Do not allow the playing field of a negotiation to become your own fear.

FACING YOUR FEAR

IT IS RATIONAL to feel afraid of confrontation. It is human, especially if the consequences of that confrontation include such possibilities as the loss of a job, loss of respect, perhaps the loss of a friendship.

Rather than deal with such discomfort, many people simply avoid the process of negotiation altogether. They accept what they are given in this world in exchange for avoiding the stress that might come with pushing for what they deserve. Other people might try to tackle the process, but they do so with fear. They are afraid to hear another human being reject their ideas and position. They are afraid to have someone tell them that they are being unfair or unreasonable. They are afraid that a person they respect might tell them they are disappointed in them. They are afraid to face possible ridicule or rage.

These are all possibilities in a negotiation. In some cases, they are probabilities. Most good negotiators will try to unbalance the other person, to destabilize him. They will try to make the other person feel illegitimate. They will try to make the position the other person presents seem clearly specious or clearly unfair. They will attempt to establish their reality as reasonable and fair and the other person's as overreaching and absurd. They will attempt, in other words, to intimidate you, and to the degree that you are afraid, they will succeed.

Therefore, the final and by far the most critical stage of preparation prior to an actual negotiation is for you to identify, confront, and resolve your fears. This requires the same brutal honesty and depth of introspection used to assess your abilities.

We all contain deeply planted pressure points of emotion, feelings that are triggered by certain characteristics or behavior in others. We may cower when someone raises his voice. We may shrink in the face of tough or profane language. Men may wilt when a woman cries. We may tense up in the presence of someone who is taller than us or someone who is of a different race or someone who reminds us of our father.

It is necessary first to recognize that you have such reactions. Then it is essential to explore where those reactions might be rooted, in order to allow yourself to control them when they begin to arise.

Think of situations where you have felt most uncomfortable in someone else's presence, instances where you have felt controlled, bullied, or intimidated, where rather than assert yourself, you have retreated or fled.

Maybe you have a tendency, when you feel threatened, to go on the attack. Or perhaps you become overly defensive.

Are you a person who places a premium on pleasing people, who feels that if you resist or take issue with someone in any way, you will lose his approval?

These are hard questions to ask oneself. They may lead to areas and issues inside you or in your past that you may never have confronted before.

Perhaps you felt neglected as a child and so you became an adult who constantly seeks acclamation and ratification of his worth. Take that tendency into a negotiation, and you will run the risk of accepting the other party's terms simply to please them, to make them happy with you.

Maybe you had a dominant father who screamed at you when you were a child, and now you turn numb whenever someone raises his voice. Perhaps you had a guilt-tripping mother, which has made you vulnerable to the slightest signs of disapproval—a sneer, a sigh, a roll of the eyes.

If any of these things are true, you will be helpless in discussions with an adversary whose intent is to destabilize you in whatever way he can. Whatever your tendencies, your insecurities, your sensitivities and emotional triggers, be assured that they will be sought out and exploited by a skilled person in a negotiation. If an employer knows, for example, that you are a person who seeks validation, he may well play the role of parent when you come in to talk about a raise. He may indicate how displeased he is with you, letting you know you have made him unhappy, making you feel that you have somehow transgressed by daring to challenge or defy him.

If you are prone to feeling responsible for the comfort of those around you, if you have that caretaker tendency, you may find yourself facing someone who plays on that weakness, who tries to induce guilt and obligation on your part to agree to his terms.

The levels of emotional manipulation are manifold in any negotiating situation. To be properly prepared, you must be aware of and able to control your own emotional needs. The last place in the world where you should be trying to satisfy those needs is in a negotiation. As much as possible, you want to walk into that first discussion—and every discussion thereafter—with your ego complete.

How can you address those weak emotional areas, fill those gaps, and control those fears?

By facing them.

If you know that you are easily intimidated by coarse language, have a friend or a colleague or your spouse play the role of such a person. As you make each point, have them respond with profanities and anger. You can only hear an obscene word so many times before it loses its impact. The same with a raised voice. If you hear it enough, at a certain point you become desensitized. The tone and the words lose their power. The same with physical intimidation. If you know that a person with a certain body type tends to unsettle you, find a friend that size or shape and have him loom over you, playing the role of an overbearing intimidator.

As for a paralyzing fear of the repercussions if you dare to take a stand, try something other than pushing those doomsday thoughts deeper inside you, where they will never stay. Try going in the other direction. Raise those thoughts, turn them over in your mind or even out loud in conversation with a friend. Consider the reality of the worst-case scenario:

If I express myself in this marriage, the other person will divorce me.

If I assert what I think I'm truly worth in this salary negotiation, I'll be fired.

If I don't offer what this guy wants for that car, I won't get it.

By staring into the jaws of incipient doom, you may well find that the worst case is actually not that cataclysmic. You may be surprised to find yourself thinking, If that's the worst thing that can happen, I'll be okay.

By considering your deepest fears and imagining them as realities, rather than pushing them aside whenever they rear their head, you may find that they are simply not that frightening. You may realize that you can live without that car, that life will go on after this marriage, that there are other jobs besides the one you have. Not that you wouldn't *prefer* to own that car or keep that job or save that marriage. But if you must compromise yourself in order to have these things, if you refuse to address your dissatisfaction or unhappiness because you are afraid of what might happen if you speak up or take issue or stand your ground, then you will make these things hardly worth having at all.

Prepare for the worst. Realize that the world will not end if you lose. Then, and only then, will you be fully prepared to win.

- You must enter a negotiation with your ego complete; this is not the place to display or fulfill your emotional needs.
- Prepare for the other party to play upon your fears.
- Identify your fears before the negotiation begins.
- Examine where those fears might be rooted.
- Ask friends or colleagues to help you become comfortable with your fears.
- Imagine the worst, accept it, then put aside all thoughts of anything but success.

4
—

THE ENCOUNTER

CONNECTING

EVEN WITH ALL the preparation and research in the world, no one can be ready for everything that will be encountered in the course of a negotiation. Things will unfold that go beyond any "game plan" you might have mapped out. The particulars of the negotiating environment, the personality of the other party, the dynamics and chemistry between him (or them) and you, the values, priorities, limitations, and capabilities of the organization or the individual you are negotiating with, unfolding events in the outside world that could have an effect on the course of your discussions—these things will only come clear during the face-to-face encounter, and no one can predict all of them.

The single most important quality that will carry you through this experience is acute awareness. You must have the ability to stay completely focused, to absorb, process, and respond to an ongoing flow of information and stimuli while shutting out all distractions. Not unlike an athlete in the heat of competition, you must be mentally, emotionally, and physically primed to read and react to swiftly unfolding and constantly shifting situations and circumstances. As with an athlete, practice and preparation help immeasurably, but when the game begins, it is time to perform, and there is no script to let you know exactly what will transpire.

The moment you walk through the door—if the negotiation is taking place on the other party's turf—you need to assess the physical setting. Is the temperature particularly warm or cold? If there are windows, is the sunlight a factor? How is the seating situated? What kind of seats are they—soft and casual? Hard and formal? Is there a surface on which to write when taking notes?

These details matter. You need to know, for example, if the firmness of a seat affects your ability to maintain a level of alertness. A deep, soft seat can have a lulling effect on some people, inducing passivity and even sleepiness. I don't think it's an accident that Jerry Jones has an office couch so plush and pliable you virtually sink out of sight when you take a seat. Talking to Jerry from that sofa is like trying to throw your voice out of a foxhole.

The traditional concept that physical positioning somehow determines authority or power—the theory that a person sitting in a more elevated seat or behind a massive desk somehow has the advantage in terms of psychological superiority—means nothing to me. But it might to you, and you need to be aware of this.

Some people have a preference for turning their heads to the right or to the left to address the other party. I happen to be more comfortable looking over my right shoulder, so I make a point of taking a seat that allows me to do this rather than have to spend hours straining my neck in an uncomfortable position.

Hopefully, there will be some period of time before you sit down during which you can take stock of such details. If you can't get it done while shaking hands and making introductions and greetings, ask the host to show you around his office. Inquire about a portrait on the wall or a book on a shelf or a photograph on the desk. This will give you time to make an assessment of the physical environment.

One of the first barriers we typically must break through in a negotiation is the armor people put up to protect themselves. It's natural to be hesitant to reveal oneself to strangers in almost any setting. It's normal to hide behind roles, titles, and carefully guarded words. This wariness is compounded in a negotiating situation, where the tendency is to begin by holding one's cards close to the vest. Anything that can be done to pierce this protective armor and begin connecting to the other party in a personal way will increase the level of trust and communication that develops between you. As the negotiation unfolds, that trust and communication will become invaluable.

One effective method to begin breaking down the barrier is to find and explore points of commonality or mutual interest. As you tour your host's office, admiring a painting or noticing a book or a photograph, it helps immeasurably if you actually know something about the subject and can comment on it intelligently and with genuine enthusiasm. This will establish some common ground between you, ground that might have nothing to do with the substance of your negotiation but can have everything to do with the nature of the relationship between you.

If this is a telephone negotiation, you can discover points of connection by asking questions. Don't be in a hurry to rush straight into the business matters at hand. Take your time. Try to find some common ground, to develop a little rapport. This is an essential point to keep in mind—that whether this particular negotiation is the only one you will ever have with this individual or whether this deal will be the first of many, the process will be much more fruitful for all involved if you approach it as a *relationship*. That is why it can help so much to lay the groundwork early in terms of mutual interests and personal connection.

This is not hard for me. I have always been voracious about absorbing the culture I live in. Books, movies, music, television, newspapers, magazines—I am constantly reading, watching, and listening to what's new, what people are paying attention to, where the trends are headed. Not only does this help me keep up with the world my clients live in, and not only does it help me connect to the individuals with whom I negotiate, but I am also genuinely fascinated by the flow of popular culture. I'm intrigued with other people's experiences and perspectives. It's not just a tactic. There is nothing fake or phony about the interest I express when I come across an item or subject I have in common with a person I am meeting in a business setting. If you are insincere, feigning interest where there is none, it is worse than showing no interest at all. If you put on an act, it will be smelled out in an instant by any moderately observant person.

That said, it is extremely beneficial to have as comprehensive a knowledge base as possible about every conceivable subject. As I have traveled over the years, I've made a point of researching each city I visit before I go there. When I arrive, I explore it a little if possible. I learn about it. And I keep up with it after I'm gone. There isn't a city with an NFL team whose issues and events I don't know about. From environmental problems in Seattle to the nature of shrimp fishing in New Orleans, from mayoral controversy in Atlanta to the senatorial situation in Minnesota—if it's important and it's happening in these places, I want to know about it. For my business, I *need* to know about it.

Although talking about the weather can seem like a cliché, it remains a handy and often compelling tool for discussion. The harsh weather we experienced in Southern California recently due to El Niño was a topic that came up in almost every business conversation I had during that time. I had a firsthand perspective to share on a subject that was national news.

The capacity to spread your web of knowledge wide enough to be able to touch something that is near and dear to the heart of the person you are meeting is an invaluable quality. There isn't a major college or university in the nation that I can't talk about in some way to a person who happens to be an alumnus. The same with movies and books—if I haven't actually seen or read them, I've read *about* them. I can't say I watch every situation comedy that is broadcast on television, but I make a point of regularly flipping through the channels so I will at least be familiar with the programs, which supplements what I have read about them. I may never have watched an entire episode of *Seinfeld,* but I know who the characters are and I understand how much that show became a part of many people's weekly routine and why it meant so much to so many people when the show ended its run.

I'm the same way about music. And politics. And about more arcane subjects, such as geography and zoology. I devour information about them because they fascinate me. But I am never surprised when the conversation in a business meeting meanders around to such minutiae as the dropoff in tourism at Carlsbad Caverns or the mating habits of bats or the manufacture of candles in New Hampshire and the other party and I are *both* delighted to find that we actually share a familiarity with the subject. In one of our first negotiations back when he was general manager of the Dolphins, George Young and I began chatting about Miami and soon discovered that we both had a deep interest in the origins and heritage of Cuban Jews. When Jim Irsay and I first met in Indianapolis, his fascination with the culture of the 1960s opened up a long conversation about our shared interest in the power and influence of rock music, especially of Jimi Hendrix, Janis Joplin, and Cream.

Such serendipitous connections make for meaningful breakthroughs, and they are not really accidents if you are an individual armed with a comprehensive base of general knowledge.

Beyond the things you just happen to know, there are also things you can specifically learn in advance of a particular meeting. The research you have done in preparation for the negotiation can pay dividends in this introductory, conversational phase as well. If you discover that the person you are meeting is into the music of Duke Ellington or that he is fanatic about fly fishing or that he worships the works of Mark Twain, then you will want to make a point of studying these subjects so that you will be able to talk about them when they come up—which they almost certainly will. It's part of my job to know that Ken Behring, the former owner of the Seattle Seahawks, has a passion for big game hunting; that Kansas City's Carl Peterson is deeply connected to UCLA; that Buffalo's Ralph Wilson owns television outlets across the country, including one in San Jose, where my first media client, Jan Hutchins, was his first anchorman; that New York's Bob Tisch owns Loew's hotels and his brother Lawrence formerly owned CBS; that Pittsburgh's Art Rooney, had he taken the opportunity to fill an empty Senate seat in Pennsylvania, might well have been Bill Clinton's running mate; or that Mike Holovak, who was general manager of the Oilers before they moved to Tennessee, served on a patrol boat in the Pacific after World War II and learned to sleep during the day and stay awake all night—a distinct advantage in lengthy negotiation sessions.

Sometimes what you learn about a person's interests might make it appropriate to bring a small present or token. If you know the person you are going to meet is absolutely nuts about sourdough bread from San Francisco, it is entirely appropriate to bring him a loaf. If you know he has a weakness for a certain type of chocolate, it makes sense to take him some if you can find it. Knowing that a transplanted Angeleno who is now general manager of a team back east is crazy about the food served at a particularly wonderful little place in Los Angeles called Tito's Tacos, we figured out a way to keep a box of tacos hot on a flight across country and brought them with us to a recent meeting. Before beginning negotiation with another NFL team, also in the East, I discovered that the daughter of the team's general manager was a big fan of the television show *Beverly Hills 90210*. I had appeared on an episode of that program in 1996 with Steve Young. It was a very tough role—I had to play myself. Because of that connection, I was able to bring an autographed photo of Jason Priestley— the heartthrob star of the program—to my first meeting with this GM, which touched both him and his daughter enormously.

Such a gift is a simple act of graciousness. It's something you would do for people who have invited you to dinner at their home, so why not do it in a situation like this? You are going to be spending hours, maybe days, maybe even months, with this person. You are going to get to know each other very, very well. An introductory token shows the other party that you care enough about this undertaking to have made an up-front effort to establish a personal connection. It helps break down the armor of distrust and caution. And most important, it is an initial step toward the next stage in the process—establishing a tone of collaboration and candor.

This thoughtfulness, by the way, extends in both directions. During the Italian meal I shared with Bob Kraft as we discussed Drew Bledsoe's 1995 contract in Boston, we both raved about some hors d'oeuvres made from an exotic type of olive. When I returned to California after that deal was done, there were several tins of those olives waiting for me, courtesy of Bob.

Be careful when accepting such gifts from the other party in a negotiation, however. They may distort your judgment or give the appearance that your acquiescence can be bought. Minor tokens for hospitality are one thing; expensive gifts and lavish entertainment are another.

A further warning about this process of first meetings and first impressions: It is important to understand the difference between sharing common interests or knowing something about someone and outright pandering. It can be easy to offend someone and raise his suspicions about your sincerity if you are overeager and try too hard to show what you know about him or what the two of you might have in common. Don't make more of these connections than the other party does. Allow the tone, length, and depth of the conversation about such subjects to be steered by his level of interest, not yours.

And don't make assumptions. Just because someone is Italian, it does not mean she likes Italian food. Just because someone is African-American, it doesn't mean you should greet him with a soul handshake. Don't make the disastrous mistake of stereotyping, and don't judge a book by its cover. To make judgments about a person based on his clothing or physical appearance is dangerous. The casually dressed person in a meeting can often be the CEO of the corporation, while the person impeccably groomed in suit and tie may be a lower-level executive with very little power. You may meet a man who is short, overweight, quiet, and not at all conspicuous, and he may turn out to be the sharpest, toughest, most capable negotiator you have ever encountered. To approach such a man with an attitude of superiority simply because you might look more physically fit or appear more powerful is to make a gross mistake.

Always assume that your counterpart is worthy. Let him show his shortcomings. But never assume them.

- Enter a negotiating encounter as an athlete enters a contest—completely prepared, acutely attuned, and ready to absorb and respond to swiftly unfolding circumstances.
- Take in every detail about the physical setting.
- Comment on some of those details; connect with the other party on a personal level; pierce his protective armor by sharing mutual interests.

- Come armed with knowledge and familiarity with as broad a range of subjects and interests as possible.
- Come prepared with knowledge of the other party's particular interests.
- Where appropriate, arrive with a gift that reflects the other party's interests.
- Don't pander.
- Don't make assumptions based on appearances.
- Never underestimate the person you are meeting.

TRUE AGENDAS

IN A BUSINESS riddled with conflict, enmity, and aggression, it puzzles many people that I have been able to maintain and develop warm, respectful relationships with the men and women I face across the bargaining table. I would argue that it is not only possible but in most cases necessary for an effective negotiator to approach the other party in a spirit of collaboration. The ability to trust one another, to develop a climate of candor and clarity, will enable both parties to reveal their true agendas. It is only when those agendas are revealed and understood by each side that movement toward an agreement can truly begin.

My first task is always to make clear that while I have my client's interests to present, I am approaching this process collaboratively and really do want to hear what the other party has to say, what his interests, position, and supporting arguments are. Conflict will come soon enough, as may ultimatums. But initially, I do all I can to make clear that I am approaching this process as a joint venture, a journey toward mutual satisfaction. Rather than viewing each other as adversaries, we should consider ourselves partners in pursuit of a fair agreement that is advantageous to each of us.

Again, every step of the process leading to this point must be based on honesty and trust in order to achieve this climate. Any form of deception, any power play based on force rather than on cooperation, will destroy the possibility of the two parties working in concert to achieve a solution that is fruitful for both of them. If trust and respect are lost, then a process of creative problem solving becomes one of protracted struggle and enmity instead.

5. Establish a climate of cooperation, not conflict.

The negotiation process in football has always been more difficult than in baseball or basketball. Working through a football deal is akin to having three bats on your shoulder in the on-deck circle, while doing baseball and basketball contracts is like dropping two of those bats before you step to the plate. The rules for football have always been tougher and more rigid than for other sports. There is no arbitration in football. Until five years ago, there was no free agency. Even with free agency, there are franchise restrictions and tender restrictions and the salary cap. And while each National Basketball Association general manager has to deal with just twelve players' contracts, and each major-league baseball GM handles twenty-five, an NFL executive has fifty-three contracts to juggle and control.

These differences affect the entire stance of the negotiation. Generally, basketball deals tend to be done more swiftly and with less rancor than other sports deals. Typically, in an NBA deal, it doesn't take long to come to a point where what we think is fair is what the team thinks is fair as well. With the NBA's cap structure setting the limits and with teams having the money to spend and only twelve players to spend it on, we tend to reach agreements relatively rapidly, while in football there is almost always a significant disparity of opinion when we begin.

Our negotiation for Austin Croshere's rookie contract last year with the Indiana Pacers typifies our NBA dealings, just as Austin typifies our type of client. He's from Santa Monica, not far from our office in Newport Beach. His family is rock-solid: His father, Pete, worked for the same company as an accountant for thirty-five years; his mother, Pat, is a neonatology nurse, who works long hours in a high-crisis setting; Austin's younger brother, Damon, will be attending Loyola Marymount University this fall, with Austin financing that schooling.

It's that kind of sharing and sense of responsibility that impressed us about Austin from the first time we met him. Before we ever did his contract, he already knew that he wanted to take a certain amount of his money and establish a foundation to help with research on Alzheimer's disease, since his grandfather has had to deal with that condition in recent years. During Austin's last semester at Providence, he asked us what we thought about his placing a full-page ad in the local newspaper to thank the people of that city for making their community his home away from home for four years. Was it any surprise that a coach like Larry Bird—an athlete and an individual with that same kind of authenticity and respect for doing the right thing—would make a player like Austin Croshere his first pick in the 1997 draft?

We and the Pacers had already talked prior to that draft. We knew they wanted Austin, and when he was still available as the twelfth overall pick, they took him in a heartbeat. It's always easier to negotiate with a team when they're happy and eager about the player they're getting. The Pacers were extremely happy to have Austin.

We talked with Bird and with Pacers general manager Donnie Walsh that same night, after they'd made the selection. Donnie is a great old-line basketball executive, a mirror of the traditional football men I deal with. He knows the game and loves the game, as opposed to the number-crunching, I-don't-know-who-this-player-is-but-this-is-what-I'm-authorized-to-do type of executive. Donnie's attitude with Austin was, Let's go on and get this thing done quickly, because we want Austin in camp next week.

Now our response could have been, "Well, we'll see about that," and we could have then dug in and tried to squeeze every possible advantage out of the deal, but we felt the same way Walsh and Bird did. We, too, wanted Austin signed and in camp as soon as possible. The league's rookie salary cap dictated the basic range of Austin's salary. There were still a couple of dozen details that either side could have quibbled over, ranging from the time frame of payouts to the nature of the guarantees, but rather than each side squaring off, taking the strongest position, and battling over every one of those points, we talked to Austin that evening, and he agreed that the important thing here was to have his first steps with the Pacers and with Coach Bird be good ones.

So the day after the draft, the entire Croshere family, along with David Dunn, flew from Charlotte, where the draft had been held, to Indianapolis. When they walked into Larry Bird's office, he was on the phone and motioned them to have a seat. Austin felt as if he were in the Oval Office watching the president talk. He was completely in awe.

Bird finished his phone call, came around his desk, pulled up a chair, took a seat, looked straight at Austin, and gave a long pregnant pause that nobody wants to fill. Then he said, "So. Are you ready?"

That was it: Are you ready?

Bird went on to share some of his philosophy with the family. He said he wanted this deal done quickly and he wanted to see Austin in camp the next week.

Larry Bird was negotiating right there. First, he was negotiating with Austin, positioning Austin to walk out of that office saying, "I want to be in camp next week." And second, Bird was negotiating with Donnie Walsh, letting Walsh know that he needed to get this deal done by the end of that week. The last thing in the world that Walsh wanted was to have his new coach—the idol of the state of Indiana—put in an awkward position by having trouble signing the first draft pick of his coaching career.

Neither side had an interest in haggling, since the NBA salary cap for rookies greatly narrowed the negotiable subjects. Basically, Donnie Walsh said, "This is what we will give. Is there going to be a problem getting this one done?" And there wasn't. We worked through the details fairly rapidly. We got everything we wanted—a three-year, $4 million contract—and they got their player in camp and ready to go. Austin's *next* contract may take more time, but this one was easy, a situation of sugar working better than vinegar for both sides.

Part of such a climate of cooperation is due to the circumstances, and part is due to the personalities. I have always believed that if you treat people in an open, honest way, they will respond. Effective negotiation is not about hoodwinking someone or hustling him. You might get away with that once or twice, but you will not be around long if that is your approach. No one will respect you. No one will trust you. No one will deal with you.

Honesty begins with being yourself, presenting yourself as you really are. I happen to be a relatively laid-back, easygoing person. My casual nature might be mistaken for weakness or pliability by a person who does not know me, and that's fine. Being underestimated is always an advantage.

One of the difficulties in any formal business setting is that people are playing roles. Their role might be that of representative of someone else—perhaps they are attorneys representing a corporation; or emissaries representing a foreign government; or general managers representing a professional football team. Or they may simply be people whose title and position prompt them to present themselves in a certain way when doing business.

Your challenge is to somehow break through that veneer, which is made even harder to penetrate by what I call speechifying—hiding behind the obfuscation of noncommittal, imprecise language. In the same way that people hide behind roles and titles, they also tend to protect themselves by speaking in vague, unclear, or perfunctory terms. Their intent—whether conscious or not—is to shield their true motivations, needs, and desires.

There may be a host of reasons why the person is clouding the issue, tossing up smoke screens to disguise his true concerns. Maybe the issue is pride: A general manager digs in his heels against signing a rookie for a certain amount but won't reveal that the reason is his concern over how it would look to the public if he were to sign a player for more than the draftee ahead of him received. The GM doesn't want to appear insecure, so he doesn't reveal his true motivation. If he did, we could accommodate him, packaging the deal so that on the surface it would not look any better than the signing ahead of it. But we can't work that out until we know that this is what he needs.

The same kind of problem confronts a fellow who asks his girl-friend to go the movies with him and she says she can't. He asks why, and she tells him she has to baby-sit. He offers to send his sister to take her place, and she says no, she has a lot of studying to do. He suggests that they study together. Again she refuses, but can now give no reason. The truth is that she has a problem with some aspect of their relationship, but she can't find it in herself to confront him with this. If she *could,* if she were able to reveal her true agenda, they could address it and perhaps resolve the problem. But as long as she is throwing out false agendas, both she and her frustrated boyfriend are wasting their time and their energy.

There are several ways to draw out someone's true agenda when that person is hesitant to reveal it. One is to turn to your research, to what you have already learned about the other party's situation and needs. Consider the car salesman who won't budge on the sticker price of the automobile you'd like. If you know he is paid by commission, which is based strictly on the purchase price, you might suggest that some extra services be thrown in, which would have no effect on the purchase price but would make this a more attractive deal for you. If you haven't done your research and know how he is paid, you might not be able to come up with this solution.

Time itself can take care of getting at the other party's core issues. Through personal interaction and an increasing comfort level, the other person's barriers will eventually dissolve, peeling away like the layers of an onion. Rather than wait for this to happen, however, you can hasten the process by asking some direct, probing questions about the other person's attitude and philosophy concerning the basic issues you'll be discussing.

I do this all the time. It's very disarming to simply say right off the bat, "Look, there are two ways we can go about this. We can spend a lot of time giving speeches to each other about our positions, or we can talk about what's really important to us here. Let me know your interests, and I'll let you know mine."

If I'm meeting with someone for the first time, I might ask him before the discussions even begin to talk in general about his philosophy of contract negotiation. It might be surprising to that person that I'm so direct, but I've found that people are eager to talk about their principles and beliefs. In my business, I've found that most general managers are quite willing to spell out their feelings about issues such as the length of a contract, the specificity of a player's responsibilities, whether there should or should not be guaranteed money. Without getting into specifics about the deal at hand, you can save a lot of time and establish some guidelines for the ensuing discussion by eliciting this kind of information up front.

Besides drawing out the other party's issues, you can also learn what resources and levels of authority will or will not be available to you. If you're an employee beginning a contract negotiation, you would want to spell out the support in terms of staff and budget that you would need in order to do this job as well as possible. You would want to ask how much autonomy and authority you would have in this position. A candidate for a head coaching position in football would want to know the number of assistants he would be able to hire, the size of the salaries he would be able to pay those assistants, and who he would have to answer to in making such hiring decisions.

Asking such questions not only gives you information you will need as the discussions proceed, but it also allows the other party to identify his own expectations, needs and restrictions—all of which you will need to know as you move toward fashioning an agreement.

Some people enter a negotiation prepared to stand on pronouncements of principle or ideology, statements of the particular issues or beliefs on which they refuse to compromise. This is not the direction you want to go in a discussion. The aim of the negotiation process is to open the pathways to possible solutions, not to lock yourselves in with limits and restrictions. If the other party has such limits, it's better to get them out on the table right away rather than learn about them later.

If you can establish this paradigm of cooperation and trust in the beginning of the negotiation, you will not only avoid groping down blind alleyways in the ensuing discussions, you will also be able to re-orient yourself at any point where the talks seem to be stalling. Having established a sense of candor and trust, you can always step back at any point in the process and say, "Look, I understand what your of-

ficial position is. But let's put that aside for a moment. I'm not holding you to anything you say right here, so let's talk about what it
would take to get this done."

Such off-the-record, nonbinding statements and discussions are
often the most valuable and productive part of the negotiation process.
But you will never have this option if you haven't established the level
of trust that allows the other person to feel comfortable revealing his
true agenda.

· Establish a tone of collaboration, not conflict.
· Create an atmosphere of frankness, honesty, and trust.
· Persuade the other party to drop pretense, roles, and "speechifying."
· Ask the other party to discuss his philosophy, values, and issues.
· Encourage him to reveal his true agenda.

THE INDUCEMENT

ONCE YOU HAVE elicited as much information as possible from the
other party about his needs and interests—his agenda—it is time to
share yours. It is time now to make your presentation, to share the
facts and reasoning you have gathered and prepared, the foundation
of objective standards and criteria that supports the proposal you intend to make.

The presentation always precedes the proposal. You need the other
party to understand *why* you think you deserve what you are going to
propose before you tell them *what* you are proposing. You need them
to see that what you are going to propose is fair, logical, well reasoned, and consistent with facts. The purpose of the presentation is to
justify what is to follow, to induce the other party to consider your
point of view, to have him see that what you plan to propose makes
sense both for you and for him, that your interests actually overlap, or
are at least compatible, and that your problems actually have mutually
satisfactory solutions.

This is one reason you began the first meeting by discussing the other party's interests, by asking him to reveal his agenda, so that you can acknowledge and incorporate those interests into your presentation. Keep in mind that behind seemingly opposing positions can lie identical, or at least compatible, interests. It's surprising how often, in negotiations, both parties want the same thing but are blinded to that fact by the positions they have assumed. Interests—yours and the other party's—should remain your focus throughout the course of the negotiation.

Besides motivating the other party to accept your reality or at least to consider it seriously, your opening presentation also provides an anchor, an underpinning to all that will subsequently transpire. When you come to a sticking point later in the discussions, the problem will almost certainly be rooted in this inducement stage of the negotiation, and you will need to go back to find out what it is. Maybe you left something out. Maybe you weren't as thorough as you should have been. Maybe you failed to take into account a critical factor. Whatever the oversight, it will reflect in the bargaining that ensues, and you will need to identify and address it when it arises.

If there is no oversight on your part, if the discussions stall because the other party is resisting something—or simply doesn't agree with it or doesn't quite understand it—then you need to go over the inducement again. You need to make your points again. And again. And perhaps again.

The presentation is your foundation, the rock of reason on which you stand. If that rock is solid—if it is accurate, honest, and reliable—it will withstand any winds or storms or attacks that might come. And rest assured that at one point or another, they will probably come.

· The presentation should always precede the proposal.
· Incorporate the other party's interests into your presentation.
· The purpose of your presentation is to induce the other party to accept your reality.
· Be prepared to return to this inducement again and again throughout the course of your discussions.

DEALING WITH A DICTATOR

IF YOU ARE dealing with powerful, strong-willed people, it is a priority—an absolute necessity—to bleed as much ego as possible out of the negotiating situation. This is rarely, however, an easy thing to do.

It is particularly difficult in the business of professional sports. This is a macho business, a macho world. I am typically negotiating with team owners who are proud, wealthy, powerful middle-aged men, many of whom were athletes themselves, few of whom are accustomed to being questioned or challenged. When you are dealing with people like that, the last thing you want to do is insult them, humiliate them, or push them into a corner. Unfortunately, it is very easy for people in positions of such power to feel that they are being insulted, humiliated, or pushed.

Many of the men and women who have risen to executive status in business have gotten there by asserting their will, showing initiative, approaching situations directly, and not taking no for an answer. They have been able to achieve things everyone said they could not.

A downside of that achievement, however, is often an inability to seriously consider opinions or perspectives other than their own. Many powerful people are so imbued with a sense of omnipotence and so determined to have everything go their own way that they see every idea other than their own as a direct challenge. The brightest, most talented people are sometimes the ones who have the most trouble listening to alternative ideas. If someone disagrees with them, their impulse is to believe that that person either does not understand the points they have made or that he is acting in bad faith.

There are people with this attitude who will literally not give the other person a chance to speak or, if they do allow the other party to say something, will instantly dismiss everything they hear. So intent are they on not giving an inch that they will instantly argue with every single point you make.

There are people whose negotiating style is to allow you to speak, but as you do, they will take issue with absolutely everything you say. They cannot sit patiently and allow you to make your position clear. Their approach is to assume a position of complete intransigence, agreeing with nothing—and accepting nothing—they hear. They interrupt. They argue. They nitpick.

One way of dealing with such individuals is to simply ask for the opportunity to make a complete presentation without interruption while assuring them that they can reserve any objections until the end and that their silence won't be taken as acquiescence.

Another method is to do something to destabilize them, something to return them to earth and make them realize that they are not in a one-way dictatorial situation here. If during your preparation for the negotiation you have been able to establish some leverage, you might want to deliver that shot across the bow as soon as the other party begins acting as if this is a monologue and not a dialogue. It can be very effective to respond to an employer who begins dictating the terms of your situation by saying, "That's interesting, because other potential employes I've talked to don't feel the same way." The fact that an alternative even exists for one party can sometimes come as a stunning revelation to the other.

It can be just as effective to address the issue of control directly. "Look," you might say to an obstinate individual. "I thought we were here to discuss both of our needs and how to reach an accommodation. The reason they call it negotiating is that there are supposed to be two parties involved. If your mind is already made up, if you're not interested in anything I have to say, then why are we even here?"

In each of these situations, the point is to head off that one-way attitude, to nip it in the bud and introduce the sense of a level playing field. If you know in advance that you'll be facing this type of individual, don't meet him in his office or on his own turf, where he is accustomed to complete control and will feel most untouchable. If for no other reason than to be shown an act of faith from him, you might ask that the discussions take place on your turf or in a neutral setting. The very act of the other party having to travel somewhere, to leave his office to meet with you, is a demonstration that he is shifting into a negotiating mode.

· Bleed as much ego as possible—yours and the other party's—out of the negotiating situation.

· Confront a controlling, dictating individual with your leverage.
· Insist that you be allowed to speak without interruption.

THE OFFER

ONCE YOU HAVE made your presentation and created the induce-ment, it is time to make the proposal, to present the offer.

The question is, Who makes the first offer?

The answer is, It depends on the situation.

In the enviable situation where an individual has multiple op-tions—a free-agent athlete would be a prime example—it makes sense to let the other party make the first proposal. In a situation with multiple bidders, you want to keep each bidder involved for as long as possible. If *you* present the first figure and it is too high, you will immediately discourage or scare away people who might potentially end up being the choice you want to make. Your aim in a multiple-option situation is to keep open as many of those options as possible. So it makes sense to let the other party begin. He may start lower than you might like, but the figures will begin climbing soon enough, be-cause of the sheer dynamics of the situation.

Those dynamics depend, as in all negotiations, on the power of your presentation, the level of inducement you are able to achieve. You want to excite people. You want them to want you—or your client or your product. You want them to *need* you. The more bidders you are able to get involved and keep involved, the higher the figure will go.

But it is not just the amount of money that matters. All the per-sonal factors that you identified during your early preparation—your values, your passion, your goals—are important as well. You may end up in a multiple-bidder situation where an employer who is willing to offer a salary of $65,000 is actually more attractive than one who is ready to offer $90,000. Other factors besides money make the first employer preferable to the second. You won't be given that choice, however, if you begin by setting a minimum of $70,000. You will have eliminated that choice, which defies a basic principle of the negotiating process, and that is that you always want to maximize your number of options, not minimize them.

Now, assuming that you are dealing not with multiple options but are facing a single buyer or seller one-on-one, the issue of who makes the first offer hinges on circumstances and on human nature. Ideally, if both parties are reasonable people who know each other well, who respect and trust each other, and who have approached the negotiation in a spirit of candor and cooperation and with very little gamesmanship, it would seem that the question of who makes the first offer would be immaterial. Both parties share essentially the same reality. They have differences, but the differences are slight. They each see the situation pretty much the same way. And so it would seem that a fair, reasonable offer by either one would be perfectly acceptable to the other. Offer made. Offer accepted. Case closed. Deal done. Everyone goes home happy.

Not quite.

One problem with this "reasonable person" theory is that it ignores the human need to feel that something has been accomplished. I believe that most people covet a sense of progress, of movement. A payer in a negotiating situation wants to feel the satisfaction of having the price drop. The payee wants to see the price go up. In each instance, that sense of movement, that feeling of progress, is sweet in itself, apart from the actual money that is paid or the product or services that have been bought.

In a deal done too soon, that sense of victory, that feeling of achievement, is missing. After all the work and preparation done beforehand, there can be a hollowness in an immediate agreement, a sense of being cheated out of the process. An athlete who trains for months for a game or event doesn't want to show up and just be given a medal or a victory without playing the game. He wants to *earn* it. He wants to put to the test the skills and abilities he has worked so hard to develop.

We all value movement. Consider a situation in which I represent a football player who feels he deserves a salary of $1 million. I walk into the negotiation, and the team immediately accepts our offer. My client now has what he wanted. But I did nothing to get it for him. He could rightfully wonder if I have done my job. He could rightfully wonder if he should not have gotten more.

If, on the other hand, the team makes an offer of $800,000, and we eventually work our way up to $1 million, I'm a big hero to my client. He has no more money than he would in the other situation, but in this case, there was ground gained. Psychologically, that can make all the difference in the world.

The person who visits a used-car lot, sees a vehicle listed for $12,000, offers the dealer $10,500, and hears the dealer say, "Great, it's yours," will almost certainly drive home berating himself for not having offered less. Even if $10,500 seems fair, even if $10,500 was what he was prepared to pay, he will be nagged by second thoughts.

There are businessmen who brag about no-nonsense negotiating— "I liked the guy's style. He made me an offer. I took it." But the fact is that this hardly ever happens. Very few people in business will simply accept an initial offer. Buyer's or seller's remorse—doubts and regrets about whether you should have offered less or more—is just too strong. Unless there is a time constraint that requires the agreement to be reached right away, you should never make an immediate deal. Better to pursue the process and see where it takes you. This is what you have prepared for.

That said, I believe that in most one-on-one negotiating situations, it is to your benefit to make the first offer. By doing so, you are the one establishing a benchmark for the discussion, a beginning point for building a reality. You are the one setting the stage, seizing the initiative. The figure you propose becomes immediately valid, if only as a starting point. The other party's response to that figure will give it a reality in itself.

The figure you propose should, of course, be justifiable. It should follow from the reasoning and evidence you have already laid out. It should be aggressive but not nonsensical. "Highballing" or "lowballing"—playing a bargaining game with outrageous numbers—is silly. You should propose only a figure supported by the facts, evidence, and arguments you have already presented. The other party may consider it nonsensical, but that will be because of his different vision of reality, not because one of you is playing games with the other.

My general rule of thumb is to make an initial offer that is more than the amount I am prepared to ultimately accept. First, I may be able to *get* that amount. But more fundamentally, I am giving both myself and the other party room to move.

Something to keep in mind when shaping a proposal is the concept of concessions. Making an offer with room to move gives you the opportunity to give up a little something here or there along the way. Your willingness and ability to concede a point are critical to the negotiating process. They show the other party that you are earnest about working toward a solution. And small concessions are often the key to making the deal.

A buyer of a home may be willing to cover the cost of title insurance or to push back the date on which he will take possession of the property if those concessions will make the deal. A seller might agree to pay for a particular repair or to move *up* the date of possession if *those* concessions will make the sale. In each case, it is a concession that finally seals the agreement. The ability to make concessions along the way can reap large dividends toward the end of the process, which is when some of the most critical moves in a negotiation are made (as will be explained in the next chapter). If, however, you have not made room for those moves in the beginning, they won't be there when you need them.

When preparing your proposal, it is critical to work out the relationships or equivalencies between various concessions and their effect on the entire agreement. It is necessary to understand beforehand how conceding or gaining a particular point can affect the equation of the entire deal. And it is necessary to have the ability to calculate those relationships instantaneously in the course of the actual negotiation.

In the case of an NFL player's contract, I need to know how every thousand dollars of signing bonus that goes one way or another affects the salary and how that in turn affects the team's economics and restrictions and its ability to pay those dollars. I need to be able to calculate discounted or deferred dollars, to translate future-payment figures into present-value amounts. And I need to be able to do this on the spot, right away. There are moments in a negotiation where a window of opportunity arises, where a concession is offered by each side and the other party is open to an agreement. That window can close in a matter of seconds. It well may be that the value of this trade-off is to your advantage. If you have to take a break, however—to figure that out, to do the math—you may lose that deal. The other party may withdraw his offer. He may simply change his mind, or he may make his own calculations and realize his error. It is infinitely more compelling to be able to immediately say yes to an offer and move on. But you will only be able to do this if you have the ability to rapidly factor figures—to add, subtract, multiply, and divide—in your head.

It is not necessary to be an Einstein. This is an ability that can be developed, like playing scales on the piano. I was not a math expert in school, and I certainly did not enjoy the subject. But I have learned through years of practice to do this kind of figuring in my head. Even a pocket calculator takes too much time, and it is a distraction. There is a delicacy to the flow of a negotiation, especially at a critical point where such concessions are offered. When that point comes, you must be prepared by understanding the interrelation between this offer and other parts of the deal, and you must be able to do the math. Instantly.

The timing of concessions is crucial as well. When and where you make them depends on the course of the particular negotiation, but one rule of thumb that applies to almost all negotiations is that you *never* want to make a large concession early, unless it leads immediately to a desirable deal. This will make you appear weak, unsure of yourself, and defensive. If your facts support your proposal, no significant concessions will have to be made. If the other party insists on such a concession, ask why. If you can respond to the answer, again with your facts, you are on solid ground and it is the other party who needs to adjust. Perhaps you can help him by revisiting your presentation.

If, on the other hand, you *cannot* respond convincingly to his objection, if his reasoning is sound and he has raised an issue or an argument you had not thought of, the concession may be one you indeed must make. Such is the price of incomplete preparation.

If you are in a situation in which the other party makes the first offer, keep in mind that in a salary negotiation, there is a fundamental difference between what an employer offers and what an employee offers. When an employer makes an offer for what he is willing to pay, he is talking about *real money*, dollars he is committed to pay. When an employee makes an offer, he is talking about nothing more than a wish, what he would *like* to be paid, what he believes he *should* be paid. At the outset, the employer's offer has a greater weight of reality to it. The burden is on you, the employee, to support *your* reality, to justify your wish with overwhelmingly convincing facts and evidence—the stuff of your presentation.

If you consider the other party's offer to be nonsensical, beyond the bounds of reasonable discussion, *do not discuss it*. Do not respond to it. *Definitely* do not make a counteroffer. That will lock you into a "split-the-difference" mentality, which is exactly what an outrageous offer is intended to do. In most cases, a preposterous offer is intended to diminish your expectation level and make you feel fortunate, in the end, to reach a point that is actually lower than what you deserve. The very act of responding to such an offer gives it validity. Don't make that mistake. The only proper response to what you consider a preposterous offer is to tell the other party—politely, respectfully, but firmly—that he is apparently not serious about this negotiation. State that you are ready to start when he is but that what he has proposed is not a beginning point.

A realistic offer from the other party should be at least 60 or 70 percent of the figure you are prepared to accept ultimately. An offer in that range indicates that the other party is serious about this process and is ready to proceed.

- In a multiple-bidder situation, do *not* make the first offer; let one of the bidders go first, and the others follow.
- In a two-party negotiation, *you* make the first offer.
- Never counter a preposterous offer.

FACING ANGER

AS I SAID earlier, you must do everything you can to bleed all ego out of the negotiating situation—if not the other party's ego, at least your own. One outgrowth of ego is anger. Often, a person with a large ego tends to be easily outraged. He may respond to what he considers your outlandishly bold offer with coarse language, a loud voice, or physical intimidation. He may try, by the sheer power of emotion, to push you into a position of inferiority, illegitimacy, sub-ordination. My reaction is not to react. I simply sit and watch it, as if it is a storm passing by in the distance.

This is the kind of moment where your emotional preparation is tested, where that psychological assessment you made of your own fears comes into play. You have got to be impervious to such an assault. You cannot react by conveying the characteristics of fear—a quavering voice, physical retreat, slumping down in a chair, a facial expression of alarm or panic. You cannot wear your vulnerabilities on your sleeve. You cannot allow someone to overwhelm your position by destabilizing you personally.

You must be able to remind yourself that this is not your mother or father. This is not the bully who beat you up on the playground back in fourth grade. This is not the teacher who berated you in front of the class in junior high or the man who mugged you last winter. This is not every authority figure you have ever needed to please.

Half the battle in facing anger is feeling no fear. Without fear on your part, the angry individual has lost his leverage. It's not unlike facing that bully on the playground. Once you accept that the worst thing he can do to you is hit you and that those cuts and bruises will heal in a short time and that it will not be the end of the earth, then you will have the courage to stand up to him. And in most cases—whether on the playground or in the boardroom—you'll find that the blustering bully backs off.

6. In the face of intimidation, show no fear.

Once your fear is gone and your courage is found, you can address the bully in the same way you addressed the dictator. Rather than wilting under his attack or rising to resist it, you can simply absorb it, hold it back up to him for his own consideration. Ask him what specifically is wrong with what you are proposing or offering that has made him so angry. Such a question, asked calmly and earnestly, gives the other party the opportunity to cool down and make his point, allowing the discussion to climb back on solid ground.

I was once negotiating over the telephone with the general manager of a team on the subject of a quarterback. The GM responded to my initial offer by going on an absolute tirade. I switched on the speakerphone to diffuse the volume and sat back. He used a certain word relating to sexual activity as a verb, noun, pronoun, and adjective in the same sentence. By the clock, he went on for almost fifteen minutes without pause or abatement. Finally, when he was done, I said, "So I take it you're not accepting our offer?"

There was a second of silence. Then came a little laugh from his end. We went on from there.

If patience and some light humor don't work, then again, a direct shot across the bow can be very effective. Calmly and without any anger of your own, you might move into the role of the parent addressing a child, telling the angry person, in essence, that he might choose to have this tantrum but that it is certainly not impressing you.

"Do you always speak to people this way?" you might ask.

Or, "Has it been effective in the past when you approached people like this?"

Or, "Do you think I hear you any more clearly when you raise your voice?"

Or, "I've never seen somebody act quite this way in a discussion. It sort of interests me."

Or, "Did I do something to offend you?"

In some situations, such responses can be effective. At other times, the proper response is *no* response. The thing to keep in mind about anger is that it is almost always a passing thing, a temporary emotion that tends to dissipate quickly, like a summer squall. Sometimes, simply letting the storm pass through is the most effective way to deal with it. Remaining calm and simply giving the other party space and time to let his anger play out is an invaluable skill in any negotiation.

Simple silence—no reaction whatsoever—can often be the most effective response to an angry or unreasonable proposal or attack. The sound of silence often allows the waters to calm and compels the other party to break the ice by following up angry words with more reasoned ones.

When Dallas had the first pick in the draft in 1989, Jerry Jones was asked if he was going to draft Troy Aikman, and he said, "He'd better drop his asking price." This was before there *was* an asking price. The Cowboys and I had not even had a conversation yet. Jerry went on about the honor of playing for the Dallas organization, saying that if he had a son who had the opportunity to play for that team, he'd tell him to take half of what anybody else was taking just for the distinction of wearing a Cowboys uniform. Never mind that the team he was talking about had gone 3 and 13 the year before.

Jerry was taking an aggressive stance, laying down the gauntlet ahead of time. It would have been easy for us to respond with anger, to say, "Who the heck do you think you are? If you don't want Troy, don't take him. Put Tony Mandarich [a highly rated offensive lineman from Michigan State] on the cover of your press book and see how many tickets you'll sell."

Instead, we chose to ignore it. We acted as if Jerry Jones had never said those words. Entering into a personal debate would have been utterly counterproductive and beside the point. The point was to reach a satisfactory agreement that would allow Troy Aikman to quarterback the Dallas Cowboys. That was all that mattered to us.

There are likely going to be times in any touchy or substantial negotiation where one party is angered by the other. This comes with the territory. Accept the fact that you risk upsetting someone—at least temporarily—when you take a stand that is different from or directly opposes his. And always remind yourself that none of this is about *you*. Whenever a sense of insult arises—whether you are representing yourself or a client—you have got to remember that this is personal. Even when the other party attempts to *make* it personal, you have to maintain the balance and detachment that comes with knowing that this is business, period. It is about the strength of your facts and your reasoning, not your personalities.

The last thing in the world that you want to do is respond to the other party's anger and aggression with your own. Besides being aware of the other party's tendency and need to dominate a discussion or to become angry and aggressive, you must be aware of and in control of your own inclination to move in those directions. Understand that there is no need to control every second of a negotiation. It is not necessary to answer tit for tat on every issue that arises. It is not necessary to have the last word on every point that is raised. It is one thing to respond in a particular way as a conscious tactic, and it is quite another to respond out of a subconscious or uncontrollable *need*.

Joining the other party in a dance of anger is almost always a sure recipe for disaster. If the person you are facing abandons the reasonable-person mode and enters an emotional state, it is essential that you not join him, that you stay detached from his anger and not allow it to trigger your own. If you get angry, you may make statements that are personally insulting or irrational, and all your careful planning will go down the drain.

It is important not to let the other party's anger and rage escalate to the point where he may let certain nonretractable statements or characterizations come out of his mouth. Do not push a losing argument to the end and allow the other party to become so fixed in his position that he can never change it. Do not allow descriptions and insults that may be especially hurtful to come out of his mouth. There are certain phrases and characterizations that can be so painful and explosive that it will never be possible to have a constructive relationship again.

There may well be instances—although they are rare—in which the other person's anger is not going to pass or his emotions are not going to subside. In such cases, you may have to face the fact that nothing constructive will be accomplished at that meeting. If this happens, take a break and suggest that you meet at a later date.

In any event, do everything in your power not to let emotion and anger derail the process . . . especially before it has hardly begun.

· In the face of anger, reveal no fear.
· When confronting anger, do it calmly but directly.
· Often, the best response to anger is silence.

THE MANIPULATOR

BESIDES OVERT ANGER and a frontal assault, there are subtler ways
in which the other party might attempt to destabilize you. More dangerous than the outright bully, in my opinion, is the clever manipulator, the person who attempts to have the entire discussion turn on
your unfairness, your thanklessness, your lack of appreciation, or your
greed.

Keep in mind that these accusations will be justified if you are not
ethical and honest in the presentation of your facts and arguments. If
you *are* ethical, if your position is based on reliable, rock-solid information and sound reason, then you should have no fear whatsoever.
Nothing inspires confidence more than standing on the ground of accuracy, reason, and fairness.

Imagine that you are an electrical engineer in your mid-thirties,
making $65,000 a year, working for a company you respect, doing a
job that excites and fulfills you. You are due for a meeting with your
boss in which your work will be assessed and your compensation discussed. It has been some time since you've had such a meeting.
You've never pushed for a raise before. You've always been content
with what you've been paid. But you have thoroughly prepared for
this discussion. Your research has shown that the fair-market value for
your services is $95,000. You arrive at the meeting prepared to pur-
sue this salary. When the time comes to talk money, your employer
puts an offer of $75,000 on the table. Why not simply take it? You
were happy before. Shouldn't this make you that much happier?

The manipulator would argue that it should.

"With this much money," he might say, "you'll be able to take that
extra vacation. You'll be able to put that new addition on your house."

"Look at what you were making when you started with us," he might say. "We're offering you *twice* what you were making then."

"Do you know how close we are to going out of business?" he might add.

It is easy to be swayed by such an argument, especially if you are representing yourself and are not accustomed to facing this tactic. It is easy to fall into the trap of comparing what you have now to what is being offered. It is easy to be lured into thinking about what that money can *do,* how many cars it can put in the driveway, how many of your children it can put through college, how it can change your life—or to compare the proposed salary to what someone else in your profession made many years before.

You must not let your thinking be turned in those directions. The discussion has nothing to do with how rich or poor you are or with how rich or poor you have ever been or with how rich or poor you might ever *be.* Those circumstances are irrelevant. So are the ways in which the money being offered might change your life. None of these things has anything to do with the issue at hand, which is: *What do you deserve?*

The husband who tells his wife he's willing to go on vacation for five whole days and reminds her that last year they only got two is attempting to position five days as a major accomplishment. But it may be that this husband has been working much too hard lately, he has starved his family of attention, and anything less than ten days is no vacation at all.

To the extent that you turn away from the question of what you deserve, to the extent that you abandon the arena of fair market value and your own comparative worth and allow the playing field to include the circumstances of your private life and personal judgments about such things as gratitude and greed, you are on the wrong playing field.

Value and compensation—those things must remain the focus of the discussion. The value of what you bring to the organization for which you work and the compensation you deserve for that value—this is what dollars measure, and this is the only context in which dollars should be discussed. The only reality that money has in a negotiating discussion is as a measuring rod, as a means of calculation. Inside the context of a negotiation, dollars only have reality and validity as a way of reflecting fair market value.

The ploy of using the seductive power of money to sidetrack a discussion is particularly common in my business, especially when I am representing a rookie. "Look," a general manager might say to an athlete fresh out of college. "You've been getting nothing but scholarship money for the past four years, and you've been happy. Now we're offering you a million dollars. A million dollars a *year*. That's big money. You'll be able to do everything you ever wanted with that amount of money. How could you possibly want *more*?"

My job in that situation is to bring the focus back to where it belongs. If I am representing Ryan Leaf in his rookie negotiations with the San Diego Chargers, we are not going to talk about how much money Ryan has or has not had in the past or how much money his family has or how many things he will be able to buy with the money the Chargers might be willing to offer.

We will talk about the value of the services Ryan has to offer. We will talk about the comparative value of other quarterbacks in the marketplace, both rookies and veterans. We will discuss how Ryan's presence will benefit the San Diego Chargers organization both on and off the football field, how the team will win more games and sell more tickets and be able to market its product more broadly and effectively because Ryan is with them. Alternatively, we will discuss how damaging it will be for the team *not* to sign their top draft pick, how the fans will react, how the press will respond, how the organization will suffer if Ryan is not with them.

One thing we will *not* talk about is how much money Ryan has ever had before or how he might spend the money he is going to now be paid. Those issues are nobody's business but his, and they are irrelevant to the negotiation.

All that matters to Ryan is what he fairly and justifiably deserves. And that is all that should matter to you.

· Do not let the other party probe such personal concepts as guilt or gratitude or greed.

· Discuss money strictly as a means of measuring value; do not discuss it in any other terms.

THE EQUIVOCATOR

BESIDES THE DICTATOR and the manipulator, there is a third type of personality that is often faced in a negotiation, and that is the equivocator.

This is the person who refuses to commit, who will not be nailed down on any particular of a deal. His strategy is to remain vague, to never commit to any one part of an agreement until the whole package is worked out.

Equivocation can be an effective response to a common negotiating strategy. Experienced negotiators will often break their ultimate goal into subcategories and get the other party to focus on and agree to each of those items separately, one at a time. A person using this strategy—party A—would concentrate and focus on each component or facet of the deal, justifying and persuading the other party—party B—to accept that term and then move on. By the time they are done, those subagreements may well have added up to a total agreement well beyond what party B intended to give. In other words, the whole has been obscured by the sum of the parts.

Once that bottom line is reached and it exceeds what party B was prepared to pay, party A can then assert that not enough money has been allocated. Both parties have already agreed that items 1 through 10 are each reasonable. If party B's budget doesn't cover the total cost of those items, then party A can take the position that that budget needs to be adjusted. More resources need to be allocated. If that means that party B has to go back to his company and ask for those resources, so be it. He has agreed that party A's position is correct.

My earlier caveat to be aware of the relationship of concessions to one another and to the total deal applies here. When discussing a particular element of a proposal, understand the extent of your po-

tential exposure and liability before agreeing to it. Otherwise you
may well be drawn by small, reasonable, justifiable commitments
into a large, overall commitment that you are unprepared or unable
to make.

This is not a danger faced only in business. As a husband and wife
discuss their budget and go through a series of twenty items, they may
agree that each item is vitally important. Clothing for their children
is vital, a roof over their heads is vital, proper food is vital, braces for
their daughter are vital, piano lessons are vital for their son, taking a
vacation is vital for the whole family. When they get to the end of
their discussion, they have agreed that every single item on their list
is completely justifiable. The problem is that the total cost of those
items is 50 percent more than the budget they have to spend. Each
part works, but the whole does not.

The equivocator will not fall into this situation. That is to his
credit. If you let him, however, he will use his tactic of noncommit-
ment to force *you* to make every commitment. He will make you bid
against yourself if you let him. You will ask him what he thinks is fair,
and he will say, "Well, what do *you* think is fair?" When you answer
with a specific figure, he will not agree or disagree. What he would
like is for you to then suggest *another* number, moving further in his
direction. He hasn't even stepped onto the playing field and you are
already backing up.

One way to respond to the equivocator is to address the issue directly. "Look," you might say. "I need to understand what your position is in this matter. What are you offering? What are you demanding?
You need to tell me so that I've got an idea of where this is going, because frankly, right now these discussions are meaningless."

Explain to him that this is a process you are both involved in. For
movement to occur, both parties need to participate. If he can't agree
to do that, he is not ready to negotiate.

· Be aware that small agreements add up to large ones.
· Don't allow the vagueness of the other party to force you into
  commitments you are not ready to make.

LISTENING

GENERALLY, WHEN PEOPLE discuss negotiating skills, they emphasize the spoken word, the capacity for persuasion, while underestimating or entirely ignoring the critical role of listening. As far as I am concerned, being an outstanding listener is, in most cases, more important to effective negotiation than being a persuasive speaker. Most true communicators understand this. They realize how utterly essential it is to *listen*.

There is a difference between listening and hearing. Hearing is a passive activity, simple reception. You are talking, and I hear you. But do I *understand* you? Am I *trying* to understand you? Or am I sitting behind the insulation of my own perspective, where your words, while I hear them, are filtered through my own needs, my own argument? Worse, do your words simply bounce like pebbles off the walls of my entrenched position?

The true listener not only hears what the other party is saying; he is intent on understanding the meaning of the words he hears. He wants—he *needs*—to know what the other party is feeling and thinking, what that person means by what he is saying and, most tellingly, what that person *wants*.

Listening is active. A good listener prefers asking questions to giving answers. It never hurts to ask questions, even when you think you know the answer. It forces the other party to clarify what he has to say, and it tests his credibility as well. You may be surprised by the response, and if nothing else, it will encourage the other party to realize that you really *are* listening, you really are interested in what he has to say.

And you *are*—or you should be. Don't be afraid to appear dumb or weak by asking occasional questions. Don't be afraid to simply say, "I don't understand," or, "Help me here," or, "I don't know" at certain points in the discussion. It's honest. It's disarming. It helps clarify the information the other person has shared. It prompts the disclosure of new information. It forces the other party to more clearly reveal his interests and needs. It reinforces the climate of mutual problem solving versus direct confrontation. Asking the other party to repeat something he has just said will not only increase the clarity of his point; it will reassure him that you are indeed listening closely.

Good listening requires utter attention, an emptying of oneself in order to receive the other. It takes a spongelike absorption and a laserlike focus. True listening requires the discipline to screen out every stimulus other than the speaker's voice and visage. This includes, importantly, your own mind. A good listener is not worried about the appointment that he has that afternoon. He is not thinking about what he needs to bring home for dinner tonight. He is not concerned about the task he left unfinished at work or at home. He is not bothered by the heat or the fact that he might have to go to the bathroom or the fact that he is thirsty or hungry. A real listener has bled himself dry of any external input or internal needs. He is fully and completely present. Nothing else exists but the human being who is speaking to him.

If you ask me for the key to any success I have enjoyed in this business, it is my ability to do this—to set everything else aside and to climb fully and completely into the moment, to open every cell of my being to the person I am listening to. It is not much different from a meditative state. Many people misunderstand what meditation is. They think it is checking out of reality, going into some otherworldly place. Quite the opposite is true. Meditation is the achievement of utter *awareness.* It is the capacity to be completely present, fully in the moment, undistracted by the meteors of thoughts and needs that constantly flash through our minds and bodies.

7. Learn to listen.

All superfluous thoughts are put aside when a good listener is on task. The time for processing and interpreting will come later, but at the moment, he is nothing but a receptor. And what he is receiving is more than mere words. A good listener has the capacity to fully absorb not only what he hears but what he sees . . . even what he smells. No detail is insignificant. He is aware of the speaker's every nuance, from his body language to his clothing to the way he breathes. What posture does he exhibit? Does he appear to be nervous or relaxed? What are his facial expressions? Does he sometimes tap a pencil, rustle paper, jiggle a knee? These little habits can be invaluably revealing as the discussions progress. You need to notice them and think about what they might mean.

If you are facing more than one person, you need to pick up on the dynamics and the chemistry between them, how each acts and looks when the other is speaking, and the interplay between them—a quick glance, a facial expression—when *you* are speaking.

As much as anything else, deep listening requires a great amount of patience. You cannot be in a hurry. You must be able to take your time. Negotiation is a process, and the key to the initial stage is being wide open in every way, gathering all kinds of information, the subtle and personal as well as the factual. Agreements are, as I have said, rarely reached early in a negotiation.

The business friends I have from Japan have told me time and again how stunned they are at the desire of Americans to please them at every given moment. They are struck by the almost unseemly haste and anxiousness with which most American negotiators they encounter want to make a deal. The Asian concept of time is that of an eternally flowing river, while the American concept seems to be closer to that of a waterfall.

The patience needed in this business involves not just the parties with whom you negotiate but with your clients as well. What does that mean? It means you have to have the ability and the willingness not just to sit through and endure but to really listen to long-drawn-out explanations by clients about something you already understand, something you may well have already heard them explain a thousand times. You might have picked up in the first two minutes everything that they have to say, and they may repeat it over and over again, and you could easily say, "Do you think I'm a moron or an idiot, or that I didn't hear you?" Or, "Do you think that the more times you say this to me, the more likely it is to occur in the world?"

But you don't say these things. You do your best not to even think them. You have to hang in there and be patient. Obviously, this person has a need to say these things, and that need alone is reason enough for you to give him your full attention—to really listen.

The worst thing you can possibly do is *interrupt*. Most people who have a habit of interrupting are not even aware of how often they do it. For some people, it is simply a need to dominate the discussion. For others—especially bright people—it is a matter of impatience. Many bright people have a hard time listening. They feel that they know where every discussion is going, where every sentence is headed, and they race ahead to their own conclusion, restlessly waiting for the other party to hurry up and get there.

Some of this is a function of ego. Good listening is just another aspect of getting one's ego out of the way, putting one's needs aside, and this is a hard thing for many of us to do. Americans as a people have such a desire to please others at every given moment. We tend to seek approval, to seek reassurance. We care mightily what others think of us. We want them to *like* us, and we want them to like us right *now.* We get swept up in our feelings of the moment, and we live and act that way, tumbling from one moment to the next, awash with our feelings and needs.

That's why as a culture we get frustrated or simply slaughtered so often in negotiations with people from cultures that have a different perspective on time and needs. The Asian cultures, for example, tend to look at time in the long continuum. While we're asking ourselves, Is this meeting producing the exact result that I want right now? Does the other person like me? they are unconcerned with such questions of immediacy. Their cultures are laced with a patience that is lacking in ours.

It's only natural, at least for most of us, to respond to pressure by obsessing about our own problems. It's normal to become self-conscious and self-absorbed under stress, and the natural outlet for most of us is verbal. The more tension there is, the more most of us try to talk our way out of it. I feel pressure like anyone else. I feel tension. But whenever I do, when I can sense it beginning to rise, I try hard to go the other direction, to forget the chaos inside me, to put my ego aside and focus on the other person.

Highly intelligent people have a particularly hard time doing this, for several reasons. One is that their ego is so large. They are prone to believe that what they have to say is much more important than what anyone else might have to offer. Anyone who disagrees with them is simply not smart enough to understand their concept or position. The instant they hear something with which they disagree, they shut down and reject anything further that the other person has to say. This is a form of defensiveness, and in terms of listening, it is disastrous. The other person might have fifteen points to make, several of which might be surprising, all of which you need to be aware of, but none of them will be registered if you pulled the plug when the first thing he said rubbed you the wrong way.

Such attitudes completely undermine the concept of good listening. They entirely ignore the fact that human beings have very different ways of expressing themselves. And they completely preclude the process of allowing another person to reveal himself. The time for positing your own position, for parrying the other party's points and convincing him of the merits of your own will come later.

Beyond the merits of enriching your own perspective, good listening has a positive effect on the other party, who realizes he is being *listened to,* and can't help but appreciate that. This is another way to build trust. By listening carefully and perceptively, it is possible to create a comfort zone in which the other party becomes more secure and more willing to reveal his true agenda. If you can listen carefully to what others consider to be critical, if you can get them to open up and be clear, to truly communicate what they want and need, they will sense that you are here to solve a problem, not to beat them and defeat them, and the traditional tone of tension and confrontation can be replaced by the cooperative paradigm that allows all parties to move forward.

My attitude in the opening stage of a negotiation has always been to nurture this comfort zone, to put myself aside and focus entirely on the other party. I already *know* what I think. What I need to learn right now is what the other person is thinking, what his feelings are, what information he has to offer—all of which will help me as the process unfolds.

· Don't be afraid to appear dumb by asking questions.
· A good listener is utterly aware of not only what the speaker says but of the way in which he says it.
· A good listener feels absolutely no distractions; he is fully and completely absorbed in the moment.

SILENCE

IMPATIENCE IS PROBABLY the single largest impediment to good listening. Closely related is the discomfort most people feel with *silence*.

We are not a society that is comfortable with silence. Ours is a culture of call and response, input and output, movement and action and noise. We keep televisions and radios and stereos on in our homes and offices even when no one is in the room to watch or listen. We have music piped into elevators, bathrooms, and the telephone line when we're put on hold.

We don't like silence, especially when we are with another person. It makes us nervous. It brings out our insecurities. It arouses the desire to placate, the need to please others. We feel nervous, we imagine *they* feel nervous, and so we rush to fill the space with sound, to break the silence and dispel the unease.

By doing so, however, we are making assumptions that could well be mistaken. The other person may simply be pausing to put a thought together. He may not feel awkward at all. By cutting in, however, we interrupt or even destroy that process. By projecting our own discomfort onto another and trying to solve his problem, we are simply creating more problems in terms of reaching a point of understanding. Your discomfort is not the other person's problem. And his—if he has any—is not yours. Deal with yourself, let him be, and leave the silence as it is.

It is hard to learn the limits of talk, to resist the urge to always respond. We rush to make our point, to state our position, essentially to get our way. But if you can stop, sit still, set yourself and your needs aside and relax, receive rather than constantly push yourself forward, it is amazing how the avenues of communication can open up.

Used strategically, silence can be a powerful instrument. After you have made a strong point, don't dilute or displace it with more words. Don't attempt to modify it or amplify it. Be silent. Let the meaning and significance of what you have just said sink in. Let the other party think about it. Give him time to draw some conclusions.

In the same way, remain silent after the other party has made a point. Don't respond right away. Don't reveal whether you agree or disagree. Often, someone who is not sure about what he has just said, who is not certain about his position, will shift in the face of silence and will amend or adjust what he has just proposed. He may sense disapproval or disappointment in your silence and immediately offer a concession in your favor—without your saying a word. Never underestimate the power of the pregnant pause.

8. Be comfortable with silence.

Understand that there are times in a negotiation where you have simply said everything you have to say. It's important at those times to be able to just let there be silence. If your discussion is being conducted over the phone and a little time passes with nothing but the hum on the line between you, be comfortable with that. If you are meeting in person and the only sound is the drone of the air-conditioning or the faint buzz of activity beyond the door, and the shadows move slowly across the office rug and a clock ticks, be at ease with that.

Again, this is a *process*. There will be points along the way where things become still. Rivers could ebb and flow, seasons could change, infants could grow into adults, but right now there is nothing more that you have to say. Not at the moment. And so it is time to just sit, in comfort, in that space made by silence.

- After you have made a point, be silent. Give the other party time to feel its effect.

Leigh Steinberg

- After the other party has made a point, be silent. Let him consider what he has just said; he may respond to your silence in a more revealing way than he would respond to your words.
- When you have reached a point where there is nothing more to say, say nothing more.

5

MAKING THE DEAL

THE COUNTEROFFER

AFTER A REASONABLE offer has been made, it is the counteroffer that sets the negotiating process in motion. It is the counter that indicates your involvement and desire to reach an agreement. It shows that you are serious about making a deal, that you are not just stringing the other person along. And it causes the other party to reexamine his proposal, to look at its terms and conditions in an evolving light. Perspectives change as the process evolves. Each time an offer or a counteroffer is made, both parties' realities begin to shift and adjust in response to the developing discussion.

This is what a counteroffer does—it tests the reality of an offer. It forces a response, not just in terms of numbers, but in terms of a rationale. It also creates a sense of involvement and investment. The deeper a person journeys into the sheer process of negotiation, the more committed he becomes to reaching an agreement. The more time and energy a person invests in the discussions, the less likely he is to pull out.

It is often necessary to have developed a more expansive set of arguments to justify your initial offer, not all of which you reveal at the beginning of the negotiation. Some of these arguments are held in reserve. This way, rather than reciting the same position over and over again, you can proceed to illustrate the fairness of your approach in a variety of different ways as you make your counterproposals.

It is also advantageous to have rebuttal aruguments prepared, which are also held back during your initial expository presentation. These rebuttal arguments consist of responses developed during the role-playing exercises you conducted in your preparation. You have antici-pated the other party's likely arguments and have come prepared with responses, which are saved until those arguments are made.

As the negotiation goes on, it is also possible, and often necessary, to develop new arguments that respond to the other party's points as they are made. During my negotiation with Mike Lynn of the Vikings over Wade Wilson's contract, we were having a discussion on the speaker-phone, and Mike was making a set of arguments about the financial difficulties of the Vikings. As he spoke, a lawyer working with me took Mike's arguments, went upstairs, worked out a detailed set of re-sponses, and delivered them to me just as Mike was wrapping up his points. I was able to respond instantaneously with detailed specifics.

This gets back to the advantage of having partners working with you on a negotiation—they can provide the instantaneous research and responses you need even as the discussion continues to develop.

Gauging and testing the reality of the other party's offer often de-pends largely on what you know about that person's negotiating style. You may have had previous dealings with this person. You should have researched his negotiating history. In either case, it helps immensely—especially in the beginning of the process—to have an idea of his par-ticular bargaining tendencies.

For example, assume that you walk into a negotiation with a salary of $100,000 in mind. An employer you would consider in the reasonable-person mode might, after hearing your presentation, make an opening offer of $90,000. Another employer might offer $40,000, which on the face of it would seem preposterous and un-worthy of a response. But it may be that this second person is just as willing to pay $100,000 as the other. It may simply be his style to make an extremely low initial offer followed by a large shift as the discussion continues. If you are aware of this, you might not be so quick to dismiss his opening as preposterous.

When faced with an extremely low offer, such as that $40,000, one tactic is to respond with an extremely high counteroffer—say, in this case, $160,000. Some people's style is to simply play split-the-difference. But there is a danger in playing this game. If you respond to what you consider an out-of-bounds offer with a similar response, it is possible that as the "trading" proceeds and you each whittle a little off your offers, the other party will reach a point still far from your goal and say, "That's it. I'm not going any higher than this. I've given and given, I've met you halfway, I've split the difference, and I'm not giving any more."

And he *has* given and given. The problem is that what he has given—the ground he has covered—is ground that has no value to you. You have vested it with value by agreeing to play this game. The danger of getting caught up in a game of sheer numbers is that numbers alone have no realism, no reality whatsoever. It is the rationale *behind* a number that makes it real. Once you abandon the rationale and begin simply trading figures, you have lost your factual footing. And you have legitimized the reality of the other party's preposterous offer by responding to it in this way. You have allowed the other party to set the expectation level. You are working off *his* number, which has no rationale.

Better to hold to the high ground of your criteria. If you consider that $40,000 offer preposterous, say so. Don't respond with a number. Respond with reason, the reason on which you have built your proposal. Don't waste time arguing the validity of the other party's unrealistic proposal. Put the focus on your own arguments. Go back through your baseline presentation. The other party might say, "I've already heard all that." You might respond, "Well, obviously not, or you wouldn't be making such a proposal."

When faced with an unrealistically low offer, always keep in mind that the other party may not be playing a "high-low" game, that he honestly may be missing the point and misjudging the situation. Your job is to bring him around, to educate him, to help him understand.

Often, the very act of refusing to offer a counter to an unreasonable proposal will push the other party to bid against himself. In response to such a proposal, rather than countering with a figure, you simply tell the other party that his offer is unacceptable. "What *is* acceptable?" he might ask. "Well, certainly not what you've proposed," you might answer. "When we get close, then we'll be able to talk about it." It is very possible that he may then offer another number, nearer to what you consider reasonable. And he has done so without your mentioning any numbers at all. This is a variation on the equivocator's stance, and it is perfectly justifiable when you are presented with an offer you consider ridiculous.

9. Don't play split-the-difference.

Tactics such as this require the confidence we talked about in the "Facing Your Fear" section. If you have been honest, thorough, and fair in shaping and presenting your position, this should provide the confidence needed to respond in this manner to an unacceptable offer. If, on the other hand, you have built your position on the shaky ground of distorted information and deceptive reasoning, you will have justifiable cause to feel fear. You will have a right to feel panic and doubt, to fixate on cataclysmic scenarios. The other party is going to test you from the moment he comes through the door. He is going to probe for weak spots not only in your presentation and proposal but in your personality, in your psyche. A seasoned negotiator facing a novice may very well throw out a preposterous offer simply to see whether the beginner caves in right away, which he may well do if he hasn't prepared himself emotionally and factually.

It is impossible to overestimate the importance of self-assurance in a negotiation. Not arrogance. Not closed-mindedness. But solid, simple confidence, a belief in your own judgment and decisions, and in the accuracy and fairness of your information and arguments.

· Use prior knowledge or research to distinguish a serious offer from a preposterous one.

· Don't play split-the-difference.
· When presented with an unreasonable offer, try pushing the other party to bid against himself.
· Do not panic; show no fear.

"ADD-ONS"

WHEN YOU DO respond with a specific figure to a reasonable offer, you have to be able to explain it. If a home owner is asking $150,000 for his house and you hire an inspector and discover that the house needs $10,000 in repairs, include this when you come back with your counteroffer. This gives the seller something to consider. It shows him that you are not just playing games, that your numbers are not merely arbitrary.

One effective way to move quickly into a cooperative paradigm— assuming that the other party's offer or counteroffer is within the realm of reality—is to accept that offer with the understanding that there remain additional side topics for later discussion. This is the one situation in which you might agree to split the difference—if there is room left for incremental additions. These additions are where you can make up the difference.

The concept here is to agree on a general acceptance of the core terms, the basic parameters. You are setting down, say, 60 percent of the floor, with an agreement that the remainder of the deal will be worked out later in the discussion. The effect is to create the feeling that both parties have been brought into the fold, that you are no longer standing apart. You now have that floor beneath the two of you. The floor is unfinished, but the sense is that the deal is essentially done, with only the details to be worked out. Once you agree that a deal is going to be made, the entire atmosphere of the negotiation changes. Instead of adversaries, the parties think of themselves as partners.

It is then around the details of the deal—that remaining 40 percent—that you focus your negotiating skills, filling the gap between the proposal you have tentatively accepted and the deal you actually want.

This is another form of the bootstrapping process I mentioned earlier. Automobile dealers do it all the time. Before negotiating, the dealer creates a new reality—namely, that this particular car is *your* car. He makes sure you test-drive it. He wants you to smell it, to feel it, to imagine what it will be like to pull up in this car for the first time in front of your coworkers or your spouse or significant other. He creates a vision in your head of how you will feel driving this car to work or taking it on your next vacation.

Once you cannot live without the car, he then begins to negotiate. After some discussion, you agree on a certain price—say $27,500. This is a price you feel comfortable with, the highest price you are willing to pay. You have essentially bought the car. You are now invested in it emotionally. All that remain are the details.

And this is where the dealer makes up his ground. "By the way," he notes, "there is a tax and license fee that have to be paid." That's $2,000. "Oh," he continues, "those mag wheels that you like so much? They're an additional $1,500." Sure, you say, that's fine. You're hooked by now. You really want this car. "And the CD player," he says, filling in more lines on the contract. "That's another $2,500." And so on.

Each incremental increase can seem relatively insignificant by itself, which is precisely what the dealer is counting on. What are a couple of thousand dollars here or there when you're talking about a $27,500 car? That's the way he wants you to see it. He's counting on that $27,500 figure staying in your head while he pushes the total price of the package up to the figure he had in mind from the beginning. By the time you drive your $27,500 car off the lot, you've actually paid $33,000 for it.

That is a classic case of bootstrapping. Even when both parties realize what is going on, it can be a very effective way to get a deal moving. Agree to the basics early, then spend the remainder of the negotiation working around the edges. This can be an advantageous way to begin a negotiation, to establish yourselves as partners in a cooperative enterprise working together toward a final solution. Rather than fighting over a central issue, you come around to the same side of the table, reach an agreement on that issue, then spend the remainder of the process as partners ironing out details.

Consider an employment situation in which you are seeking a salary of $100,000. Your employers have made it clear that they cannot go higher than $85,000. The fact may be, because of budgetary constraints or other factors, that they truly cannot pay a salary higher than that. This is where creativity comes in.

Fine, you say, you'll accept the $85,000. But you add that there are some other benefits you'll need to discuss. They say okay. The salary, which was their fundamental sticking point, has now been taken care of. You have given ground in that direction, and they acknowledge that. They are open now to talking about those "benefits."

You suggest a company membership over at the country club. They say sure.

And a company car?

Why not?

And an expense account?

No problem.

How about another week of vacation?

Sounds reasonable.

By the time you're finished, the value of the total package may well be more than the $100,000 salary you wanted. You're happy. And your boss, who is signing off on that salary of $85,000, is happy as well.

If you are offered such a contingent agreement in the midst of a negotiation and you are not comfortable with the process of add-ons, say so. Some negotiators want nothing to do with bootstrapping. As far as they are concerned, the deal you make is the deal you've got, period. No extras. No add-ons. No open ends. If there is anything that has not been mentioned, it has to be mentioned *now*, not later. Otherwise there is no deal.

If this is the way you feel, make it clear. Don't allow yourself to be set up for add-ons you won't accept.

· When you make a counteroffer, always provide a rationale.
· Consider making a basic agreement, with the understanding that particular points remain to be discussed.
· Focus on those points to earn your advantage.

CONCESSIONS

NEGOTIATION IS A process of give-and-take. No experienced negotiator expects to get everything he wants. Once an offer and a counteroffer have been made and the discussions proceed, concessions will become a key factor. They keep the process moving, they create a sense of cooperation, and they give each party a feeling of achievement, a sense of movement. Knowing that concessions must be made, the effective negotiator, as explained in the previous chapter, has planned ahead what he might give up, as well as when and how he might give it.

An important dynamic to understand about concessions is the difference between the substance of what is being conceded and the emotions that come with each concession. One party may move $200,000 across the table in the course of a deal, but the way that money is moved can make all the difference in the world. One large move of $200,000 is *not* equal to twenty smaller moves of $10,000 each. The person making those twenty small concessions will likely feel that he's giving much more than the person making the one large move. It is the *feeling* of giving in—the act itself—that tends to matter most in the negotiation process. Knowing this, you can orchestrate the concessions you make, as well as those you receive, to work in your favor.

One basic principle of concessions is that you want to minimize the significance of the other party's concessions and maximize the significance of your own. Each time the other side gives something up, accept it and immediately move on to the next point. Don't allow his sacrifice to achieve any stature. Each time *you* make a concession, however, elongate the gesture, prolong it, draw it out as if you have just ceded the major point of the twentieth century.

> **10. Emphasize your concessions; minimize the other party's.**

Ted Phillips, the general manager of the Chicago Bears, is a master at this. He is incredibly well organized, to the point that he sits down for a discussion with a flip chart of index cards, each card spelling out the details, ramifications, and relative value of every possible clause that might come up in the discussion, from incentives to bonuses. When a particular clause is mentioned, he flips to that card and immediately breaks that point down into six subpoints, each of which he has a position on. He will grudgingly concede each point you are able to win. The substance of each point might be relatively insignificant, but Ted makes you fight for every nickel and dime. The feeling, because of the struggle, is that you've won a major victory, a huge concession, when in fact what he has given up might not be that much at all.

Using concessions in this way is a very effective tactic. Concessions can also be used as bait. You can build an emotional position by reluctantly yielding points you actually care little about in order to then be given the point you really want. Remember Br'er Rabbit pleading with Br'er Fox not to throw him in the briar patch, when in fact that was precisely what he wanted the fox to do? This is a similar strategy, and it can be particularly effective when dealing with a person whose ego demands that he be a winner.

There are people who will battle in a negotiation over each and every point you make, no matter how small or large. They will take issue with everything you say, simply on principle. The weakness with a win-every-point person is that in his zeal to argue each detail, he often loses sight of the overall negotiation. He can't see the forest for the trees. Rather than join him in this game, you can use it against him.

Say, for example, you are an employee in a salary negotiation, facing a win-every-point boss. You are discussing your compensation package. There are five or six parts to the package. The only part that really matters to you is getting three weeks of vacation rather than the two you now receive. Your parking space matters hardly at all, but you argue for it first, and you argue hard. You make your boss earn it. Let him feel that he has won that first point, point A. Do the same with points B, C, D, and E. Then, when it comes to point F—the vacation—grudgingly let him give you this one . . . which is the only one you really cared about in the first place.

One more thing to keep in mind as far as concessions are concerned: Always stay keenly aware that there will come a point at the end of the negotiation where you are close to an agreement but not quite there. Almost invariably at this point, one party or the other will be ready to close the deal in exchange for a final concession. A key step in the closing stage of a negotiation can be the offer of this one last concession, "if it will make the deal."

Knowing this, you will want to save something to give at the end. You will want to keep that final concession in reserve.

- Grudgingly yield points you care little about to set up the concession of a point you desire.
- Save key concessions for the end of the process.

DEADLINES

NOTHING INTRODUCES A sense of crisis like a deadline. This can be good for motivating movement, bringing closure to the process, forcing a resolution. It can be counterproductive, however, if the parties are not ready to make that resolution and wind up with a less than satisfactory agreement—or if they cannot come to terms and the deadline arrives and they wind up with no agreement at all.

A deadline can bring out the best, or worst, in a negotiator. When the clock is ticking, when people's pulses start racing, when their hearts start beating, when the job seems impossible, when it looks too unwieldy, too daunting to ever achieve, this is when a talented negotiator earns his money.

A few years ago, my partner David Dunn and I commenced a negotiation with the New York Knicks that put us in a beat-the-clock situation more intense than any we have ever faced.

The player in question was John Starks, who had become our client midway through his career. John's story is legend around the NBA—how he left basketball after playing at Oklahoma State, how he worked for a time bagging groceries in a supermarket, and how he came back to the sport, first playing his way into the CBA, then winning a job with the Knicks, where he established himself as an NBA All-Star and now serves as one of the league's best shooting guards. John understands, in a way that many players do not, the transient and fleeting nature of a professional basketball career. He appreciates what he has. But he also understood that the original contract he had signed with New York, for an average salary of $1.2 million a year, left him underpaid once he had climbed into the upper echelon of the league's guards, many of whom were making three or four times that amount.

Matters became complicated by the fact that even as we were sitting down in November 1994 with Dave Checketts and Ernie Grunfeld of the Knicks to work out a new contract for John, the NBA was arriving at the end of its labor agreement with the players. The league was very determined that the new collective bargaining agreement would be a more stringent one, with tougher rules against large "balloon payments" in contract extensions, rules that would directly affect the deal we were trying to do for John. A moratorium by the league on all new contract extensions was set to go into effect at exactly 5 P.M. on a Tuesday afternoon that month. Serious discussions had begun less than a week before then. So what normally would have been a negotiation that would have occurred over a couple of months became a deal that was pushed up against a backdrop of days—and, as it turned out in the end, minutes.

Luckily we were working with Checketts, then-president of the Knicks, who is one of the most talented executives in sports and entertainment. Dave and Knicks general manager Ernie Grunfeld came in with the let's-get-this-deal-done attitude that is, as I have said, more common in the NBA than in the NFL.

The Knicks had almost all the leverage here. If they chose, they could simply have forced John to play the next three years of his contract with the existing terms. But Dave and Ernie really understand players' feelings. Ernie was a star player in college and then in the NBA. Unlike in football, where a couple of dozen players on each team have key roles during a game, in the NBA there are just six or seven, so intangibles—such as chemistry among teammates and an individual player's emotional balance—become extremely important.

Dave and Ernie understood this. They wanted John to be happy. They agreed that he was undervalued. The issue became how much to pay him. That Saturday we sat down to discuss numbers. The Knicks proposed a four-year extension for $2 million a year. We wanted a two-year extension at $7.5 million a year. We had a large gap to close. And the clock was ticking. The NBA did not care what problems we or the Knicks had. If this contract was not signed and at the league's offices by 5 P.M. on Tuesday, there would be no deal.

The next day, Sunday, the Knicks played and we didn't hear from Dave and Ernie. Now we were beginning to wonder. But then so were the Knicks. It is often possible to confuse lack of contact for some substantive shift in the course of the negotiation. When one does not hear from the other negotiator, paranoia can ensue and a variety of horrendous scenarios may be imagined. In this case, it was simply a matter of taking a day off. Monday night we began talking again, and by Tuesday morning we agreed on the fundamentals of a three-year $14 million extension, with half of that sum coming to John in the form of a first-extension-year balloon payment.

Now, however, it was a mere matter of hours before the deadline. We were helped immensely by the fact that Dave and Ernie approached this in the spirit of not contesting each and every technical point for all its possible permutations. We cut through what ordinarily might have been a great deal of disagreement. Still, we were discussing a significant amount of money here, and there were numerous complex details that demanded to be addressed.

We were scrambling—David Dunn and I on the phone in our L.A. office, Checketts and Grunfeld on the phone in New York—while John waited in his hotel room at the Regency in Manhattan. Noon passed—3 P.M. New York time. We were rushing now. Both we and the Knicks knew that this contract had to be right. But we also knew that it had to be *done*.

At 1:15—4:15 New York time—we were still hammering it out. Now we were looking at the fact that this contract not only had to be finished but that it had to be *filed*. This meant it had to be signed by John, who was on his way to the Knicks' offices when he called us on his cell phone to say he was stuck dead-still in rush-hour traffic on Park Avenue.

This was horrifying. It was 4:40 now, New York time. With no time to spare, John pulled to the curb, ran into Madison Square Garden and upstairs to the Knicks offices, where the secretaries had his contract ready to sign. He signed, and the contract arrived over the NBA's fax machine at 4:58—two minutes before the deadline.

Another instance of negotiating under the gun occurred in 1996, with the negotiation of a contract adjustment for Merton Hanks, the Pro Bowl free safety for the San Francisco 49ers. Merton, a bright and colorful athlete best known for his signature postinterception dance, was determined to have a restructuring done on his contract by the beginning of that season. Come opening day, the contract still had not been completed.

As the pregame festivities began, 49ers president Carmen Policy and I met in a windowless room adjacent to his luxury suite in 3-Com Park, the 49ers stadium. We watched on television as the game began, even as we continued negotiating. I was determined that this deal would be done by the time the game ended.

Carmen, a charming, articulate NFL insider, has one of the most optimistic, resilient personalities I have ever encountered. That resilience showed in this situation. Time after time over the next couple of hours, the negotiation bogged down over the size of Merton's bonus. We broke off again and again, with Carmen retreating to his box to check in on the game. After every breakdown, he would return and we'd push on.

By the end of the game, we had reached an agreement: a seven-year, $22.4 million contract with a $4.75 million signing bonus. As the 49ers ran off the field, Ed DeBartolo, the owner, stood at the edge of the locker room greeting each player individually. When Merton came running in, Ed, who is as enthusiastic an owner and as close to his players as any executive in professional sports, hugged him and said, "You not only won the game, but you've got an amazing new contract. And we're happy to pay every penny of it."

That was an instance of a self-imposed deadline with a happy end-
ing. Normally, though, I am not particularly fond of deadlines. I believe in allowing the dynamics of the negotiating process to lead to a
resolution. Sometimes, as in the Starks negotiation, a deadline is an
unavoidable reality. In most cases, however, it is up to the parties
themselves to establish if and when there is a deadline. In such cases,
the issue that matters most is who controls that decision.

One circumstance in which I can understand a deadline being necessary is the multiple-buyer situation, in which several parties are bidding for a product or service. In the NFL, a free-agent player being
pursued by several teams is, of course, such a situation. Each team
needs to know quickly whether it can sign a particular player or
whether it has to go in a different direction—because while the team
is considering this deal, other deals are being made for other available
players and the number of alternatives is shrinking.

In such a situation, the parties need a clear, well-defined structure
of the bidding procedure, and they need a deadline. People will not
bid against each other forever. They simply will not do it—it violates
the reasonable-person paradigm. They need to know there is an end
to the process, and they need to know when that end will be. Otherwise they will feel manipulated, strung along, and sucked dry.

In the case of a two-party negotiation, I have no problem with a
deadline if both parties have agreed to it. There might be a good reason to set a deadline before a negotiation begins. As long as both parties agree and are aware of it, that's fine.

There can also be times where it is appropriate to set a deadline in
the midst of a negotiation, in order to introduce that sense of back-
against-the-wall crisis, to ensure that a deal gets done. When we were
negotiating Jake Plummer's contract with the Arizona Cardinals, we
could see that it was very likely that Jake would have a strong shot at
becoming the team's starting quarterback right away. This was a rare
opportunity for a rookie, but in order for it to happen, he could not
afford to miss a second of training camp. So we told the Cardinals'
negotiator, Bob Ferguson, that we had to set an artificial deadline of
a week before camp to get this deal done. That way, if any com-
plications arose, we would have room to deal with them without

damaging Jake's chances to become a starter. Ferguson accepted, we did the deal in plenty of time for Jake to report to camp, and he did indeed wind up as Arizona's starting quarterback.

Again, though, this has to be a mutual decision, agreed upon by both parties. And it must be adhered to. Setting a deadline and then ignoring it, letting it pass, destroys the credibility of that decision and makes it impossible to have confidence in any deadlines you might set thereafter. As with the boy who cried wolf, it is not wise to play with phony deadlines.

What I cannot abide is being faced with a deadline that is created and imposed by another party without my participation and agreement. This is something I am rarely willing to accept. To me, it is insulting. If we mutually agree upon a deadline, that's fine. We can accept it or reject it together. But to impose a deadline before the process begins or to introduce one when the discussions are not developing as one party might like is clearly an attempt to control the situation. It defies the spirit of a mutual undertaking, of a collaborative process.

Unfortunately, this sometimes happens, and there may be little you can do to resist it. Again, this becomes an issue of power and leverage. The fact may be that you are facing a person with more power than you, who at some point in the process announces that this is taking too long. He's had enough. You've got till tomorrow to make a decision. Or you've got until quitting time today. Or you've got fifteen minutes. Or he needs your answer right now.

This is yet another form of intimidation. And this is yet another situation in which you must stare doom in the face and not allow fear and anxiety to overwhelm you. It is undeniably disturbing to be told that the company may have to go with another employee or that a customer may have to buy someone else's product or that a home owner may have to sell his house to someone else or that a football team may look for another player instead of your client. But you cannot capitulate. You must stay focused.

Have faith in your research, in your preparation, in your presentation, in your proposal, and in *yourself.* The fact may be that you have no other options. The fact may be that you will have to accept this deadline. But if you must accept it, stand your ground in doing so. Explain to the other party, calmly and reasonably, that you feel this is unfair. Tell him you will abide by his conditions but that the setting of this deadline defies the good-faith spirit of the process.

If forced into a situation where an unfavorable deal is impossible to avoid, make the term of that deal as short as possible. And tell yourself that it is time for you to direct your energies toward a new situation—whether it is finding another job or a different house or seeking another football team for whom your client can play.

- Always provide a deadline in a multiple-party bidding situation.
- In a two-party negotiation, both parties should mutually agree on a deadline.
- Do not allow the other party to dictate a deadline.

PACE

THE PACE IN a negotiation is an element that can be orchestrated to a certain extent. There may be points where it is to your advantage to speed up the proceedings, and there may be times where it is in your best interest to slow things down. Much of this depends on an analysis of who is feeling the pressure. Generally, if the pressure is on the other party, you will want to prolong that situation and slow things down. If the pressure is on you, you would most likely want to quicken the pace and move on.

In most buyer-seller situations, the pressure is on the seller. One sign that he is feeling pressure is if he begins pushing hard for a conclusion, for a decision. If you find yourself in such a situation—buying a car would be a prime example—take it slow. Know that time is on your side. You are in control, not the salesman. If he is pushing you to make that purchase, walking away can be an effective tactic. That may be the time to say, "We're just not making any progress here. We'll have to talk about this another day," knowing that another day will be an excruciatingly long time for him to wait. Such buyer-seller deals rarely get worse when you walk away. And the chances are high that the terms will improve when you return.

The strength or weakness of your position can dictate the pace as well. If you have hit a stage in the discussion where you feel that some vulnerability in your position might be revealed, you would naturally want to speed up and move on to another point. If, on the other hand, you are on solid ground and in a good position to motivate the other party, you may want to stay where you are and spend more time on that particular point.

Another element to consider is momentum. In a hot deal that is rolling toward fruition, the last thing you want to do is take a break. If you need to do any research, number-crunching, or retooling, this is the time to call on your partner or your support staff. This is *not* the time for you to stop the discussion and do such work yourself. If things seem to be falling into place and you appear to be headed toward an agreement, keep it going—keep it moving. If you've been working for weeks to get the other party simply to meet with you and you've finally gotten together and you've successfully got him focused and thinking about your proposal instead of the ninety-seven other things he's got on his agenda, the last thing in the world you want is to end or interrupt the process—because once you stop, it may be three weeks before you get your next meeting, and you'll be starting all over again.

When things are going your way, *keep* them going. And be careful about revealing your emotions. Don't appear overeager. Don't reveal your delight. If the other side has just offered a proposal that will make the deal for you, you may feel giddy inside. Do not show it. Any glee on your part will only make him doubt what he has just agreed to.

Keep control of your emotions.

Always keep control of your emotions.

- If the pressure is on the other party, slow things down; if the pressure is on you, speed things up.
- Never stop when momentum is on your side.
- Don't reveal your excitement when things are going your way.

PERSEVERANCE

VERY FEW NEGOTIATIONS are resolved immediately. In my profession, most are complex, involved, and drawn-out. They often last for weeks or months, and sometimes even years. My negotiation with the Atlanta Falcons over Jeff George's quarterback contract extended from 1995 through 1996. Beyond what seemed like hundreds of hours of phone calls with the Falcons, I made seven different trips to Atlanta during that time.

Over the course of an extended process like that, I may have to revisit an issue over and over and over again. This requires tremendous patience and persistence, as well as physical stamina, resilience, and perseverance.

If ever there was a situation that called for perseverance, it was the 1997 negotiation for Bruce Smith's contract with Buffalo. Bruce, a highly intelligent and sensitive veteran, who is the most dominant defensive player of our generation, is clearly headed for the Hall of Fame. This deal involved redoing Bruce's previous contract, which had been signed just before the advent of free agency in 1993. Three seasons after signing that contract, Bruce was looking around the league and seeing salaries explode through the ceiling. Players at his position who were less talented than he were signing for salaries far greater than his. Not only that, but when the Bills had been confronted with salary-cap limitations in 1995, Bruce had agreed to renegotiate his 1996 salary, actually taking a $600,000 *cut* in order to allow the team to more easily meet its needs by signing other players. Not only was Bruce dismayed that the Bills were fighting so hard over his new contract, but he felt further angered by the fact that the team seemed to be ignoring the sacrifice he had made for it the year before.

We and the Bills worked for fourteen months on that situation. The talks broke down when Bruce chose to hold out from camp. He made several emotional comments to the press that upset and alienated the Bills' owner, Ralph Wilson. Ralph, who I consider a good friend, refused to meet me face-to-face at any time during these discussions. He said he valued his relationship with me too much to jeopardize it by becoming involved directly in these talks. All my direct dealings had been with Buffalo's general manager, John Butler. But by the weekend of the NFL's opening day, I knew I needed to see Wilson.

So I flew to Buffalo, with no promise from Wilson that he would even meet with me. I had just undergone minor surgery on my forehead, which had left my face somewhat swollen. When I arrived in Buffalo and met Bruce and Thurman Thomas and several of their friends for dinner that Friday night, the first thing Thurman said was, "Hey, it's the Elephant Man!"

At another time that might have been funny, but I really was not in much of a mood to laugh. I felt sick. I was exhausted. I was not eating well. I missed my family. I was 2,500 miles from home. I checked into a bleak motel room, awaiting a phone call from an owner who had not even agreed to see me.

This was one of those points where it would have been easy to say the situation is hopeless. But I didn't think of giving up. Resilience and perseverance are fundamental qualities of an effective negotiator. He has to have the capacity and the willingness, as well as the patience, to see beyond the circumstances of the moment. He has to be able to look beyond what someone is saying, especially when that person states over and over again that he has gone as far as he can. An effective negotiator has to believe that no matter how hopeless the circumstances might seem, there is still some way that he will be able to reach an agreement with the other party.

If there was ever a time that that belief was tested, it was that weekend in Buffalo, which wound up with me finally sitting down with Ralph Wilson two hours before kickoff on Sunday afternoon and reaching an agreement just moments before the Bills took the field to begin their 1997 season.

The need not to get discouraged, no matter how bleak things look, is paramount. It takes a certain amount of faith, in yourself and in the process. Sometimes your faith must extend beyond the bounds of the particular negotiation in which you are involved. Sometimes it is knowing that no matter what happens in this particular negotiation, you are going to live to fight other battles on other days that can provide needed ballast in a seemingly hopeless situation.

Remember, though, that there is a difference between patience and inaction. Patience is understanding that you have correctly analyzed the situation, the personalities, and the positions, that you have made all the right moves, and that time is now the only thing that will make the difference. With the inner calm and confidence created by knowing that your tactics, your responses, and the rightness of your course are sound comes the capability to sit for hours with complete silence or to wait for days with no response from the other side.

This is not, however, a good thing to do if the discussion is simply dragging, going on too long, and headed in a bad direction. Staying with a situation like that, without making adjustments and righting the course, is not patience—it's an inability to react to an impending disaster.

Assuming your course is correct, sheer physical stamina can become a necessity. The success of a negotiation may hinge on your ability to stay sharp, awake, and focused after six straight hours—or eight, or twelve—of detailed discussions with the other party, every element of which has to be absorbed and processed by a brain that cannot afford to be faltering from fatigue.

This is where the anticipation, planning, and preparation of your physical needs come into play. What is your circadian rhythm? When are you most and least alert during the day? Do you get drowsy following a meal? When you are hungry, is that all you can think about?

Questions like these must be considered and addressed beforehand. You do not want to be in a situation where a breakthrough has occurred, progress is rapidly being made, and you need to take a break for dinner or a nap, or you have to go to the bathroom. Momentum, when you have it, is more important than any of these needs.

Some people become agitated and restless if they haven't exercised. They need those endorphins in their system for the calming effect. These people should work out before they enter a meeting. Others feel that they have a better edge when they are slightly tired, a little bit gnarly and angry. This type of person should do whatever is necessary to have that edge when he enters the room.

Be aware of your own tendencies. There are people who unthinkingly overstimulate themselves by drinking large amounts of coffee;

they need to step back and assess how that coffee is affecting their behavior. There are people who smoke cigarettes to the point where they become extremely distracted; they need to consider what that habit does to their decision-making abilities. There are people who like big lunches, who devour carbohydrate-laden meals and then become drowsy in the afternoon; they need to be aware of what that food is doing to their mental acuity and physical strength.

There are times, of course, when all the preparation in the world cannot prevent discomfort. Circumstances beyond your control may occur that might cause you to become unfocused or disturbed. You may feel fatigue and hunger if a discussion has drawn on for hours longer than you could have imagined. The temperature in the room may be extremely high, inducing drowsiness. The setting may feel closed-in, claustrophobic, as was my situation in that underground Kansas City bunker. In such instances, it is perfectly acceptable to take a break, to go get a caffeinated beverage to wake yourself up, to go get something to eat if you're hungry, or to take a walk outside if that might refresh and restore your ability to concentrate and focus.

I am often teased for carrying rice cakes, carrots, MET-Rx bars, and Evian in my briefcase during a negotiation. But those items come in handy when it's not possible to take a break.

The greatest danger in any elongated and physically uncomfortable negotiation is that the desire to end the discomfort becomes a factor in the decisions you make. It's late, you're tired, you're hungry, you're in a city far from home, you miss your family—it is very natural to find yourself thinking about these things more than the subject at hand. But beware. Such thoughts are the enemy of focus and concentration. To the extent that you are feeling vulnerable, pressured by needs, and looking for relief, for a way out, you are setting yourself up to lose all that you might have worked for up to that point.

First, you must recognize these feelings in yourself. You must be aware that your concentration is beginning to drift, that you are thinking about how wonderful it would be to be back home in bed or watching a movie or making love with your significant other. If you find yourself having such thoughts, change the environment immediately. Stop the discussion. Take that break. Go for that walk. Visit the bathroom. Do whatever is necessary to restore your focus and concentration.

If such relief is impossible, or if you are at one of those momentum points where any interruption at all might be counterproductive, your discomfort will remain in place. In this case, you must summon the physical and mental discipline necessary to control your discomfort, to set your needs aside and continue. Somehow you must gather the resources to control your body and your mind, to not allow any of these very real physical needs to interrupt the process. When you have entered that crucial, delicate stage of a discussion where things are finally coming to a head and an agreement is in sight, you must allow nothing—but nothing—to get in the way.

Stamina has never been a problem for me. I have the ability—I guess it is in my genes—to stay up all night and still negotiate with absolute accuracy in the morning. I actually become sharper rather than duller as time goes by. I know myself well enough to realize that I always have a bit of a slowdown around 10 or 11 P.M., but then I shift into overdrive for the next three or four hours. Like a running back who is strongest in the fourth quarter, who gets most of his yardage late in the game, when everyone else is fatigued, I often make my most progress toward the end of a long discussion. Unfortunately, I should add, my three-year old daughter, Katie, my seven-year-old son, Matt, and my twelve-year-old son, Jon, seem to have inherited the same qualities.

I have been blessed with extraordinary stamina. But that is not to say I don't ever feel extreme physical discomfort, a screaming need for relief. In the summer of 1993, I was negotiating with the New England Patriots for Drew Bledsoe's rookie contract. I took a break to attend the wedding of one of our NBA clients, Greg Anthony, in the Bahamas, then joined my family for a short vacation in New Orleans and Disney World before flying to Boston to finish the talks with the Patriots over what was taking shape to be the largest rookie contract in NFL history.

It was the Fourth of July when I arrived that night in Boston. I could see fireworks outside my hotel window, the John L. Williams orchestra was on the television, playing patriotic music . . . and suddenly I felt sick. Not just sick but violently ill. I became nauseated, dizzy. My bones ached. All in all, it was the worst I had ever felt in my life. It turned out that I'd been hit with a particularly virulent strain of flu. But I didn't know that at the time. All I knew was that I had to somehow get up in the morning, finish the last details on this contract, and be done in time for the press conference the Patriots had scheduled that day.

I could barely drag myself out of bed the next morning. I felt weak as a baby. I was still vomiting. If ever there was a situation where a level of unearthly transcendence was required, this was it. So I summoned a thought that has become a mantra for me over the years, a revelation that came to me years ago, while traveling as a young man. I was in Mexico City when I came down with dysentery. I had been intent on visiting the great pyramid outside that city and climbing to the top. This was to be the highlight of that trip, possibly the only chance I would have in my lifetime for this experience. I decided I was not going to let my sickness stop me.

The pyramid was mountainously massive. And steep. The climb seemed endless. The heat was stifling. The bodily effects of the dysentery were overwhelming. But I kept going, telling myself over and over that years from then, any memory of how sick I felt would pale beside the power of the memory of reaching the top of that pyramid.

And I was right. The sensation of sitting atop that ancient archaeological wonder, with what looked like the entire planet stretching out below me in all directions, remains one of the most startling, dramatic experiences of my life. As for how sick I felt, I have to think hard to remember that.

This is what I remind myself of whenever my body or my spirit is tested. Whenever pain or distress or any form of discomfort begins to feel overwhelming, I focus on the goal of the climb, the reward that awaits at the top. I tell myself that no matter how bad I feel right now, no matter what I'm going through at the moment, when this is over, the memories of the hardship will be eclipsed by the sweetness and rewards of success. And I also remind myself, in such circumstances, that my petty discomforts or inconveniences are inconsequential compared to the majority of people in this world who struggle day in and day out with hunger, disease, physical disability, or political repression.

I reminded myself of all these things that morning in Boston as we closed the deal and held the press conference.

Then I excused myself to go throw up.

- Know the difference between patient awareness and blind inaction.
- When your body or spirit is strained, focus on the rewards your success will bring.

DEADLOCK

ONE FUNDAMENTAL FACT of negotiating is that the other person almost always sincerely believes he is right. Two people of good conscience can, with the best intentions, come to diametrically opposed points of view on a particular issue. Negotiation is a process of communication, of bridging the gap between those views. When there is a breakdown in the process, when the discussion comes to a grinding, or screeching, halt, it is almost always because there has been a breakdown in communication. Both parties are no longer listening. They are no longer considering the fact that their own best interest depends on understanding and somehow accommodating the interests of the other side.

Often, the reason this happens is pure passion. The inexperienced or overcontrolling negotiator can so fervently believe in his position and his argument that he becomes unable to compromise. He is so consumed with certainty about his position that he becomes self-righteous, to the point where he considers any disagreement to be an affront bordering on sacrilege. By the time such a person has finished proclaiming his position and his principles, none of which he will adjust, there is no room left to negotiate.

Being ethical involves not only a belief in your own position but also an earnest desire to consider and understand the other party's belief in his position. If you are so entrenched in the fairness of your arguments and conclusions that you refuse to even consider the possibility that there might be other approaches and arguments that are equally fair, then you are *not* being fair to the other side. And you are not being faithful to the process of effective negotiation.

This was what I experienced with the Packers' Chuck Hutchinson during our 1985 negotiation for Ken Ruettgers. Hutchinson opened that discussion by saying, "Well, you know we just can't pay a higher signing bonus. We don't believe in it. That's money that's at risk, you know. We may never see it back. We just can't do that.

"And what we do pay will have to be spread out over a number of years, because we don't have that kind of money to pay up front. We don't care about present value or discounted dollars—that's your problem.

"As for this high a salary for a rookie, we can't do this. We can't pay you what a veteran would get. That would set a bad precedent. It would create dissension.

"And no incentive clauses. What do you think we're paying him for in the first place?"

And on and on. By the time he was finished, there was nothing left to negotiate. Which is what I told him.

"Well," I said, "if all those things are true, if every single one of those factors is equally important to you, then you're not ready to make a deal in the National Football League."

Chuck laughed and allowed that he had "some room" to make adjustments, and we eventually made that deal. But people can sometimes park themselves in a hole by setting such rigid parameters that there is no room left to maneuver.

Closely related to this is the person who becomes so fixated on the figures he has calculated during his preparation that he becomes unable to move the slightest distance from those numbers, even when that slightest distance might make the deal. This person becomes so unrealistically stuck on his goal that he lets a positive result go by without recognizing it. When he is offered a glass that is $15/16$ full, all he sees is a glass that is $1/16$ empty.

People fall into this kind of fixation all the time. A buyer negotiating for a car is close to a deal, the car is a good buy at the price being offered, but the buyer won't budge from the number he had in mind when he arrived on the dealer's lot. An employee is looking at a job offer on the table that is good and solid, but he makes himself miserable by fixating on the one benefit not included in the package. Instead of measuring what they have achieved in the course of the discussion, on the movement that has been made in their favor, these people can only see the parts of the deal that have fallen short of their goal. Yes, there are limits that must be set, points that are noncompromisable, minimum and maximum standards that outline your position. But within those limits, anyone entering a negotiation must understand that it is highly unlikely that he is going to get everything he wants. Sometimes people can get so caught up in the process that they lose sight of this fundamental fact. Sometimes they can become so enmeshed in the microtechnical points of their proposal that they lose sight of the purpose of the deal. The sales representative making $20,000 who has just been offered $45,000 may risk letting the entire deal fall apart because she insists that management pay for her parking space, which it refuses to do.

Back in 1987, Cincinnati Bengals general manager Mike Brown and I let a dispute over $30,000 in a contract totaling $1.4 million allow a rookie to miss most of training camp. Because of that delay, the player's career was never as successful as it might have been. After coming back in 1992 and having a similar experience with another rookie player, Mike and I learned our lesson. When we *next* came together in 1994 to negotiate defensive lineman Dan Wilkinson's rookie contract, people were predicting a long, acrimonious holdout. But both Mike and I had seen firsthand the damage a deadlock can do, so we got started early on this one. Within a couple of weeks we had Dan signed, much to the surprise of many people. Many of our other rookie clients since then, whom we have been able to get signed and into camp on time, have had an immediate impact on the field. Our high-round draft choices from 1997's rookie class alone— Warrick Dunn, Jake Plummer, Darrell Russell, Tony Gonzalez, Derrick Rogers, John Allred, and Juan Roque—all made major and immediate contributions to their teams, not in small part because they began their careers on schedule.

It is always a tough call to decide when to keep fighting for a better deal and when to stop pushing and accept what you've been offered. I'll talk more about this in the "Endpoint" section. But I will say now that it is imperative, especially at a point of deadlock, to remember that your goal in any negotiation is to come away with the best deal possible. Better to be happy with a car you can drive than to push on to the bitter end in a game of chicken that leaves both you and the other party sitting in smoking, ruined wrecks.

During the height of the Cold War era, when the United States and the Soviet Union each held the power to destroy the other with nuclear weapons, there was a term for the ultimate head-on collision: MAD— mutually assured destruction. If one side pushed the button, so would the other, and everyone would lose. The assumption was that this would never happen, but it is a frighteningly dangerous assumption to make. In any deadlocked situation, it is tempting to assume that the situation will get no worse than the stalemate that exists. But the fact is that it can get worse, much worse. Offers can be pulled off the table. Jobs can be taken away. In the case of societies, as the history of mankind has shown, slaughter and death can ensue.

The inability to imagine disaster often invites it. This is something anyone involved in a deadlocked situation must remember. But it is something easily forgotten when both sides become consumed with righteousness and rage. This was precisely what happened with Kevin Greene and his holdout with Carolina. It was what happened with the students and police at Berkeley in 1969. It is important always to control your anger, but never more so than in a deadlocked situation. Assume that both of you are standing at the edge of a cliff. You want to do everything you can to move away from the cliff, not fall off it. If there is ever a time in the process where it is imperative that you keep the discussion going and keep it focused, it is when your backs are against the wall. That is not the time to allow your frustration and anger to come through.

Unfortunately, this is precisely the time when those feelings often do arise. It's easy at this point to throw up your hands and let out deep feelings that have nothing to do with the issue at hand.

"*Not only are you not paying me what I deserve,*" the exasperated employee might finally say to his boss after hours of discussion that have led to an impasse, "*but you're the meanest [blankety-blank] I've ever worked for.*"

It may feel sweet to let those emotions out, but the damage is inestimable. The discussion might as well be over at that point. Even less pointed generalizations—"You *never* do this . . ." or "You *always* do that . . ."—are destructive and counterproductive. This is not the time for judgment of any sort. The compulsion to lash out and accuse can feel strongest in time of deadlock. This is natural. It is human. It happens to everyone. There are going to be moments when you feel that the tide is running against you, that this just isn't fair, that you've had enough and you're not going to take any more.

You don't have to take it. But you've got to stay on track. You cannot allow your emotions to wash away any possibility of a solution. If you feel yourself getting too angry, if you can sense that you are losing control of the situation, take a break. Go to the bathroom. Go for a walk. Do anything necessary to allow yourself to gather your emotions.

Show some self-control. Understand that this moment will pass. You don't want to be muttering in your beer for years to come about how you screwed up. You don't want to flog yourself for the rest of your life for saying something you wish you hadn't.

Show a little patience, a little stamina, a little wisdom and strength. Hang in there. Believe in the process. Know that things can get better, and they will.

Not only must you remind yourself of this, but there will come times when you need to remind the other party of these same things. It is not uncommon in a long negotiation process for people to become discouraged. When faced with a seemingly insurmountable schism, they may begin to despair—either for show or in actuality. Sometimes, you may *want* the other party to feel this way. There are times when this is the right mentality for that person to be in, when this is the only way he will possibly adjust his view of reality. You may want him to go home and contemplate the fact that he has no choice but to shift his position. You may want him to squirm a little with that feeling. That might be the only way he will change.

There are also times where the other party may say, "That's it, we can't make a deal," and—*boom*—he just walks away . . . and you let him. Because you know he'll be back. You know he is not truly quitting. This is a tactic on his part, and you can see that, so you let him go.

But in most cases where the other side stiffens, locks down, and begins to despair, your priority will be to encourage him, to buck him up, to lift his spirits and help him fight that feeling of hopelessness. Your goal here is to restore a sense of a cooperative enterprise, the feeling that you are in this together and you are going to find a way out together.

Consider a salary negotiation in which the employer feels that the discussions have hit a wall. "Wait a second," you might say, stepping back and surveying the situation. "I want to work here. You *want* me to work here. All we have to work out is the money. And we *will* work it out."

Lure him back in with a reminder of how close you are to a solution. "Look," you might say, "we're $5,000 apart here. It's not the largest amount of money there's ever been in the world. We'll figure out a way to do this. We're *going* to figure out a way."

Such a mere testament of faith and commitment can ease the tension and conflict and get you back to conceptualizing your future together.

Humor can also be effective. When we were doing Jim Harbaugh's rookie contract with the Bears in 1987, we were close to an agreement, but we were still stuck on a couple of issues. We had spent many days trying to get the deal done over the phone. At one point Ted Phillips and I began talking at 6 P.M. San Francisco time and went straight through to 11 P.M., at which point my partner Jeff Moorad took over on our end of the phone and kept going with Ted while I went home to sleep. When I got back to the office at 7:30 the next morning, they were *still* talking. They had gone all night. That's the kind of stamina Ted Phillips has—as does Jeff.

But that discussion did not produce an agreement. We still had no deal, and training camp was about to open, which weighed heavily on my mind. Mike Ditka, who was coaching the Bears at the time, had a long history of absolutely blasting players who missed camp. We had to get this deal done. So Jim and I got on a plane and flew to Dubuque, Iowa, which was the closest airport to the Bears' training camp, at a place called Platteville. We didn't call ahead. We just went.

When we arrived, I phoned Ted Phillips from the airport and told him we were there.

"Where?" he asked.

"In Dubuque," I said.

"Well, you're not signed," he said. Rules forbid unsigned players from being in training camp.

"I know," I told him. "But you and I need to meet. We'll have Jim stay in a hotel or something."

So Ted sent a car to pick us up. On the way to his office, Jim and I began joking about Chicago and gangsters and Al Capone, and then I had an idea. I asked the driver to make a quick stop at a shopping center, where we bought two Super Soaker water rifles. When we arrived at Ted Phillips's office, we walked through the door and let him have it.

That prank was an act of sheer impulse. If I had it to do over again, I would find a prop with less deadly and tragic connections than guns—but my intentions were light and silly, and Ted Phillips took it that way. We all had a good laugh. Then Ted and I did the deal, and Jim Harbaugh was in camp the next day.

Something to keep in mind as a negotiation appears to become stalemated is that a no from the other side is rarely permanent. Almost every negotiation begins with a series of nos. That is the nature of negotiation; that is why you are in this situation in the first place—because there is a gap between your positions. The challenge is to somehow bridge that gap. With time, with the exchange of information, with listening, and with adjustments in each side's proposal, almost every no can be transformed into a yes. Just remember that there is rarely, if ever, a way to reach a yes without making your way through a minefield of nos. That is the nature of negotiation. That is the nature, really, of life.

When does no truly mean no? That is the million-dollar question in many human endeavors. To answer it, however, you may have to stare down an ultimatum. You must be prepared to face doomsday scenarios and even open threats intended to undermine your confidence and test your stability and strength. Don't let an ultimatum unnerve you, and resist the temptation to answer an ultimatum with one of your own.

Ultimatums are a last resort. I don't believe they should ever be turned to until the very end of a process, after every possible avenue has been explored. As soon as you issue an ultimatum—*"I guess I'm going to have to go somewhere else"*—or as soon as you answer the other side's ultimatum with one of your own, you're locked into a battle to the death. You had better be sure it is truly the end of the process, because ultimatums are like deadlines—they mean nothing if they are announced and then ignored.

When the other side issues an ultimatum, when you are confronted with that great emblazoned phrase *"Take it or leave it,"* you must not wilt in fear. You must not say to yourself, My God, I'm going to get fired. My kids will be on the street. My wife will have to go to work. I'll be humiliated. If you have properly prepared, you will be ready to respond to such an ultimatum with something other than fear. If you are not prepared, if all you can think about are your vulnerabilties and the consequences of threats, then you should accept the first offer you are given. Because there is no way you will stand a chance in a negotiation.

When presented with an ultimatum in the beginning of a discussion, you must confront and question the other party's willingness to be reasonable and to actually negotiate. If he has no such willingness, all the negotiation skills in the world are useless. Your goal then becomes, as I have said before, to do all you can to change or get out of that situation.

If, however, an ultimatum is issued well into the discussions, keep in mind that you would not have reached this point if the other party did not have needs of his own invested in the process. It is easy, at a point of deadlock, after hours or days of discussions, when you are fatigued, frustrated, and faced with a take-it-or-leave-it threat, to say,

"Fine. I'll just take it." But you must resist that temptation, no matter how strong it is. There will come a point in every negotiation where a line is drawn and a decision must be made, but you must not allow that line to be dictated by your own frustration or fear. This is not the time to cave in. This is where you need to remind yourself how important this is to you.

It is not just an ultimatum that may tempt you to yield too soon. When I was negotiating wide receiver Mike Sherrard's contract with Dallas in 1986, Joe Bailey, who was representing the Cowboys, made one of the oddest proposals I have ever heard. We were up against a deadline, with the team getting set to leave for London, where it would begin its preseason exhibition games. We were still $300,000 apart on Mike's deal, and we couldn't seem to settle. Finally, Bailey called with a suggestion.

"Let's flip for the difference," he said.

He was serious—$300,000 on the toss of a coin. Bailey was ready to move on. He didn't want to bother with this anymore. I called Mike with the proposal, knowing what his response would be.

"Is he *serious*?" Mike said. That money might not have seemed like much to the Cowboys, but it meant a lot to Mike Sherrard. We continued the negotiation and wound up with a four-year, $1.425 million deal—a package much closer to our figures than we had been at the time of Bailey's suggestion to flip a coin.

It is at those times when it is most tempting to quit that you need to be able to tell yourself to hang in there.

- Don't become so fixated on the specifics of your position that you lose sight of the entire agreement's value.
- In a deadlocked situation, never assume that things can't get worse. They can.
- Encourage the other party when he begins to despair that this deal won't get done.
- If you know your position is secure, don't worry when the other side walks away. He will be back.
- Keep a sense of humor.

BREAKING THROUGH

BREAKING OUT OF a deadlocked situation often begins with actual physical movement—literally changing the environment in which you have become stuck. If each side is doing nothing but repeating its position or proposal over and over again until the dialogue sounds like a broken record, it is time to lift the needle. Take a break. Go for a walk. Go to lunch. Ask the other party to join you.

Leave the negotiation behind for a while. Talk about something else—maybe a movie you saw last weekend or a book you just read or the golf course you both played last weekend. If you both have children, talk about school or the kids' teams—anything to reconnect you as people, to put both of you back in touch with each other as human beings rather than speechifying adversaries. Often, simple small talk can provide the necessary counterpoint to tension and can make room for a fundamental shift in the course of a negotiation.

When you return to the discussions, shake up the setting. Do something—*anything*—to adjust the dynamics. It might be something as simple as changing the way the seating is arranged. Perhaps, if you have been meeting as a group, you might suggest that you break into one-on-one pairs. Or maybe something more dramatic is required. If you've been conducting your discussion on the telephone, it might be time to get on a plane and fly to meet the other party in person.

Sometimes it will be you, not the other party, who is in danger of becoming discouraged, of falling prey to hopelessness. This is the time when you need to take a break and recharge. Do some physical exercise that gets your endorphins flowing. Place a phone call to someone who gives you positive energy. Maybe your spouse. Maybe your children. A friend. A colleague. When your perspective has become so focused and locked in on one subject, it helps immensely to be reminded of the context of your world outside that room. A simple act of refreshment can be just the thing to restore your resiliency.

Beyond sheer emotional support, you may want to call on the people in your life for input about strategy and ideas. If you are negotiating by yourself, it can help immeasurably to have friends or coworkers whom you can call on as sounding boards when you feel stuck. They may be able to talk with you about strategy or help interpret a situation and provide fresh thoughts and possible solutions.

Choose someone whose intellect you respect and whose judgment you trust. I have a staff of twenty such people that I can turn to whenever I need them. At the lowest point of that weekend in Buffalo with the Bruce Smith deal, when it did not look as if I was going to get a meeting with Ralph Wilson, I called David Dunn back in L.A., and he said, "Hey, look. The sun is shining out here. Everything is fine. This is going to get done. Don't worry about it." Simple words, but that was exactly what I needed to hear to jolt me back on track.

More than once, my clients have provided a boost when my spirits began to ebb. During a tough negotiation I recently completed with the Dallas Cowboys for Troy Aikman, I called Troy and said, "I don't know if this is ever going to get done." "Leigh," he said. "*I'm* not worried, so why should *you* be? I've got complete faith in you. I picked you because I believe in you. I know you'll figure this out." You can't put a price on a words of support like that.

In a deadlocked situation, besides reaching out for support, you might also reach out for information and insight from people familiar with the other party. It may be that another executive knows this negotiation is going on, has had dealings with the other party, or even is part of the same organization and would be willing to offer new information about the other party's situation, strategy, and thought process. This, of course, requires great delicacy. You must be sure the person you contact is someone you can trust. You don't want such a conversation to backfire, with the other party discovering that you are "investigating" him. That could kill the whole deal right there.

Even more risky—but sometimes necessary and often very effective—is reaching out to people who can directly influence the other party. In my business, this could be as simple as getting another general manager to call the GM with whom I'm negotiating and tell him, "Hey, this is a good deal; don't let this guy get away." Or having fans write in, urging the owner to sign this guy.

In each of these instances, I'm looking for points of impact—friends, colleagues, the press, the public—who might be able to influence the other party and shift the course of the proceedings. This can, however, be hazardous. The elements of ego and pride are always involved here. People do not want to feel manipulated. They do not want to feel used. So you must use extreme caution in attempting to influence the process through outside parties.

If you are in a salary negotiation, you could easily ask another executive with whom you have a close relationship to put in a good word for you. But beware of involving individuals whose status is higher than that of the party with whom you are negotiating—especially that party's own supervisor or boss. Going over the other person's head, or even appearing to bypass him, can be devastatingly disrespectful and insulting. No matter how frustrated you might be, to appeal directly to that person's superior will make him feel disregarded, and make him implacably furious. There have been many times in my career where I have been involved in a negotiation with a general manager and have felt it necessary to speak to an owner. But I always make that appeal through the party with whom I am negotiating, through the general manager himself.

Never go over someone's head. This will make him even more unwilling to work with you. If he is forced to do so, he will do it grudgingly and you will have made an enemy for life.

Going to the press can be just as dangerous. In my business, public perception is a powerful weapon. NFL teams depend upon their relationship with their city, their community. These are the people they represent, the people they serve, the people they need. Most owners and team executives pay close attention to and are sensitive to what they read in newspapers or see on television or hear on radio about their organization. Most players, though they might deny it, pay close attention to the press as well.

The media can be helpful in influencing the other side, but my approach to dealing with the press differs from that of many of my colleagues. There are people in my business who virtually conduct their entire negotiation through the press. Like lawyers trying a case through the newspapers, they share their information and arguments with reporters, hoping to pressure the other side through the weight of publicity and public opinion.

I think this is the wrong direction to go. You don't want to embarrass anyone in a negotiation. You don't want to make someone look bad. People who feel their dignity has been abused may do something destructive—in the case of my business, they may not sign a player, even though it is in their best interest to do so. In any negotiation, I believe it is important to understand its delicacy and the necessity of keeping the dynamics private. It is one thing for one party to criticize or attack another in a private discussion; it is quite another to do it in public. The former might involve bruised feelings, which are quickly recoverable; the latter involves losing *face,* which can do much more lasting damage.

It is almost always preferable to keep any negotiation as private as possible, limiting the dynamics to the parties directly involved. The only comments you should make to the press are those that will encourage the other party and improve the climate and direction of the discussions.

I learned this lesson years ago. I was involved in a horribly drawn-out negotiation in 1979 with the owner of the St. Louis Cardinals for the services of a player named Theotis Brown. The owner, Bill Bidwill, was a tough, hard-nosed, old-school football executive. He couldn't stand the idea of agents. He was personally insulting to me. We weren't getting anywhere in our discussions. Out of sheer frustration, I began to argue our case in the press. I made a convincing pitch, a plea of sorts, that brought support from all sides—from writers, from the fans.

But not from Bill Bidwill. The more colorfully, vividly, and persuasively I argued my case to the city of St. Louis, the more resistant Bidwill became in our discussions. I began to realize that it did not matter if the entire world stood behind me and told me I was right. Being right was not the issue. There was no outside arbitrator or judge or great scorekeeper in the sky who was going to step in and say, "Yes, Leigh, you're right. You *win.*"

Only one person's opinion mattered, and it was that of the man who was going to be writing the check. The worse I made him look, the more I had fans climbing all over him, the harder I pushed his back to the wall, the less likely we were to reach an agreement.

Bill Bidwill and I were eventually able to make a deal, but not without a monumental struggle, including an epiphanic moment in a St. Louis hotel room. A Cardinals team executive had come to discuss the agreement, and we were deadlocked on a particular point. Theotis was sitting off to the side, biding his time by lighting matches and flicking them into a trash can.

At a certain point, the executive proclaimed that "hell would freeze over" before he accepted our proposal. At that same instant, one of the matches Theotis had lit missed the trash can, landed at the bottom of the window, and set the curtain on fire.

Well, I thought to myself, now we're going to get a firsthand look at hell.

- If the discussion has ground to a halt, shift gears—change the subject; shift the setting.
- Use your colleagues and friends for reassurance and advice.
- Never go over someone's head.

SHIFTING DIRECTION

IF YOU CAN see that someone is absolutely adamant about resisting your proposal and you have presented it in every way you can possibly think of, if you have tried every imaginable strategy and tactic to influence him to shift and he is still not budging, then you have to back off and adjust your proposal itself. Pull back, retool, then begin pushing again, but from a different direction.

Never push a losing argument to the end. When no looks like it really means no, when pushing any further will bring the discussion to an end, back off. Think of another argument, another possible solution, a different way of dealing with the objections the other party has. You have played the game one way up to this point. Now it is time, gathering everything you have learned during the process itself and combining it with everything you already knew, to come up with something fresh.

11. Never push a losing argument to the end.

This is precisely what provided the breakthrough for Drew Bledsoe's rookie contract with the New England Patriots in 1993. When I met with then Patriots owner James Orthwein to discuss that deal, we faced a new factor in the salary cap. To complicate matters even more, Orthwein was giving strong indications that he was either going to move the team to another city soon or sell it.

What we wanted to achieve with Drew's situation was the salary and signing bonus we thought he deserved within the constraints of the cap, without draining the Patriots' resources and without limiting Drew's future potential and possibilities. We had to have a long-term contract in order to receive the bonus Drew deserved. But signing a long-term contract with an owner and team in such an unstable situation presented its own set of problems. Somehow we needed to figure out a way to give Drew some options if and when the Patriots' situation suddenly shifted.

Our solution—a product of hours of cap study by Scott Parker, Jeff Moorad, and David Dunn—was to create a concept called voidable years. As part of the six-year, $14.5 million deal we negotiated with Orthwein, we included a clause that voided that contract if Drew started at least ten games in his third season or if he started a total of at least forty games over the course of his first three years. In either of those cases, he would become a restricted free agent and we would negotiate a new contract.

We had little doubt, knowing Drew's abilities, that he would start those games. He was on a pace to do so when we renegotiated his deal. The voidable-years clause was, in essence, an escape hatch, providing Drew with an option if the team's circumstances dramatically shifted. Meanwhile, Orthwein did indeed sell the Patriots, passing on the Bledsoe situation to Bob Kraft, who faced the renegotiation of Drew's contract as one of his first challenges. That was the situation Bob and I faced when we came together for that 1995 negotiation. "Voidable years" was what got us there. It was a novel breakthrough, our way of solving a situation that could have led to deadlock.

There are limitless ways to find such solutions in any apparently deadlocked situation. With a home purchase, creative methods of financing can be used to solve the dilemma of a buyer being unable to produce the requisite down payment. Perhaps the seller can take back a second mortgage or a bridge loan can be arranged. There are an unlimited number of creative ways in which anyone can restructure a contract to accommodate the other party's interests and objections and to break a deadlock. An employee might include specific incentive or bonus clauses based on future performance. Or it might be in his better interest, depending on his vision of the future of himself and his company and the industry as a whole, to include a clause that calls for a renegotiation if his performance reaches a certain level.

This was what we did with Troy Aikman's rookie contract. At the time that the $11.2 million deal was signed, it was a sensation. Some people saw it as a signal of the end of the sport as we know it, a familiar response every time a new record amount is paid to a player. The fact was—and we could see this coming—that Troy's contract became outmoded almost immediately, as other players' deals leapfrogged his. We had not built a renegotiating clause into Troy's contract, because we received so much money for signing that that would have been inappropriate. But we did get an assurance from Jerry Jones that he would take a look and review it if circumstances shifted. Circumstances did shift. And Jerry did sit back down with us to renegotiate Troy's deal in 1993. The result was a new $50 million contract, which once again set the quarterback standard.

If all else fails, if you have exhausted every possibility and there is no new insight, no new argument, no new concept or idea left that might break the stalemate, you can always appeal to emotion. Your final option may be to break away from the objective sphere and address the emotional connection between the other party and you or your client.

This was, in the end, what provided the breakthrough in the Bruce Smith negotiation. After fourteen months and all he had been through, Ralph Wilson was numb to our objective criteria. He was sick and tired of it all. He finally agreed to sit down with me in the Bills' offices at Rich Stadium the morning of the team's 1997 opening game. But he was openly upset with Bruce's behavior during his holdout and he was angry that we had not immediately accepted his last best offer, which had been made a month earlier and which Bruce was now willing to take.

"Leigh," Ralph said, "you know how I feel about you. But in terms of this thing, the offer is off the table. This is it. I've been pushed too far. I'm not doing it."

There was not much I could say to that. So I began talking with him about how he was doing with the lease on his stadium. We went over a couple of marketing ideas. I told him how I hated franchises leaving one city for another, but if he ever thought that he had to leave Buffalo, I said, he should consider coming to Los Angeles.

We chatted like that for a while and then we came back to the issue. Ralph remained adamant.

"I gave you your opportunity," he said. "This is more money than I should ever be paying. Bruce is thirty-four. He's had injuries."

I listened. I did not respond. Ralph needed to say these things. He needed me to hear them.

When he was finished, I said, "Ralph, you were willing to offer this money."

"Yes, I was," he said. "And you guys tried to gouge me."

I didn't take issue. I didn't argue.

"I understand," I said. "But this can't be the best way for the relationship between Bruce Smith and you, a relationship that has gone on for all these years, to end."

"But the things he's said . . ."

"Yes, I understand. But here's the best defensive player in football, a sure Hall of Fame selection. Besides, this is *your* Bruce Smith. You guys have been through heaven and hell together."

At this point, Ralph threw up his hands.

"I'm sorry," he said. "You guys can just think about it."

"What," I asked, "is there to think about?"

His frustration and disgust rose back up again.

"Well," he said, "if there is nothing to think about, then I guess this discussion is over."

I stood up and began to leave. I knew that if I stepped out that door, it would truly be the end.

"Ralph," I said, turning around, "this is nuts."

"You're right," he said. "This is just ridiculous. Besides, I don't even know what I've offered. I've forgotten the precise terms."

This was what I had been waiting for. Now we were onto the issue. Ralph was exasperated, very upset, but now, finally, the door was cracked open. Something—the issue, at least—was back on the table. Ralph was making it clear that he was at the end of his rope, but what mattered most was that he had not yet let go of that rope.

"Here is what was proposed," I said, and I wrote the terms out on a piece of paper.

He scanned it. He didn't say a word. Then he pulled back from the table.

"Look, Leigh," he said, drawing a deep breath. "I've got to get to the game."

He stood up, the piece of paper in hand.

"This says 3.9 in salary," he said, pointing at a figure that represented what Bruce would make in the third year of our proposed contract. "I could never pay 3.9. That's a ridiculous salary. I could never pay that. It's got to be less."

"Like what?" I asked.

"Well," he said, pausing a second. "Take a million dollars off of it."

"And put it in the next couple of years?"

"Yes, but it can't be 3.9 that year."

That was fine. It was the package average—$4.7 million a year over the six-year course of the contract—and the signing bonus that concerned Bruce, not the salary for that specific year. Derrick Thomas had signed a deal with the Chiefs earlier that year that averaged $4.5 million, making him the highest paid defensive player in the game. Bruce wanted that status back. For me, it was the signing bonus that mattered most.

"Okay," I said.

It was close to twelve-thirty now, time for Ralph to get up to his box for the game.

"Well," he said, "do we have a deal?"

"Yes," I said. "Do you want to document?"

"No. My word's my bond, you know that. Do we have a deal?"

"Yes."

"Great."

And so it was done: a six-year $28.2 million contract—including $6 million to sign—that made Bruce Smith the highest salaried pure defensive player in the NFL.

Always, *always,* remember that while negotiation is about ideas and rationale and criteria and logic, it is most of all about people. And people have feelings, which must never be forgotten.

· Never push a losing argument to the end.

· When no looks like it means no, shift your strategy.

· If possible, when all else fails, appeal to emotion.

THE ENDPOINT

NOW COMES THE moment of truth. How do you ever end a nego-tiation? When does no really mean no? When is enough enough? When is it time to close a deal?

The answers to these questions rest on a combination of your re-search, your awareness of context and timing, your knowledge of the other person's negotiating history, your ability to read his verbal and physical cues, and the intuition that comes with experience.

First, the research. When you sat down before the negotiation began and shaped your proposal and set your limits, you should have come up with a range of figures. At the high end was the ideal pro-posal, which became your initial offer. Below that was a figure or po-sition closer to your actual goal. And then there was your bottom line, the absolute minimum you would accept. If you calculated those figures correctly, accurately, and fairly, they should have served as a gauge throughout the process. They should have been a compass of sorts. Checking those figures with what is on the table when it looks as if you are near the end will tell you how acceptable a deal you are looking at.

Next, you have to ask yourself if you are in the ideal negotiating zone. Have you done everything you can to steer, pull, or push the other party to make his best offer? Have you maximized your leverage? Have you used every possible means to put maximum pressure on the other party? Is there anything else that you could introduce into the situation that might have an effect? Is there anything else transpiring in the outside world that might matter to the other party—a shift in his company's fortunes, a downturn in the market, a good comparable deal taking place somewhere else, a bad comparable deal, a change in rules or regulations that might entirely shift the direction of your discussion?

When you come to a point where, in your judgment and with all the information you have, it appears that the situation has peaked, that it can only disintegrate from here, that the only change at this point will be in a downward direction, that it might be possible to push for more but the consequences might not be worth it, that pushing the other party any further might cause you to lose ground, then that is the point where you pull the trigger and make the deal.

This takes confidence in yourself and in the work you have put into the process. You need to feel that you have indeed done your research thoroughly and completely. You need to know that you have used every possible technique to maximize your leverage. You need to have faith that you are reading the other person's limits clearly. With the knowledge that you have done these things correctly comes the confidence and courage to make the deal.

This is the point in the process where concessions can become critical. As I have said, it is important from the beginning to leave yourself the latitude to make a dramatic move at the end. You may have yielded a number of points over the course of the discussion, but when you are close to an agreement, your willingness to make even a small concession can matter much more to the other party than any larger point you might have yielded earlier in the process. It can make all the difference in the world to be able to say at this juncture, "If it will make the deal, I would be willing to . . ."

If it would make the deal . . .

These can be powerful words at this point. They can be just the words to give you an agreement.

If it finally looks like you have a deal but you want to be certain that you are making the right decision, run it past someone whose opinion you trust and respect. Before giving your agreement, you might want to "shop" the decision to a colleague or to someone else whose opinion you respect, to get his perspective on it.

In the end, though, the call is yours. In the end, only you know what is doable and what is not.

· Allow the other party to make a final concession, if it will make the deal, and be prepared to make such a final concession yourself.
· If you are unsure of your decision to make the deal, "shop" the decision for other opinions.

PERSPECTIVE

I HAVE BEEN representing athletes for almost a quarter century, longer than some of them have been alive. During the course of that time, I have developed deep relationships—friendships and partnerships—with many of the executives with whom I do business. We have done dozens of deals with one another over the years. There has been contention and struggle. There have been misunderstandings at times. But in the end, not unlike a marriage, we have stayed together, moved forward, and grown. That kind of shared experience over time results in a foundation of trust and respect that is immeasurably valuable.

But that kind of trust must be earned. I understood this when I did my first deal twenty-three years ago. A basic premise of my entire career has been the knowledge that I will be working with the same people again and again. That means I am always thinking not just about the deal I am making right now but also about a given player's future deals. It means I see the other party as a potential partner, not as a foe to be vanquished.

If it were not for the team owners, I would not have a profession. If they did not feel that they could operate at a profit, we would not have an industry. I may believe that a player deserves every penny he is paid, but that is only half the equation. The other half depends upon whether the *owner* believes he can profit by making that payment.

These are not showdowns. In the end, they are collaborations. We each have an interest in the success and health of the other. I need and want professional sports to survive and thrive. The various leagues need a steady supply of quality players who are quality people. Each side has something to offer the other. Each side depends on the other.

In any industry in which repeat business is done with the same parties, there is always a balance between pushing the limit on any particular negotiation and making sure the other party—and your relationship with him—survives intact. This is not to suggest that you subordinate your interests to his. But sometimes it is in your best long-term interest to leave something on the table, especially if the other party has made an error that works to your advantage.

No one likes being taken advantage of. We are all human beings. We all have the potential to make a mistake. No matter how much each side stresses preparation, there is no way to consider every factor in a negotiation. There may be times during the process where one party realizes he has made an error in calculation or in interpretation and may ask that that point be revised. There may be times where terms have been agreed to but the other party then sees a mistake and asks you to let him off the hook. You don't have to do it. You could stick him on that point. But you need to ask yourself, Is it worth it? Is what I have to gain here worth what I will lose in terms of this person's willingness to work with me in the future? In most cases, the long-term relationship is much more valuable than the short-term gain.

Sometimes the other party may make a mistake and not *know* it. There are times when the GM or owner I am dealing with makes a major error in his calculations or commits a major oversight, and I can easily take advantage of that and just nail him.

But I don't. He shows me his jugular, and instead of slashing it, I pull back. I might even point out his error. Because if I do crush him, he will eventually realize it. And although I might make a killing on that particular deal, I will also have killed our relationship and, very likely, any possibility of future agreements. Or it might be that the person's mistake costs him his job, in which case someone else might take his place—who is much rougher to deal with and is intent on paying me back for taking his predecessor to the cleaners.

12. Develop relationships, not conquests.

What goes around comes around. I have always believed this. As surely as your foot is on someone's neck today, with the capacity to crush it, someone else will have his foot on your neck at some point in the future. To believe otherwise is sheer arrogance.

In any business or personal relationship, your reputation is a critical factor. To be unduly greedy, to cheat, to steal, to take unfair advantage is to put your reputation at risk. It can be tempting to become so caught up in what can be gained in the deal at hand that you lose your ability to consider the future. People often get the sense in a significant negotiation that if they can just make this one big deal, their whole life or career will be set. Rarely is this true, no matter how big a deal they have made. Life goes on. The time will come when another deal must be made, another problem must be ironed out, another difference must be discussed. And if you have betrayed someone's trust, if you defied his good faith in order to make that major deal, that trust and good faith will not be there when you need it again. Not only will the person you betrayed not trust you, but your reputation will have reached others, and they will not trust you, either.

A good reputation is difficult to earn. It is easy to lose. And once it is lost, it is almost impossible to regain.

- Look ahead; remember that you will both return to the table again.
- Sometimes it pays to leave something on the table, as an investment in the future.
- Never compromise your reputation.

THE CONTRACT

ONCE YOU HAVE reached a final agreement, the negotiation is not over. That agreement must be put in the form of a contract.

This process requires as much care and attention as the discussions that led up to this point. What one gains during the course of discussions can often be lost in the drafting of the documentation. Points that seemed crystal-clear when they were spoken, concessions that each party believed he had made, can somehow lose their precision or simply not show up in the draft of the contract. When the contract is drawn up, there may appear significant differences between what you thought you agreed to and what is described in the document.

This does not mean that someone is trying to cheat. The problem is most often one of clarity in communication. The process of communication is very subjective. What I think I hear when you say something might be very different from what you are actually saying. I may agree to it, thinking you meant one thing when you actually mean another. In a negotiation, these differences may not be clarified at the time an agreement is made. They often do not appear until the contract is drafted.

This can be jarring to someone who is not prepared for it. After all the energy and effort that have gone into the discussions, it can be both deflating and unsettling to have to go back and essentially argue many of the same points all over again. It can be painstaking and excruciating, especially after all the effort that has already been expended. But it is absolutely necessary. Sloppiness here can undo everything you have accomplished up to this point.

The temptation to hurry through this process can be great. You are tired. You are ready to get this over with. You have already experienced the surge of celebration that comes with reaching an agreement. Now you just want to wrap it up. But you must resist weariness or impatience. This is the very point where you need to take the most care and be at your absolute sharpest.

The other party may not feel that way. He may be in no mood, after this long, laborious negotiation, to do anything but sign. He may become angry if you begin to question and contest points or words that need clarification. This was exactly the stage of the process that Bill Oldenberg was unprepared for at the end of that Steve Young–L.A. Express negotiation in 1984. But you must not allow the other party's impatience, or your own desire to complete this process, rush you into compromising terms and specifics you struggled hard to win. It can be tempting to say to yourself, Well, this isn't the exact wording I wanted, but we've got the deal. I'll live with it. That wording may well come back to haunt you later. It may well leave you with a deal significantly different from the one you think you are getting.

In 1997 I arrived in Tempe, Arizona, to wrap up a deal with the Cardinals for running back Larry Centers. The principal terms had been agreed to. All that was left was for the contract to be reviewed.

When I arrived, the Cardinals' executives were clearly eager to get this signing done quickly. As Larry and I sat down to go through the documents, we could feel the Cardinals people becoming edgy and apprehensive, wanting us to hurry up. That had the effect of making Larry reticent. No one likes to feel that he is being pushed into something.

As time passed, I discovered why there was such anxiety on the part of the team officials. Expecting an immediate signing, they had scheduled a press conference to take place five minutes after our arrival. Not only that, but they had filled a downstairs auditorium not just with writers but with a hundred or so fans, all waiting to give Larry this huge Arizona welcome. It was a wonderful gesture from the team and the community. But the fact was that there was no way we would have been ready that soon. Simply reading through the document was going to take over an hour. If there were any problems, it would take longer. Finally, after about an hour and a half, we finished, signed the contract, and went downstairs to meet the audience. But not without a great deal of anxiety on the part of the Cardinals and some puzzlement on the part of the crowd.

One caveat to keep in mind about contracts is to beware of oral agreements. There are times in my business, because of the relationships I have developed over the years with a number of owners and general managers, where I will accept a GM's or owner's word on something in order to make the deal. During our negotiation for Troy Aikman's rookie contract with Dallas, Jerry Jones said to me, "Look, you know it's not going to be in our interest to have an unhappy Troy Aikman down the line. If these figures turn out to be grossly off, you have to assume it will be in our interest to make some changes. In other words, I'll take care of Troy Aikman."

I knew I could count on that. This is something unique about negotiations in the world of professional sports. Unlike negotiations in other industries, where confirmation letters flow back and forth as discussions proceed, in professional sports it is possible to announce a signing and fly to a city to close a deal without actually having signed a single piece of paper. The agreements made during the course of sports negotiation discussions are almost always oral. But they are also dependable. When the team GM or president on the other send of the line says, "It's a deal," it is invariably a deal.

In almost every other business or industry, however, it is risky to trust an oral agreement. The question you need to ask yourself when faced with such verbal assurance is, Does this person have a track record of making such modifications if market circumstances or employee performance changes? Or is he someone who absolutely sticks to the precise terms and conditions on the contract?

Unless you are almost certain that you can trust him, assume that the latter is true and insist that any and all promises or agreements be put in writing. In virtually every contract of any kind, there is a clause that reads "Other Agreements," in which all supplements or addendums are included. This is where you want to get that verbal promise in writing. Don't make the mistake of trusting the automobile dealer who says, "Look, if you don't like this car, just bring it back." If you leave the parking lot and the car is a clunker and you bring it back and the salesman says he doesn't know what you're talking about, you won't have a leg to stand on legally. A judge will hold up that contract you signed and say, "I don't see anything here that says you could bring the car back."

Even in situations where the salesman means what he says and truly does intend to follow through on his word, keep in mind the fact that he might not *be* there when and if you return. He might be fired. He might die. He might take another job and move away. Any number of things could happen.

Get it in writing. Every point or promise that you are counting on—get it in writing. And have a lawyer review the contract if you have any questions at all about its terms and conditions. If that seems like too much of a hassle, talk to any of the countless aggrieved parties who did not take the time or effort to do this. Ask them if it is worth the trouble. They will tell you.

Get it in writing. Always get it in writing.

· Misunderstandings may not appear until a contract is drafted.
· Get it in writing.

CLOSURE

THE DOCUMENTATION IS done. You have signed the contract. The deal is complete. Now is the time for you and the other party to come together in acknowledgment of what you have achieved. Now is the time for a celebratory act, something to commemorate the experience you have shared and the agreement you have finally reached.

You may go out to dinner together. You may have a small ceremony. When we finished the deals for safety Darren Woodson and fullback Daryl Johnston with Dallas, Jerry Jones staged a ceremonial signing in his office with champagne, and souvenir keepsake pens and a videotape made of the event. This gave a sense of closure and positive definition to the process.

This is the perfect point for an act of graciousness on your part. If the other side has yielded significant concessions during the process, you may want to put something back on the table, as a way of acknowledging their effort. Drew Bledsoe's donation to the Bob Kraft Foundation after our 1995 signing was such a gesture. So was Steve Young's contribution to the Edward DeBartolo Foundation following his most recent signing with the 49ers. This is a way of saying you recognize the commitment the other party has made to you. It is a tangible acknowledgment of the mutuality of your interests and of the fact that you are walking forward as partners.

Beyond celebrating with the other party, this is the time to rejoice for yourself, and, if you are representing someone else, with your client. Beware at this point of second thoughts or regret. There is always the danger after a negotiation is done of thinking about errors that were made, arguments that might have been presented more effectively, points that you may have missed, a multitude of ways in which you might have done a better job and gotten a better deal. Such thoughts only serve to diminish and sour the sweet taste of what you have achieved. It is too late for such thoughts. You need to remind yourself that you did the best you could do. If the deal turns out to have been less than it might have been, carry that knowledge into your next negotiation. But do not let it damage your positive feelings about this one. Don't obsess over "should haves" and "could haves."

And don't let outside circumstances and developments diminish your sense of achievement. If you just sold your house for $95,000 and two weeks later a neighbor sells a similar property for $105,000, does that make you a fool to have made the deal you did? No. You did the best you could under the circumstances you faced. Understand, too, that you never know what the realities of another situation are. You may not fully understand its terms. There have been many times where I have signed a player to a contract and soon thereafter came word of another player signing an even better deal. Something I always remind my clients is that we don't know the terms and specifics of these other contracts. A deal that on the surface appears to be one thing can, on closer inspection, turn out to be quite another. There was a report last year that a top draft pick had signed for an astronomical amount of money compared to a player we had just signed. But we came to find out that the figure quoted in the newspapers included a $10 million salary for the last year of a multiyear contract—money that that player will never, ever see. That $10 million year had been added on to the contract to artificially pump up the package value for public relations purposes.

A dynamic to understand about almost any deal is that as a general rule, the people who are paying the money tend to understate or de-flate the amount that they paid, while the people receiving payment tend to exaggerate what they received. So don't put too much stock in the talk overheard at a bar or around the water cooler. Those "facts" are rarely accurate.

Once your deal is done, savor your success. Think about what you might do with the extra money you are now receiving in salary. Imagine the fun you are going to have driving that car you have just purchased. Walk through the house you have just bought and think about the ways in which you and your family will make it your own.

Look ahead, not behind. And be prepared to begin all over again when the time for the next negotiation arrives.

· Commemorate the closing of a deal with some kind of ceremony.
· Look ahead, not behind.

The Twelve Essential Rules
of Negotiation

1. Align yourself with people who share your values.
2. Learn all you can about the other party.
3. Convince the other party that you have an option.
4. Set your limits before the negotiation begins.
5. Establish a climate of cooperation, not conflict.
6. In the face of intimidation, show no fear.
7. Learn to listen.
8. Be comfortable with silence.
9. Avoid playing split-the-difference.
10. Emphasize your concessions; minimize the other party's.
11. Never push a losing argument to the end.
12. Develop relationships, not conquests.

Epilogue

NEGOTIATION IS ABOUT change. It is about redefining and re-shaping one's life in large ways and small. It is about movement—in one's career, in one's home life, in one's personal relationships.

Change is rarely comfortable. It is rarely convenient. It is a process that invites doubt and uncertainty. It is an experience that almost always includes fear—fear of the unknown, fear of risking what one already has.

It is human nature to cling to the comfort and security of what we know. It is natural to want to hold on to and protect the things we have—a job; a house; a relationship. There may be problems with all of these things, but we have them. To try making them better may well involve the risk of losing them altogether. And so we tend to lock down, to remain in our comfort zones.

Compounding the fear of change is the pace of our day-to-day lives. Between the demands of our jobs and our families, we tend to move from crisis to crisis, with an overwhelming sense that it is all we can do to keep our heads above water, to simply survive. We have little time for reflection. We have little time to stop, sit still, and consider the possibility that some kind of change might be necessary in our lives.

It is easy in this kind of hurry-scurry environment to slip away from where we really want to be in our job, our family, and our personal relationships. It is easy in a stressful, demanding world to stray far from our intended course and not even know it.

The question we need to ask ourselves is, Do we *want* to know it? Do we *want* to make our lives better, or would we prefer to leave them as they are? If we are truly happy with the way our lives are, then there is no need to change them. If we are not, however, then we must be able to gather the courage and the resources to make those changes.

This is what the skills and the process of negotiation can provide.

Rather than approaching a negotiation as an unpleasant experience of tension and uncertainty, it is more appropriate to see it as an *opportunity*.

An opportunity to examine and assess our lives.

An opportunity to clarify our goals and desires.

An opportunity to define or *re*define the quality and direction of our careers, our companies, our families, or our relationships.

Few of us are fixed, finished people. Few of our lives are just where we want them to be. If they are, it is unlikely that they will remain that way. Life is about change. It is about growth. It is about constant movement and adjustment in response to continually shifting circumstances.

With that fact in mind, it is possible to consider each negotiation we face as a crossroads, as a time to stop, look around, and pull out the map of our life. We may be off course. Our destination may have changed. Or we may be exactly where we belong.

In any event, a negotiation forces us to take stock, to assess our situation, and to challenge both ourselves and the people involved in our lives to address and resolve issues that should not or cannot be ignored.

The ability to negotiate in a skillful manner can fundamentally alter the course of one's life. Beyond any particular agreement, the process of negotiation can unlock potential and promise in each of us that we might never have imagined.

Integrity—the word means "completion." This is what the courage and ability to negotiate properly and effectively can do in our lives. It can complete them.

And that is a kind of winning that leaves no losers.

Index

About the Authors

LEIGH STEINBERG has been a sports lawyer for twenty-four years. His law firm, Steinberg & Moorad, represents over one hundred athletes. A frequent national radio and television guest host and analyst, Leigh was the technical adviser to the film *Jerry Maguire*. He lives in Los Angeles.

MICHAEL D'ORSO is an award-winning journalist and the author of nine books, including *Like Judgment Day: The Ruin and Redemption of a Town Called Rosewood* and *Rise and Walk*, written with former New York Jets defensive end Dennis Byrd. His work has appeared frequently in *Sports Illustrated*.